The Nebraska Indians

— and —

Fun and Frolic with an Indian Ball Team

THE MCFARLAND HISTORICAL BASEBALL LIBRARY

1. Cobb, Ty. *Busting 'Em and Other Big League Stories* (1914). 2003

2. Axelson, G.W. *"Commy": The Life Story of Charles A. Comiskey* (1919). 2003

3. Ellard, Harry. *Base Ball in Cincinnati: A History* (1907). 2004

4. Richter, Francis C. *Richter's History and Records of Base Ball, the American Nation's Chief Sport* (1914). 2005

5. Lanigan, Ernest J. *Baseball Cyclopedia* (1922). 2005

6. Evers, John J., and Hugh S. Fullerton. *Touching Second* (1910). 2005

7. Rice, Grantland. *Base-Ball Ballads* (1910). 2005

8. Claudy, C.H. *The Battle of Base-Ball* (1912). 2005

9. Kelly, Mike "King." *"Play Ball": Stories from the Diamond Field and Other Historical Writings about the 19th Century Hall of Famer* (1888). 2006.

10. Anonymous and Noah Brooks. *The Great Match* [1877] *and Our Base Ball Club* [1884]*: Two Novels from the Early Days of Base Ball,* volume editors Trey Strecker *and* Geri Strecker. 2010

11. Green, Guy W. *The Nebraska Indians* [1900] *and Fun and Frolic with an Indian Ball Team* [1907]*: Two Accounts of Baseball Barnstorming at the Turn of the Twentieth Century,* volume editor Jeffrey P. Beck. 2010

12. Salsinger, H.G. *Ty Cobb: Two Biographies— "Our Ty: Ty Cobb's Life Story" (1924) and "Which Was Greatest: Ty Cobb or Babe Ruth?" (1951),* volume editor William R. Cobb. 2012

13. Joss, Addie. *Addie Joss on Baseball: Collected Newspaper Columns and World Series Reports, 1907–1909,* compiled and annotated by Rich Blevins. 2012

The Nebraska Indians — and — *Fun and Frolic with an Indian Ball Team*

Two Accounts of Baseball Barnstorming at the Turn of the Twentieth Century

by GUY W. GREEN

volume editor JEFFREY P. BECK

The McFarland Historical Baseball Library, 11
Gary Mitchem *and* Mark Durr, *Editors*

McFarland & Company, Inc., Publishers
Jefferson, North Carolina, and London

Library of Congress Cataloguing-in-Publication Data

Green, Guy W.
The Nebraska Indians; and, Fun and frolic with an Indian ball team : two accounts of baseball barnstorming at the turn of the twentieth century / by Guy W. Green ; volume editor Jeffrey P. Beck.
[Gary Mitchem and Mark Durr, series editors]
p. cm. — (The McFarland historical baseball library ; 11)
Includes index.

ISBN 978-0-7864-4359-8
softcover : 50# alkaline paper ∞

1. Nebraska Indians (Baseball team)—History. 2. Indian baseball players—United States—History. I. Powers-Beck, Jeffrey P., 1964– . II. Green, Guy W. Fun and frolic with an Indian baseball team. III. Title. IV. Title: Fun and frolic with an Indian ball team.
GV875.N3G74 2010
796.35709782—dc22 2009049604

British Library cataloguing data are available

On the cover: The Nebraska Indians of 1898 with founder Guy Green in the back row at the far right (Photograph from the collecton of Jeffrey P. Beck)

Manufactured in the United States of America

McFarland & Company, Inc., Publishers
Box 611, Jefferson, North Carolina 28640
www.mcfarlandpub.com

To Marjorie with all my heart

Acknowledgments

I wish to thank Gary Mitchem of McFarland, who recommended this project to me. I am grateful to him for his enthusiasm and to his staff for their industry. Equally indispensible have been Kelly Hensley, my interlibrary loan librarian; Tom Fehr, my resource librarian; Jon Dunkle of SABR's Minor League Committee; and Daniel Sutton, my student assistant. Christian Ferrer and Prudhvi Maguluru have been of technical assistance in scanning photographs for this project. Rosa Portell of the Stamford Museum, Stamford, Connecticut, and Ian Todd of Toronto have also encouraged me in this work. I am deeply appreciative of Ian for sharing his photographs of the Beltzers' Nebraska Indians teams from Max Towle's scrapbook with me. Thanks are due to my colleagues, Robert Davidson and Kevin O'Donnell, for their encouragement, and to my department chair, Dr. Judith Slagle, and my boss, Dean Cecilia McIntosh, for their support of this project. Most of all, I thank my beautiful wife, Marjorie Beck, and our daughters (Alex, Emily, Christie, Ellie, Emma, and Maddie) for their love, without which, no such project would be worthwhile.

Jeffrey P. Beck

Table of Contents

Editors' Note

This volume brings together Guy W. Green's writings about the Nebraska Indians baseball teams of the early 20th century, including *The Nebraska Indians* (third edition, 1903) and *Fun and Frolic with an Indian Ball Team* (fourth edition, 1907). A third publication, Green's article "Experiences with an Indian Ball Team" (1908), appears in the appendix. With the exception of the Foreword and Acknowledgments — duplicated in the two historical booklets but run here only once, with *The Nebraska Indians*— the text for all three has been faithfully reproduced, including any peculiarities of spelling and punctuation. The pagination has been adjusted to fit series specifications.

A small number of the illustrations from *The Nebraska Indians* and *Fun and Frolic* regrettably could not be reproduced to a high standard. They have been included nevertheless, on the grounds that their contribution to the overall historical value of the writings is indispensible.

The series editors gratefully acknowledge the assistance of Ryan Chamberlain and Gary Sarnoff, who tracked down missing pages from *The Nebraska Indians* and provided improved copies of that booklet's drawings. Thanks are also due the Bibliography Committee of the Society for American Baseball Research, whose members volunteered to compile the index.

We extend our deepest gratitude to Jeff Beck, who not only wrote the historical introduction for this volume but provided a number of photographs of Green and his players, furnished the text for *The Nebraska Indians,* and even keyboarded the article that runs as the appendix. The book has greatly benefited from his expertise, generosity, and hard work.

Gary Mitchem *and* Mark Durr

Introduction by Jeffrey P. Beck

"The famous Nebraska Indians," "the fast Indian nine," and "The Nebraska Indian Base Ball Team — Only Ones on Earth," the newspapers read. Guy Green, an attorney, journalist, businessman, Presbyterian evangelist, and one-time Western League baseball team owner, is remembered most today as the founder of the Nebraska Indians, the most vibrant of the Indian barnstorming teams early in the twentieth century. Between 1897 and 1912, when Green owned the team, hundreds of cities and towns in the U.S. witnessed the popular cast of players recruited from federal boarding schools and reservations in Nebraska, Kansas, South Dakota, Oklahoma, and other parts.

The team under Green was highly entertaining and successful. While averaging more than 150 games per season in almost as many towns, Green's team won more than 70 percent of their games. Two American Indian pitchers who played for the team, Winnebago pitcher George Howard Johnson and Choctaw pitcher Arthur Lee Daney, eventually made the major leagues; a third, John Levi, was an athlete of major league ability, and a number of former Nebraska Indians played in the minors. Occasionally, white major league players such as Sam Crawford, Charley O'Leary, Les Mann, and Peaches Graham also played for the Nebraska Indians.

Green chronicled and promoted the team's success in two dime pamphlets that he sold as concessions, *The Nebraska Indians: A Complete History* and *Fun and Frolic with the Nebraska Indians*. This edition makes both pamphlets and Green's 1908 feature article "Experiences with an Indian Ball Team" available in one place for the first time. This introduction will detail further Green's tenure as the team owner, his writing style as the author of the pamphlets, and the legacy he left for the team, which continued to play into the 1930s.

Guy W. Green

Guy Wilder Green was born 1873 in Ottawa, Illinois. He and his family moved in 1880 to Stromsburg, Nebraska, where he and a sister grew up. At age 14, the young man was soon numbered among Stromsburg high school's first graduating class, in 1887.[1] Of medium stature, Green was a multi-sport athlete, but he was better known to his peers as a witty speaker. Green enrolled at Doane College in Doane, Nebraska, in the fall of 1887 and graduated in the spring term of 1891, with a bachelor of science.[2] The small college was to develop a formidable football tradition, and Green boasted that he played on the school's first football team in 1890.[3] He also played baseball at Doane, where he was captain of the team, played basketball at the University of Nebraska and the University of Iowa, and briefly ran track and played baseball at the University of Iowa.[4] Somehow Green managed to balance his athletics well with his career plans, as he was admitted as a law student to the University of Nebraska, graduating in 1897 with a bachelor of law degree.[5] At the annual law school banquet in June of 1897, Green, always convivial and expressive, served as toastmaster: "Mr Green has the reputation of being one of the brightest men in the class and it was fitting he should take the lead. His eloquent words in the introduction of the gentlemen who responded to the toasts were happily received by his auditors."[6]

Typically, Green referred to his athletic career in droll and self-deprecating fashion. He said that he threw out his arm while playing catcher at Doane, and "ever since 1892 my arm has contained as much glass as the scrap pile of the queensware store."[7] Green's love for baseball, though, abides throughout his writings. He dedicated his *Complete History* to the man "whose sporting pulses beat so high / He walks three miles to see a game of ball.... / Attracted by the magic words, 'Base Ball.'"[8] And he wrote: "I cannot remember a time when I was not interested in base ball.... I consider it the king of athletic amusements."[9] Although Green led his teammates as baseball captain at Doane, he said his first stint as a local team manager came in Stromsburg in July of 1895. Again, Green tells the incident with humor: "About this time a fortuitous thing happened to me. The manager of the local baseball team was sent to the penitentiary for horse stealing and, since I seemed to possess a good many of the departed citizen's characteristics, the players asked me to take his place — not in the penitentiary, but as manager of the Stromsburg team."[10] Green's brief tenure as manager of the town team not only gave him a foretaste of his future career, but it also gave him a crucial insight into the drawing power of an American Indian baseball team.

Team Founding

It happened that the first game Green arranged for the Stromsburg team in July of 1895 was with the Genoa Indian Industrial School, a federal Indian boarding school thirty miles away. In his *Complete History*, Green emphasized his affinity to the Genoa team: "Before the summer was over, I knew most of the Genoa boys.... I frequently attended their dances. I even played on the team once in a while."[11] The first game in Stromsburg, however, struck Green as a revelation, the kind of experience that makes entrepreneurs giddy: "I observed that even in Nebraska, where an Indian is not at all a novelty, a baseball organization composed of red men drew everyone who was alive. When the Indians came to Stromsburg, business houses were closed and men, women and children turned out en masse to see the copper-colored performers corral the festive fly and chase the elusive grounder. I reasoned that if an Indian base ball team was a good drawing card in Nebraska, it ought to do wonders further east if properly managed."[12] Green tells the same story in "Experiences with an Indian Ball Team" even more colorfully: "The people came out in hordes. Cripples, who had not been out of the house since the Smith hanging in Osceola in '88, paid their money to see the game."[13] From that July game came his determination to organize the Nebraska Indians traveling exhibition team, but the birth of the team would have to wait almost two years for his graduation from law school in June of 1897.

Organizing the Nebraska Indians meant corresponding with players and management at nearby federal Indian boarding schools and Green "gathered the team together from Santee and Genoa, Neb., and from South Dakota and Kansas."[14] The boarding school superintendents were understandably worried that Green's travelling team would go bankrupt, leaving the native players stranded far away from school or home, or that the players would leave school permanently to pursue unsavory semiprofessional careers. Green noted: "They [the players] were willing to enlist under my banner but the government officers, under whose control the players lived, were not enthusiastic in their support of the enterprise."[15] He thought briefly of abandoning his project, but having secured the services of a number of players from Haskell and Genoa, he pushed on. The team played and lost its first game against the strong Wahoo, Nebraska, town team on June 21, but managed to defeat the town team in Freemont, Nebraska, in its second game, and to win one of two games against the University of Nebraska in Lincoln. Green had not yet formalized his team's name and identity. It was called "the 'All Nebraska' Indian Ball Team" in the *Freemont Weekly Herald*, "a band of Indians from Nebraska and Kansas" in Lincoln's *Evening News*, and simply an "Indian baseball team" in the *Nebraska State Journal*.[16]

Still, from the first games the team played, they exhibited traits that would become trademarks of Green's Nebraska Indians. The team was met by large and enthusiastic crowds that often whooped at and rooted for the American Indian players; the Native players were fast runners and fine athletes, though not always strong on defense; the Indian roster was supplemented by talented white players that Green also recruited (in this case, Wahoo Sam Crawford, later a big league star with Detroit); and the players often engaged in gags that delighted the crowds: "They seldom caught a ball or stole a base without making some elaborate gesticulations intended solely for the spectators." The first squad included two sets of brothers, the Keelers (who were twins) and the Dupuis (who looked remarkably alike), and "their favorite amusement was to have the baserunner and the man coaching [third] so nearly alike in appearance that the catcher often mixed them up and tried to put out the wrong man."[17]

The summer schedule of 1897, though brief, was perhaps the toughest slog in the team's history and the only losing season under Green's management (they won 21 games, and lost 26). During that first season, the team travelled entirely by horse and wagon: "We first took to the rocky trail of public amusement in wagons. I had two lumber wagons, six horses, a bale of hay and a dog as my complete traveling outfit."[18] The travel arrangements, which included sleeping in the wagons and bouncing down dirt roads, day and night, left the players exhausted. Green wisely decided to travel by train in his later campaigns, hire wagons when necessary to carry team luggage, and camp in tents on local ball fields between destinations. While train travel greatly improved the team's performance, the Nebraska Indian's status as an exhibition team, playing always away from home, was a daily challenge. Even in later seasons, the team faced many reminders of "the rocky trail" of the first season. As in 1898, when the team made a rugged forty-mile horse-drawn ride in Missouri, the wagon miscarried, and the players had to pull the horse and wagon out of a muddy culvert.[19] Or as in 1900, when the team was forced to travel from Cedar Rapids to Solon to Iowa City, Iowa, by horse and wagon: "They were being hauled by a four-horse team.... When the party reached Solon one of the horses took sick and out about file miles made a plunge and dropped dead. Another horse was secured from a farmer and the party brought into town"[20]

Athletic and Financial Success

Despite the travails of the first season, Green had seen the large crowds and fanfare he anticipated for his team, and he planned a longer campaign in 1898, playing more than 100 games and venturing from Nebraska, through Missouri, into Iowa, into Illinois, and back. As usual, he put it humorously: "I waited for some time, expecting a few offers to manage teams from the National League, but as none came, I took to the road again the next year and the team has been gratifying the American people ever since."[21] This time, Green retained some of his best players from the 1897 squad, including George Long, the talented Winnebago second baseman, and he had greater success recruiting players from the federal boarding schools. Early in the season, he signed the big Shawnee first baseman Jacob Buckheart, who had played for Carlisle Indian in 1897, and had "the strength of an ox,"[22] an athlete of professional ability who would continue with the team for three seasons. The team also benefitted from Green's promotion of it in local newspapers. When the team played Waymore at the beginning of the season, the local paper referred to it as "the famous Indian nine."[23] As the tour progressed to Auburn Park, Illinois, Green's team witnessed a crowd of over two thousand, and when they played Gilchrist, Illinois, "An immense crowd came to see the second game. People drove over fifty miles.... When the gates were opened the crowd almost swamped the ticket sellers and swept the ticket takers off their feet."[24] The team was an athletic success, with a record of 81–22, and the acclaim was growing [Figure 1].

Figure 1: The Nebraska Indians of 1898. Green appears at rear right in a dark suit, and his partner John DeYoung Smith at the rear left in a light suit. The team's best player, Jacob Buckheart, sits cross-legged at the bottom left. *Jeffrey Beck.*

Green discovered in 1897 that hiring the best ball players from Carlisle, Haskell, and Genoa Indian schools improved his team remarkably, and he recruited there with increasing frequency in the coming years. Future Nebraska Indians teams included Chauncey Archiquette (a long-time player at both Haskell and Carlisle), Charles Roberts (a first baseman at Carlisle), White Boy (a star pitcher from Genoa), Emil Hauser (a football and baseball star at Carlisle), Charles "Wahoo" Guyon (a three-sport athlete at both Haskell and Carlisle, who played catcher), George Howard Johnson (a tremendous Winnebago pitcher who played briefly at Carlisle), Jesse Youngdeer (a centerfielder for Carlisle and friend of Jim Thorpe), Walter Nevitt (a pitcher and third baseman at Haskell), Eli Stover (a football and baseball star at Haskell), and Thomas Reed (an infielder at Haskell).[25] As Green's recruiting and team management improved, so did the team records. The Nebraska Indians went 108–35 in 1899, 90–53–1 in 1900, and 135–26–1 in 1901. The team's most ambitious and successful season was 1903, when Green ran two Nebraska Indians squads, a western squad managed by Dan Tobey, and an eastern squad managed by Green himself. The two squads combined for a remarkable record of 267–57–1 for the year [Figure 2]. As the Nebraska Indians' tour extended to the East Coast, and the team continued to win, Green's players began to be recruited by other professional teams: "Manager Guy Green ... lost three of his players: O'Leary, shortstop; Snow, pitcher; and Ketchum, outfielder; having received offers from professional clubs."[26] The greatest of Green's Native players was Johnson, who would pitch for Western League teams for five seasons before signing with the Cincinnati Reds and Kansas City Packers in the major leagues.[27]

Nebraska Indians Team Records	
1897	21–26
1898	81–22
1899	108–35
1900	90–53–1
1901	135–26–1
1902	136–26–1
1903	123–24–1 (Western)
1903	144–33 (Eastern)
1904	149–25–1
1905	163–27–1
1906	151–31–2
1912	101–27
1914	101–25–3
1915	77–15 (partial record)
1916	108–53
1925	.658 winning percentage
1931	93–41

Figure 2: The Nebraska Indians' available team records. Most of these records come from *Fun and Frolic*, but are supplemented with information from newspapers and team postcards. The 1915 season record is of games played through August 12, according to a report by the *Lincoln Daily Star*.

In addition to recruiting the best Indian players from federal boarding school teams, Green also occasionally hired white players of professional ability, especially in April and September, just before and just after the minor league season. So Wahoo Sam Crawford, the Hall of Fame outfielder for the Detroit Tigers, played with the team briefly in the beginnings of the 1897 and 1898 seasons. And Charley O'Leary, the wide-ranging shortstop for Des Moines Western League team in 1902, joined the team for games in Iowa, Illinois, and Ohio in late September of 1902. He would later play in the major leagues for Detroit and St. Louis and coach for New York and St. Louis.[28] George F. R. "Peaches" Graham also played briefly with the Nebraska Indians in 1901 before playing for the Chicago Cubs and Boston Braves.[29] Even after Green sold the team, the Beltzer brothers would continue the tradition of signing both Native and white players of major league ability. The team was becoming an athletic success and a financial success as well.

This was the heyday of wild-west shows, and Green's team played expertly on the public fascination with indians. Like the wild-west shows, the team created a circus atmosphere to whip up excitement for the baseball games. Green sent notices to his opposing managers well in advance of games, with advertisements for local papers, emphasizing the team's originality ("the only ones on earth") and Indian identity ("genuine red men") [Figure 3]. Before multi-day engagements in larger towns, he also circulated handbills or posters of the team, and organized what he called a "good ballyhoo." Green would have his popular player-manager Dan Tobey, dressed as a clown, leading players in buckskin and headdresses through the town streets in a parade to the ballpark.[30] Postcards of Tobey and early Nebraska Indian players illustrate the practice, and photos of the team taken in the 1910s show that the Indian parade to the ballpark continued under the ownership of James and Buck Beltzer [Figure 4]. Green's two pamphlets and postcards of the team (in what is purported to be native dress) were also sold as concessions at games and contributed to the team legend. After the team's first game in a town, they would pitch tents on the field and create an encampment, reminiscent of the wildwest shows. Stromsburg's *Headlight* described the sight: "The team is composed of genuine indians.... Then, too, they camp right on the grounds where they play and live in true savage style."[31]

The athletic success of the team and the public fascination enabled Green to expand the team schedule in 1899 and succeeding years, until the

Nebraska Indians regularly played more than 150 games a season from Nebraska to Chicago to the East Coast (New York, Maryland, Washington) to the South (Kentucky, Georgia, Tennessee). The idea of the Indian encampment allowed him to save money on lodging and to book doubleheaders on weekends and summer holidays. In later seasons, the team lodged more frequently in hotels, although doing so depended on the hospitality of a hotelier and overcoming prejudices against the Native players. Green was also a keen negotiator with local managers, always seeking more than half of the local gate receipts for the team's games. A writer for the *Tecumseh Cheiftain* opined, "They are under the management of a man named Green, who is in the base ball business strictly for the money he can get out of it."[32] And the *La Crosse Tribune* complained, "The Nebraska Indians of Lincoln, Neb., are after a game with Madison. The Nebraska manager, however, wants 75 per cent of all the receipts."[33] Green himself recalled a game set in River Falls, Wisconsin, which he refused to play because of a crowd of "deadbeats and deadheads" trying to watch the game without paying. [34] In fact, the following paragraph appeared printed on the Nebraska Indians team letterhead: "Under no circumstances will we play for a smaller general admission price than twenty-five cents. This must be paid by everyone both men and women.

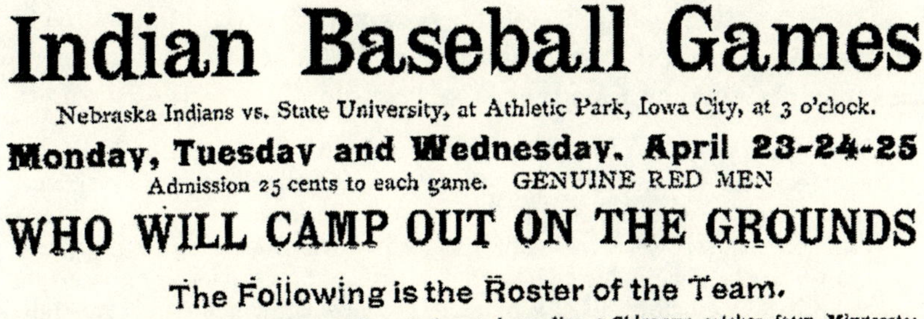

Figure 3: Advertisement, *Daily Iowa State Press,* 24 April 1900, 8. *Jeffrey Beck.*

If the game is worth seeing it is worth paying for."[35] Green later maintained that he made $5,000 a year from the Nebraska Indians alone, a considerable annual income at the beginning of the twentieth century.[36] The "rocky trail of amusement" was becoming quite profitable.

In these years, Green kept an office in downtown Lincoln with his law partner, John DeYoung Smith, but he was often on the road much of the summer with the Nebraska Indians. He married Wilhelmina Erickson, a Swedish girl from Stromsburg, on October 28, 1900—after the conclusion of the baseball season—and began a family at his home on E Street in Lincoln. But Green continued actively on the road with the team at least through 1907, when Dan Tobey, a fine athlete and a brilliant promoter himself, began to take on additional duties. Green's hands-on management was crucial not just for the financial success and growing national reputation of the team, but for the development of his two baseball pamphlets. In order to promote the team, Green had hand bills, advertisements, stationery, cabinet photographs, and postcards printed, and in 1899 he began writing his two baseball pamphlets about the team. Contracting with the Woodruff Company in Lincoln to print them, Green published the first editions (3,000 copies of each) in April of 1900 for the new baseball season.

Although *The Nebraska Indians: A Complete History* was much longer, both of Green's dime pamphlets shared the same genesis. Both sprouted from the same eager fan questions about the team, and, in fact, Green repeated the same introduction in both books. He wrote:

> During the years that I have been connected with the "Nebraska Indians" as manager I have frequently felt the need of a book like this one. Everyone seems to be curious concerning the origin of the team, its history and its probable future. Wherever we have played I have been assailed with questions of every imaginable character. "What gave you the idea of organizing an Indian base ball team?" "Where did you get acquainted with your Indians?" "How long have your boys been with you?" "How many games have you played and how many have you lost?" "Do you ever have any trouble with the Indians?" "What is the history of your players?" "Is this the only Indian team that has ever traveled?" I have listened to these and numerous other inquiries a thousand times if I have heard them once. It is with the intention of answering these questions that this little book has been written.[37]

So Green compiled both books to answer these questions. *The Nebraska Indians: A Complete History* tells how Green conceived the idea of the team,

Figure 4: The Nebraska Indians in their parade to a ballpark, circa 1915. ***Max Towle Scrapbook. Courtesy of Ian Todd.***

its early history and development, and how the team traveled and fared. *Fun and Frolic* focuses more on humorous anecdotes of the team's most colorful players and of the difficult and absurd situations they encountered in many small and inhospitable hamlets. In both works, Green attests that he has "endeavored to confine myself strictly to the truth," but his idea of truth surely admits a great deal of absurdity and humorous exaggeration. The author retells many of the same humorous stories (e.g., the missing "che-ild" in Murphysboro, Illinois, the bombing of Coke in Kahoka, Missouri, the beating of Tobey by a nonagenerian, etc.) in *The Nebraska Indians: A Complete History*, *Fun and Frolic*, and "Experiences with an Indian Ball Team," but each work reads quite distinctly.

The Nebraska Indians: A Complete History

Organized chronologically, *The Nebraska Indians: A Complete History* is a much plainer, blow-by-blow work, telling the major events and record of each season in turn. It is also much longer, including some of same anecdotal materials as *Fun and Frolic* in its final chapters. The seasons, which Green calls "tours," are recounted year by year and state by state, as in "our 1897 tour though Iowa," "the Illinois tour," and so on, with a roman numeral for each chapter. Green bounces journalistically along each season, from

Lincoln to another Nebraska town, and then on to other states. Overall, the emphasis in the history tends to be on the team's achievement of athletic and financial goals. For instance, a key moment early in the history is the team's victory against Gilchrist, Illinois (a team previously unbeaten at home), in 1898, which proves both the team's athletic power and drawing power. And he begins his account of 1899 factually, explaining that the team began its season earlier than before (in May rather than in June) so that they could play more college teams before the end of the college baseball season in early June. While *The Nebraska Indians: A Complete History* often lapses into plodding lists of games and scores, it does often stop to note the team's real accomplishments, especially at the beginnings and ends of seasons.

Whereas humorous anecdotes dominate in *Fun and Frolic*, such tales appear suddenly in the midst of game accounts in *The Nebraska Indians: A Complete History*. So in Chapter XII, the most important sporting bulletin is Buckheart's grand slam that leads to the team's surprising victory against the Payne, Ohio, team in 1899. However, Green's own knack for humor upstages the account with an anecdote from a game in Plymouth: "During this game one of the spectators, who was somewhat the worse for liquor, became very demonstrative and in the fifth innning, when the Indian left-fielder, Hopinkah, ran down to first base, the intoxicated gentlemean hurried out to the line and kicked him. Quick as a flash the burly redskin whirled, knocked his tormentor down by a well-directed left hand blow, then went back to his base as if nothing had happened. The crowd rose *en masse* and cheered the Indian."[38] The author may wish for the reader to remember the glorious victory against Payne or that "my team was the only one which bested Matthews during the entire season of '99," but it is instead Hopkinah's dispatching of the drunk on the foul line that sticks in one's memory.

While the score reports of *The Nebraska Indians: A Complete History* can be tiring, the book contains a great deal of detail about the playing conditions, recruitment of players, and day-to-day play of the Nebraska Indians. Little of this detail is available in the author's other works. For example, in reviewing the 1899 season in Indiana, Green quotes from the Richmond, Indiana, daily newspaper concerning Buckheart: "Their first baseman was a wonder and when the ball was thrown to him it was like throwing it into a box car or into a barn door."[39] Likewise, we learn facts about leftfielder Ed Davis, infielder George Long, the pitcher Whiteboy, the shortstop Ogee, and other players that are not mentioned in *Fun and Frolic*. We also learn a great deal about the Nebraska Indians' competition — that they played against teams that hired major league pitchers such as George Mullin and Ad Gumbert, and the Carlisle star pitcher Jacob Jimeson. And there are the amusing tidbits too — we learn that after the Nebraska Indians demolished the Kahoka, Missouri, team, "the Kahoka magnates had begun to tear down their fence and were going to turn their ball park into a cow pasture."[40] And after Green got into an angry disagreement with an official scorer in Keokuck, Iowa, he was described in the local newspaper the next morning as "a noisy unknown" who "spewed out ... rhodomontade" on the diamond.[41]

But if season after season of game scores makes for wearying reading, Green seems to have recognized the problem in the later chapters of *The Nebraska Indians: A Complete History*. Starting in Chapter XXIX, he breaks up the narrative with a series of "amusing incidents," and Chapter XXX dispatches with the 1902 season quickly by listing in columns teams they played, and Chapter XXXI launches into more tale-telling about the notorious ruffians of Murphrysboro. At this point, along with the decided shift in manner and tone, readers will also recognize many of the stories retold in *Fun and Frolic*. It is as if the author started deliberately to write a journalistic chronicle and, the raconteur inside him refusing, he then launched reflexively into his favorite tales.

Figure 5: One of many stylized team logos that appear in *A Complete History*, with Green's trademark phrase "Only Ones On Earth," 24. *Jeffrey Beck.*

While in all *The Nebraska Indians: A Complete History* reads as a rather scattered literary work, the author was apparently quite satisfied with it. As with *Fun and Frolic*, Green published his portrait on the book's paper cover, evincing his pride of authorship. After an initial printing of 3,000 copies in April of 1900, he expanded the pamphlet for a printing of 10,000 copies in April of 1902, and he expanded it again for a printing of 10,000 copies in April of 1903. The third and final edition, which is reproduced here, was elaborately illustrated with team logos and stylized Western Indian portraits [See Figure 5]. Green also, always the business man, arranged ads with the Brunswick Company of Chicago and Spalding Sporting Goods of St. Louis. And he included his own ad for additional copies of the books at a dime apiece: "Don't forget the 10c. That is a mighty essential thing."[42] His own estimation of his literary work was typically modest ("I am sure you can find worse reading, even though, I doubt not, you can find better"), but he took efforts to make it a shrewd financial venture.[43]

Fun and Frolic with an Indian Ball Team

The reader sees from the cover illustrations and first pages of *Fun and Frolic with an Indian Ball Team* that this is quite a different work. While the fourth edition does include all the team's "Official Records" from 1897 through 1906, by way of appendix, the focus is not the team's athletic achievements but its humorous misadventures, comic struggles, and absurd antics, as well as its most colorful players, and the often crass and prejudiced spectators. One notices immediately that the printer's font is much larger than in *The Nebraska Indians: A Complete History*, and the illustrations done by an artist named E. Smeltzer are in manner of stereotypical cartoons rather than stylized drawings. The grossest of these caricatures is on the cover itself, showing the Native players dressed in loinclothes, moccasins, and eagle-feather headdresses, dancing wildly while holding bats, balls, gloves, and knives [Figure 6]. Meanwhile, some comic fans climb a ballpark fence, apparently frightened out of their wits by the Nebraska Indians.

Rather than proceeding chronologically, *Fun and Frolic* proceeds topically. Its twenty-five chapters are not numbered, but each begins with a bold-faced heading. The order is essentially random, although the early chapters focus on Green's remarkable American Indian players, starting with the most colorful player, "Nakomas." Later chapters tell of bizarre accidents, the team's long-time player-manager Dan Tobey and its burly baggage man Sandy Leach, and the difficulties the team confronted in prejudiced strangers and unruly fans. Given the random order, the book can be read from beginning to end in little time, but it can also be sampled, with the reader skipping from heading to heading or cartoon to cartoon. So, the short chapters usually begin with an attention-grabbing phrase. Sometimes Green picks an astounding detail: "One time in Apple River, Illinois, I ran across a ball player who had neither arms nor legs."[44] Sometimes he starts with a tart aphorism: "If it were not for the fact that the ordinary man wants something for nothing, get rich swindlers would go out of business."[45] Sometimes he begins with an intriguing question: "What is the biggest piece of luck you ever saw in a base ball game?"[46] And, whatever the weaknesses of *Fun and Frolic*, Green does an impressive job of captivating the reader's attention.

Figure 6: The illustrated cover of Green's *Fun and Frolic*, 4th ed., with Green's portrait and a grotesque cartoon of the players. *Courtesy of Ian Todd.*

Although the introduction stresses the "truthfulness" of the pamphlet, the accounts in *Fun and Frolic* stretch truths beyond the implausible. The story of Nakomas, the Wyandotte who was "the oldest redskin ball player alive today," is typical of Green's penchant for exaggeration. Starting with the facts of Nakomas's age and scarred body, Green goes on in tall-tale fashion, claiming that his players would all beat their spikes over Nakomas's head to knock off mud, and other Wyandottes would cut pieces of flesh off of Nakomas to survive the winter, which he would regrow every spring. Likewise, Green claims that Nakomas was a miraculous spitter with chewing tobacco: "As the train pulled out, Nakomas would carefully locate the object of his humorous experiments, open his face and emit a cataract that looked like the tail of an amber comet."[47] What we have here is not a factual profile of an athlete and ballplayer, but a skein of humorous embellishment around a caricature.

Similarly, when Green describes his right fielder Powless, who actually did play for the team in 1903, he exaggerates the player's defensive miscues into epic haplessness: "He played right-field, and seemed to think it was part of his duties to fall down every time a ball came into his territory. If he ran fifty feet to catch a fly, he skated ten more on his face after he had nabbed the horse hide." Green goes on to say that in one game, "he lay gracefully on his back and speared a fly with his spikes," and the illustrator Schmeltzer pictures him doing so.[48] He finishes the story of ultimate baseball absurdity by telling of Powless's fall into a well during a game, and he does so in the backwoods vernacular of a tramp named Buck Adams. Here the point is not to describe a player's weaknesses accurately, but to make a far-fetched comic strip of them for the guffaws of a knee-slapping audience.

Contemporary readers are quite likely to find their chuckles at Green's jests interrupted by cringes at racial stereotypes and insensitive language. Although the author was progressively educated and genuinely concerned for his Native players, he was not beyond engaging in some of the popular stereotypes of his day. So in his portrait of Juzicania, a Yaqui center fielder on his 1906 team, Green summons up the stereotype of a Western savage: "I hesitated a long time before I added Juzicanea [*sic*] to my Team. He was the meanest looking Indian I have ever seen. He wore his hair long, surveyed everything with piercing black eyes, and when he came down the street people moved to the edge of the sidewalk and apprehensively watched him pass."[49] Such stereotypes are exacerbated in *Fun and Frolic* by the racial caricatures in the illustrations, and the uses of "red skins," "red men," "aborigines," "savages," "copper colored," and like terms. Similarly, Green describes his players dancing in a schoolhouse near Boone, Iowa, as "contorting savages," making "the walls rattle with their savage songs and dances."[50] And Green and Smeltzer combined for an ugly piece of racism in the chapter on Juzicania, when Smeltzer depicted a fearful waiter in black-face caricature, and Green wrote that the man's "Ethiopian intellect was hopeless unhinged."[51]

While one can easily respond to such depictions with disgust, they hide an important point: Green had deep respect for the athletic abilities of his

Native players, and he believed in them as players and people. In fact, when he bought a Western League franchise in 1908, he began moving his best Nebraska Indians players to his minor league team, the Lincoln Greenbackers, and the very best of them, pitcher George Howard Johnson, eventually made the major leagues. When interviewed in 1909 in Sioux City, Green showed real concern about the treatment of his Native players, and he singled out the heckling that Johnson often faced while pitching:

> Johnson, my Indian twirler ... pitched for my Nebraska Indian team three seasons. During that time we played an average of 150 towns annually in the United States and Canada. That makes 450 towns. Johnson is now pitching his second season in [the Western League]. He has never yet stepped to the mound to pitch a game anywhere on earth that three things have not happened. Numerous local humorists have started what they imagine to be Indian war cries; others have yelled "Back to the reservation," and the third variety of town pump jester has shrieked "Dog soup! Dog soup!" If you were at the game Tuesday you heard this. If you see him pitch in Pueblo or Sitka or Kamchatka you will hear the same thing. You would think people would get all that kind of patent inside stuff out of their systems after awhile, wouldn't you? But they never do.[52]

While Green obviously profitted from the small town fascination with American Indians, he by no means accepted many of the popular prejudices. In fact, the most consistent targets of satire in *Fun and Frolic* are the local constables and citizens who bear outlandish prejudices against Nebraska Indians players.

Green sometimes encamped his team on ball fields because hoteliers often refused his team rooms, and he and his players were continually harassed by local officials on baseless charges. He tells many anecdotes about the xenophobia that his players faced, especially in his chapter "Among Strangers." Green noted that if a "violation of the law occurred in a city while we were visiting it ... the local sleuths [would begin] convening in solemn conclave and deciding that 'them darned Injuns' are the guilty party."[53] The author goes on to a cite a series of such absurd incidents:

- In Indianola, Iowa, the city marshall investigates whether they have absconded with a piece of bacon from a local smoke house.
- In Murphysboro, Illinois, a frantic mother fears that the "red men had kidnapped her 'che-ild.'" Meanwhile, the child has returned home from a nearby huckleberry patch.

- In Center Point, Iowa, the mayor appoints "a large force of special police" to guard the town while the Nebraska Indians are staying there.
- In Collinsville, Illinois, a Native player who ventured away from the team camp is arrested on suspicion of burglary, although no burglary has been committed in the town.
- In Kokomo, Indiana, the police chief claims that the Nebraska Indians are bold criminals and "your red Men should be called down, and called proper," although, again, no crime has been committed.[54]

And the stories continue. Green never ceases to marvel at the buffonery of locals when confronted by strangers: "People never entirely rid themselves of the feeling, which, in ancient times, impelled them at the approach of a stranger, to raise the drawbridge and flood the moat."[55] In the cases involving the Nebraska Indians, the fear is compounded by racism. Although Green was no Mark Twain, he did share Twain's contempt for small town mobs and their fear of strangers: "The pitifulest thing out is a mob."[56]

In addition to the tales of his players, several good anecdotes in *Fun and Frolic* concern the Nebraska Indians' player-manager Dan Tobey, the blond-haired and blue-eyed Irishman who often pitched for and always promoted the team. Tobey, who had been a baseball and football player for the University of Nebraska, would travel with the Nebraska Indians during the summer and pitch for Pasadena of the California League in the winter. He would go on to become a legendary ring announcer in Los Angeles. Vera Hirt described him as "always funny and full of wit" and having "more pep and fire than the average six men his age."[57] Likewise, Green said: "Tobey is a mine of energy. He drops into a town at 10 o'clock in the morning, is acquainted with everybody inside an hour, and at noon is liable to be eating lunch with the mayor or a leading preacher."[58] In one chapter, "The Tramp Pitcher," the author tells how Tobey disguised himself as a vagrant and appealed to Green in front of the local manager, speculating that the Nebraska Indians could beat the Iliopolis team even if he, a tramp, were pitching. Before a large, buzzing crowd, the disguised Tobey did beat them, and after the fifth inning, he pulled off his tattered jacket to expose his Nebraska Indians jersey to the delight of the spectators.[59] In another vintage Dan Tobey anecdote, Green repeats in Tobey's own words: "When I paid my hotel bill last night at Riley [Kansas], $18.75, the proprietor fell into a swoon.... He started to bend over like a person having a fit; he kicked the desk a hell of a jolt and closed his eyes, his face all wrinkled up." Tobey, it seems, often kidded Green about giving hoteliers a heart attack by paying a bill.[60]

While *Fun and Frolic with an Indian Ball Team* (also titled *Fun and Frolic with an Indian Ball Team* in some printings) was a shorter and more light-hearted work than *The Nebraska Indians: A Complete History*, it proved even more popular. Green printed 3,000 copies for the first edition of 1900, 10,000 of the second edition of 1902, 10,000 of the third edition of 1904, and 20,000 of the fourth edition of 1907.* The author's photograph appeared prominently on the cover of the dime pamphlet and also in a frontispiece alongside his players in a team photograph of the Nebraska Indians. Many of the surviving copies of *Fun and Frolic* are from the fourth printing, which was first republished by Amereon Press in 1992 as part of its classic baseball series. The fourth edition is also reprinted here.

"Experiences with an Indian Ball Team"

The last and perhaps the most satisfying of Guy Green's writings about the Nebraska Indians was a lengthy feature article for the *Nebraska State Journal* that was published in December of 1908. It is printed here as an appendix. Like *The Nebraska Indians: A Complete History*, the account begins chronologically, but like *Fun and Frolic*, Green's piece focuses on humorous tales. The description of the first season, with the team bouncing down rocky roads with pots, pans, dogs, and food in a converted lumber wagon, is especially vivid. And the "dime novel" account of Emil Hauser, also known as Waseca, a football star at Carlisle who played on the Nebraska Indians, is especially colorful and not found in either of the previous works. Hauser, who played catcher on the 1906 team during part of the season, broke his ankle at a game in Carrolton, Kentucky, and stayed there to mend while the team travelled on.

> During his second day there a sweet little society lady who had been writing papers on the noble red man for the woman's club, dropped in to see

*Editor's note: I have never been able to find a first or second edition (1900, 1902) of *Fun and Frolic*. Since Green included material from *The Nebraska Indians: A Complete History* in the 1904 and 1907 editions of *Fun and Frolic*, it is possible that the first two editions did not exist as separate publications. Thanks to Dan Bretta for mentioning this possibility to me.

> how the aborigine was prospering. She carefully untied the "Four X" flour sacks with which Emil's foot was wrapped, soaked it copiously with tears of sympathy and a horse liniment which cost three dollars a gallon at the corner drug store, and went away. The next day she returned to again look after the patient, and this continued until Hauser wore a haunted expression most of the time and trembled whenever he saw a man go by with a gun. One day as Hauser was enjoying his afternoon doze..., the big husband of the Indian's admirer burst into the room with an assortment of bright new oaths and a consignment of firearms that made a civil war museum look as tame as an exhibit of agricultural implements. He shoved a gun, the barrel of which looked big enough to sleep in, up against Emil's palpitating dinner and told him to fly fast and far. Emil flew. He flew on foot, by wagon, by horseback, mule back, steamboat and train until he reached us where we were sojourning somewhere down in Tennessee.[61]

As in *Fun and Frolic*, Green's account is exaggerated for the sake of humor, as he mingles deliberatley inflated circumlocutions with gritty details. Here again he chooses unfortunate phrases like "noble red man" and "aborigine," but the anecdote does bespeak the suspicion and prejudice that his Native athletes faced in their travels. The feature piece (published with portrait photographs of Green and Tobey, a Nebraska Indians team photograph, and a photograph of the team on parade in Baltimore in 1907) appeared when the team was at the height of its fame, and the author's disposition seems remarkably wry and sunny. The tone is both nostalgic and bright, infused with the best of Green's humor.

"My New Foe"

In the October 1901 issue of *Lippincott's Monthly Magazine* (a major Philadelphia magazine that published Walt Whitman, Rudyard Kipling, Oscar Wilde, and Arthur Conan Doyle, among others), a sonnet entitled "My New Foe" was published by Guy W. Green. The poem was written in iambic pentameter and in perfect Petrarchan form by someone who knew sonnets and had an affinity for the manner of Elizabeth Barrett Browning. The formal language and tormented speaker of the poem have nothing of the breeziness and humor of *Fun and Frolic* or *The Nebraska Indians: A Complete History*; in fact, only the baseball author's later career as a Presbyterian evangelist and the religious themes of the sonnet would seem to make his authorship a possibility. The poem is interesting inasmuch as it characterizes the speaker's secret sin as a Friday within himself (that is, a Native stranger or Caliban), which he discovers in a moment of isolation. The sonnet is printed here as a poem of doubtful authorship.

> WHEN Crusoe trod the beach upon that day,
> Sweet peace went with him, and the earth had grown
> To seem a paradise; he walked alone
> In calm content until, within the way,
> The print of some strange foot before him lay.
> 'Twas then he felt that rest for aye had flown,
> And knew that henceforth he must guard his own
> Like one besieged who holds a foe at bay.
> To-day, upon the tablet of my soul,
> I found the trace of an abhorred sin
> That I have feared and dreaded these long years;
> And though my life may reach its chosen goal,
> I must, like Crusoe his rude cell within,
> Await my new-found foe in pray'r and tears.[62]

Green's Other Barnstorming Teams

In addition to his Nebraska Indians, Green organized two other barnstorming teams that toured throughout the Midwest: Green's Japanese Baseball Team in 1906 (also known as the Mikado Japanese Baseball Team) and Green's Native Hawaiian Baseball Team in 1913. He also investigated the possibility of touring with a Cuban team. In the winter of 1906, he made "an extended trip to Cuba for the purpose of organizing a ... team" but soon discovered that the best Cuban players were often of mixed race or black, a fact that promised to complicate any tour of the States. Green abandoned his plans but had again proven himself far-sighted in recognizing the interest of American fans in watching baseball players of other races, ethnicities, and cultures.[63]

In the fall of 1905, inspired by the success of the Nebraska Indians and the recent visit of the Waseda University team to the United States, Green contracted with Tozan T. Masko, a well-respected Japanese player in St. Louis, Missouri, to recruit an exhibition team of Japanese players.[64] The recruiting efforts were considerable, and Masko and the Mikado team were celebrated in *The Japan Times*: "Mikado's Japanese baseball team was organized during 1905 by Tozan T. Masko. Every Japanese player is full-blooded Japanese.... There are in Japan 265 middle schools and thirty-five universities at which baseball is played. Mikado's team is composed of the pick of the players from these institutions, and they have crossed the 4,000 miles of Pacific ocean in order to reach America for this tour."[65] The team began their 1906 season in the early spring in Nebraska with practice before undertaking their tour, with Dan Tobey serving as a traveling secretary and player for the team and Masko leading the team as a player-manager. Green commented that "the men composing the squad are the pick of these institutions, and each will draw a big salary for his services."[66] *The Lincoln Evening News* listed the lineup for the 1906 team: Katz, catcher; Toyo, pitcher; Saito, pitcher and outfielder; T. Uyeda, first baseman; J. Uyeda, second baseman; Naito, third baseman; Kitsuke, shortstop; Nish, outfield; Kawashima, outfield; Kimo, infielder; and Masko, pitcher and manager.[67] The team was scheduled to play games in Nebraska, Kansas, Oklahoma, Iowa, Illinois, and North and South Dakota.

Curiously, Green mentions the Japanese team only once in his pamphlets, in sideways fashion, in telling the story of Tobey and the hotelier in Riley, Kansas. Perhaps this was because after the 1906 season Masko parted ways with Green and served as owner-manager of the Mikado team himself for several more seasons. It was quite clear, however, that Green left a definite stamp upon the team. The "rules" that Masko printed on the Mikado team letterhead, emphasizing the team's right to gate receipts, were taken *verbatim* from the Nebraska Indians team letterhead:

1. Under no circumstances will we throw a game. Leaving entirely out of consideration the moral aspect of the question, dishonesty with the public is bad business policy.
2. Under no circumstances will we play for a smaller admission price than twenty-five cents. This must be paid by every one, both men and women. If a game is worth seeing it is worth paying for.
3. We positively will not admit free of charge the relatives or friends of ball players, managers, magnates, stockholders or officers. We are not running a charitable institution.
4. We positively will not admit at any stage of the game children who are unaccompanied by their parents. Children must be pretty small to get by our ticket taker....
7. We carry our own tickets for both gate and grandstand. We sell

and you take. When you are ready to settle count the tickets you have taken in, figure your share of the receipts and we pay you instantly.

8. We always reserve the right to use two umpires, one of whom will be furnished by us....
10. We are willing to furnish you all the free advertising matter you can use to advantage. But don't expect us to pay for putting it up. You ought to have enough to look after that yourself.
11. Settlement must be made for each game as it is played. We positively will not wait until the end of the series.[68]

Some writers have noted Masko's skillful entrepreneurship in managing the Mikado team, but they have neglected to note that Masko followed Green's team rules and example, learning exhibition team management from a ticket-booth master.[69] The Mikado team, now known as an early Issei (first-generation immigrant) team, won the Northwest Japanese Baseball championship in Seattle in 1911 and continued to play into the 1920s.[70]

Less successful as a barnstorming attraction, apparently, was the Hawaiian baseball team that Green organized in 1913, as few records exist of the team. It too seems to have been inspired by another foreign team, in this case the Chinese baseball team of Hawaii, which made headlines for its tours of the United States in 1912 and 1913. The "Chinese Nine," managed by A. Arkana, was a college team of Chinese players from Hawaii that defeated most of its U.S. college opponents, wowing fans and enduring a gruelling schedule.[71] This time Green travelled to Hawaii in the winter of 1912 and recruited players himself from colleges and semi-pro leagues. Dan Tobey, in his last stint with a Guy Green team, was the road manager, and he described the Hawaiians as "expert swimmers and musicians" who played the game of baseball with "remarkable brilliance and dash."[72] The team began its tour in June and played into September. *The Lima (Ohio) Gazette* referred to the team as "intelligent savages who performed great stunts with ball and bat in their native haunts before being brought to the United States by Colonel Green."[73] Such prejudiced appraisals of their teams were hardly new to Green and Tobey. Overall, the team failed to compete with the headlines generated by the Chinese team, and Green's final baseball venture lasted only a single season.

The Lincoln Greenbackers

At his pinnacle as a baseball magnate, Green was the owner of both the Nebraska Indians and the Western League franchise (Class A) in Lincoln. He purchased the Lincoln club from James "Ducky" Holmes on September 28, 1907, and became, for the first time, a baseball owner with a home field, the M Street Park.[74] While the Nebraska Indians may have been a more profitable business, ownership of the Lincoln team meant Green had moved into the small circle of midwest business men who were prosperous enough to serve their cities as baseball magnates. Green pledged to make the Lincoln franchise, now known as the Greens or the Greenbackers, successful, and part of his plan was to use his most talented players from the Nebraska Indians, including pitcher George Howard Johnson and infielder Billy Smith. He also signed another Native player, former major league outfielder Frank Jude, to his team, and hired Billy Fox as his manager. Green opened the 1908 season with great fanfare. "Get ready for the big show," the *Nebraska State Journal* reported, "Guy W. Green, president of the Lincoln club, announces a rather imposing program for initial day. The game is to be preceded by a parade in which the Lincoln and Sioux City players are to make the rounds of the principal streets of the Nebraska capitol seated in tallyho coaches. At the head of the process, also in coaches, will be the new state band, which will later regale the cranks [i.e., fans] with harmonious music at the park. Governor Sheldon is down on the program to pitch the first ball."[75] Not only was Green initiating his season in Nebraska Indians fashion with a parade, but he was clearly exhibiting his local pride as president and owner. In fact, in the 1909 season, he would violate his own money-making principle out of public spiritedness and offer free game tickets to up to 8,000 Lincoln public school students with attendance certificates.[76]

No longer traveling with his Nebraska Indians, Green, however, was faced with the daily headlines in *Lincoln Evening News* and *Nebraska State Journal*, which did not always speak well of his Greenbackers. For the first season since 1897, he was confronted by a middle-of-the-road team (they finished 74–73 in 1908) and some disenchanted fans. A Lincoln sports-page poet gibed:

The Greenbackers

There was a "Guy," he came to town —
We guess he came to win —
But for a while it looked as if
His chances were "durned" slim,
When "Jack" and "Bill" and "Gag" and "Fen"
Who always had been it,
Right up till thirty days ago
Could seldom make a hit.
The fans were sad as every day
They rooted all in vain,
While ciphers on the big black-board
Told how each hope was slain.[77]

And while the verse depicted Green's team more bleakly than their league record indicated, it was clearly a different kind of business from exhibition baseball. As the 1908 season concluded in early September, the team was left with dwindling attendance and no hope for the league penant. Green briefly considered cancelling the final games against Pueblo, but relented to fan pressure: "Guy Green announced yesterday that the Lincoln club would play out its full home schedule ... even if there are only a dozen persons at the park."[78]

And if 1908 was somewhat disappointing for the Lincoln fans, 1909 was extremely so. The pitching staff was thin and hitting was anemic, and the team began to fade early in the standings. The Greenbackers would finish with a 61–89 record, beside Pueblo in the cellar of the Western League. Although Green again began the season with good fan support, the crowds were dwindling quickly when he decided to sell the team in July of 1909. Green claimed to the newspapers he had made of profit of $3000 by July of 1909, but the prospects looked poor when the team was purchased by Don Despain and Lowell Stoner on July 8. The paper stated that "Mr. Green is to retire to devote his full time to the direction of his Nebraska Indian club."[79] There was some irony in that determination, however, as Green would soon find the landscape changed considerably for the Nebraska Indians.

The Sale of Green's Nebraska Indians

Although the Nebraska Indians continued to play well in 1909 and 1910, with Dan Tobey still in charge as player-manager, changes were impending that would make ownership of the team more difficult. First, the most prestigious of the federal Indian boarding schools, Carlisle Institute, ended its baseball program in January 1910. The superintendent, Moses Friedman, decided to cancel the program because talented players so often dropped out of the school when they signed with teams like the Nebraska Indians. Also, and equally important for Carlisle, the play of talented Native athletes with professional baseball teams endangered the amateur athletic status of the school's famous runners and football players, as Jim Thorpe would later rue. So began the movement to deemphasize baseball at the federal boarding schools, which would catch up with Haskell Institute some years later.[80] Second, and much closer to home, was another trend in professional baseball: the organization of town teams into professional leagues with ties to the National Association. One notices clearly in the sports pages of the 1910s that the Nebraska State League and the Missouri-Iowa-Nebraska-Kansas League (MINK), for instance, received coverage in columns that once had been the columns of devoted to the Nebraska Indians. Both were Class D leagues in the National Association, and both began in 1910 with ten Nebraska teams represented between them. Significantly, the Nebraska State League teams included Seward and Fremont, two of the Nebraska Indians' favorite competitors early in the baseball season, and the MINK League included Auburn, another long-time opponent.[81] Furthermore, the National Association of Professional Baseball Leagues (commonly known as minor league baseball) made its own strictures and financial assessments concerning exhibition games.

Dan Tobey returned from California in the spring of 1910 with some promising Native athletes he had recruited on the West Coast, and he began working out with the team in Crete, Nebraska, where they scrimmaged Doane College. But at about this time the Lincoln paper was reporting signs of trouble: "Don Despain had a half notion to book the Indians for an exhibition bout at the local park for next Friday, but decided to leave the date open."[82] Lincoln's M Street Park was usually a big early season gate for the Nebraska Indians, but not so in 1910. Then, in an even more disturbing development, the Seward team cancelled its game against the Nebraska Indians after Green had already collected ticket receipts. He was forced to return the gate money. While playing in Auburn, Nebraska, Green then received the most troubling news yet — a telegram from the National Association secretary, J.H. Farrell, stating that if he wished to play his game against the Auburn team, he would be required to pay $100. He did pay the fee but said that he did so "under coercion." [83] Secretary Farrell also chose to fine Green $100 for violations of National Association rules and to censure his conduct in the National Association bulletin.

Overnight, the Nebraska Indians went from being one of biggest drawing cards that could come to a city like Freemont or Auburn to a pariah club that minor league teams feared to play. The newspapers were siding with the minor league teams (who saw strong independent teams as unwelcome competition) in squeezing out coverage of the Nebraska Indians. Green saw the writing on the wall for the Nebraska Indians in 1910, but it wasn't until the end of the 1911 season that he was able to arrange a sale. The same team that had drawn crowds in thousands in Chicago, Indianapolis, and other cities was now struggling to draw crowds in the hundreds. Green was also struggling to make payroll for the team.

In January of 1912, Green sold the Nebraska Indians to James E. Beltzer of Lincoln, for a mere $400, and he filed both federal and state lawsuits against the National Association and the Western League. Defendants in the suit included Secretary Farrell, the individual members of the national arbitration board, and Western League president Norris O'Neill, whom Green argued "damaged plaintiff to the extent of $50,000, and as a result Green was unable to secure games for his club the following year, being forced to sell his team." For the loss in the value of his team and his own damaged reputation, Green asked an additional $50,000, making it a $100,000 suit.[84] He was indeed serious about the lawsuit, serving O'Neill in Don Despain's offices in Lincoln, but Green was (in this case) on the losing side of baseball history.[85] Over the long term, the development of minor league baseball helped marginalize semi-pro and exhibition baseball teams such as the Nebraska Indians.

The Beltzers' Nebraska Indians

On Thursday morning, January 18, 1912, the *Nebraska State Journal* announced: "James E. Beltzer of Arapahoe, formerly a University of Nebraska baseball player, completed arrangements with Green to assume the sole management of the Nebraska Indian baseball team for the coming year."[86] The sale to James Beltzer gave new life to the team, although it would never again have the kind of financial success it enjoyed under Green. James was a pitcher for the University of Nebraska team during the 1903 season, and he briefly owned another American Indian baseball team, known as the Oxford Indians, during the summer of 1908, with a partner named Quigles (or perhaps Quigley).[87] A surviving photograph shows the Oxford Indians dressed in fringed buckskin with bats held high, and it is clear from the photograph that James Beltzer hired many local white players as well Native players for the team.[88] The team soon gained a bad reputation in the press, however. A game in McCook, Nebraska, ended with a fan brawl: "Play was obstructed by spectators and [the] game discontinued."[89] In early June, the report in the *Hebron Champion* was even more troubling: "Comment on the game is unnecessary. Whoever plays with the indians may look for a dirty game."[90] But whatever James Beltzer's management troubles in 1908, by 1912 the *Nebraska State Journal* described him as "a capable man for the business end of the game," and the Nebraska Indians were his.[91]

Partnering with James was his younger and more famous brother, Oren "Buck" Beltzer. Buck was an athletic standout, playing half back and kicker for the University of Nebraska football team and third base for the Nebraska baseball team from 1905 to 1909. He captained both the football and baseball teams for the Cornhuskers in 1909. In 1910, he was the player-manager of the Grand Island team in the Nebraska State League, and his athletic prowess earned him a tryout with Connie Mack's Philadelphia A's in the spring of 1911, though he did not stick with the team.[92] While James Beltzer arranged the initial purchase of the Nebraska Indians, both he and Buck appear in the team photographs, and by 1914 Buck appeared in news stories as manager of the team. Buck's Nebraska baseball and football teammate Pip Cooke also played for the team in 1914 and served as assistant manager.[93] All three were linked closely to University of Nebraska athletics, and perhaps the single greatest difference from Green's teams to the Beltzers' teams was that the latter were more strongly identified with the Cornhuskers.

During the 1912 season, however, the team continued to play using trunks and team logos that bore Green's name, and were often still labeled as "Green's Nebraska Indians" in newspaper reports. In 1914, the team photo, with both Beltzer brothers, appeared in the *Reach American League Base Ball Guide* as "Green's Lincoln, Neb., Nebraska Indian Team."[94] In fact, as late as 1917 a sports story reported, mistakenly, that "the Indians are under the management of Guy W. Green."[95] And, to their credit, the Beltzers continued some of the most successful elements of Green's management: they played games in small towns excited to see the team; they staged player parades; they traveled the country from coast to coast; they charged 25 cents admission (sometimes 35 cents for better seats); they sold team postcards; and they encouraged town team managers to publish advertisements in their local papers. Also like Green, the Beltzers recruited successfully from federal American Indian boarding schools. Jessee Youngdeer of Carlisle and Thomas Reid of Haskell played on the 1912 team, Moses Poolah of Haskell played on the 1917 team, and Eli Stover of Haskell played on the 1918 team. Like Green, the Beltzers occasionally hired white players of professional ability. In 1912, for instance, Les Mann, a future major leaguer with the Boston Braves, appeared in an August boxscore for the Nebraska Indians.[96] And in 1913 it was Joe Brady, a big southpaw from Washington, D.C., who briefly pitched with the team before signing a minor league contract with the Oshkosh club in the Wisconsin-Illinois League.[97] Like Green's teams, the Beltzers' teams won, regularly outclassing the town and amateur teams they faced.

The Beltzers' Nebraska Indians, however, did have a different personality from Green's teams, and it is evident in team photographs. Instead of the dark baseball jerseys with white N.I. or Nebraska Indians lettering that Green's teams sported, the Beltzers purchased jerseys that had the appearance of buckskin and were heavily fringed on the sides of the arms and legs. They also touted their players' traditional Indian names — Big Chief, Comanche, White Bull, Whitehorn, Little Deer, Sweetgrass, for example — whether real or assumed. The team under the Beltzers was described more often as "red men" and "injuns" in the press, apparently as a result of the owners' desire to play up the exotic identities of the players. Ironically, though, the Native players on the Beltzers' teams appeared to be, even more often than on Green's teams, nattily dressed students from federal boarding schools [Figure 8].

Like both Beltzers and Cooke, the players had ties to the University of Nebraska. Bill Hosek, a Cornhusker in 1912 and 1913, played for the Nebraska Indians in 1914 (batting .300 in 130 games) and in 1915. Max Towle, the Cornhusker quarterback in 1913, joined the Nebraska Indians in 1915 as catcher, and he assembled a photo scrapbook that is an important source of

Figure 8: Three players from the Beltzers' 1915 team in Livermore, California. ***Max Towle Scrapbook. Courtesy of Ian Todd.***

information about the team.[98] The Towle scrapbook shows the new uniforms, the extensive travels of the team (from Lincoln to Paola, Iowa, to Fort Marion, Florida, to Livermore, California), the balance of Native and white players, and the horseplay of Towle and his friends. In one photo, two white players in bedsheets, wearing headdresses, appear to wrestle.[99] The increasing use of Nebraska players and dilution of Native talent did, however, present a clear problem for the team. As Cedar Rapids' *Evening Gazette* reported: "The Nebraska Indians baseball team ... includes some pure white pale faces."[100] And so one finds the Beltzers' teams playing before smaller crowds, playing less talented teams, and, ultimately, making smaller profits.

A number of the Beltzers' American Indian players were noteworthy athletes of professional ability. One remarkable player was William W. (Bill) Watkins, a lanky right-hander, born in Shoshone, Nevada, and of Shoshone ancestry, who played with the team for five seasons, from 1914 to 1918. Watkins had pitched for the Central League's Erie and Fort Wayne clubs in

1912 and 1913, respectively, but was signed by the Beltzers for 1914 and proved to be one of the team's best pitchers. "Much is expected of Watkins, the Indian slinger," wrote Waterloo's *Evening Courier* in 1915.[101] He was often referred to as "Chief Watkins" or "Big Chief Watkins" in press accounts [Figure 9]. His minor league career would continue into the 1920s with Chicago area teams, as Watkins played professional and semiprofessional baseball for forty years altogether.[102] Another such player was Tommy Natum, who played second base and shortstop for five seasons, from 1912 to 1916. In one game report in 1915, Natum "poled three hits. One of his drives was a triple, being interposed when the Indians had three runners on the paths."[103] Another long-time fixture for the Beltzers' was Cherokee first baseman Scotty Sweetgrass, who also filled in as catcher and outfielder, playing for the team on and off from 1912 to 1918. A game report in the *Atlanta Constitutio*n in 1915 read, "Sweet Grass led in the hitting for the Indians with a home run."[104] A talented infielder and pitcher, Moses Poolaw (or Poolah), was a Choctaw student at Haskell whom the Beltzers recruited for the 1917 team. He was leading the team in hitting in July, when superintendent H.B. Peairs at Haskell ordered him to return to the school. Poolaw would later pitch for the Southern Association's Little Rock Travelers club in 1921.[105] And last there was Ben Green, who played with the team in 1916 and signed the next season with the Janesville Janes in the Wisconsin-Illinois Leagues in 1919. The *Janesville Daily Gazette* celebrated: "Green will be useful in more ways than one. He is a bearcat personified at the bat. In stiff practice he bunted or knocked out a long hit, just as he chose, and irrespective of the wishes of the hurler.... Green is a ball player through and through. He can hit, field, run like lightning and knows the INSIDE of the game. Watch him!"[106]

In the six seasons that they owned and managed the team, the Belterz' extensive schedules and impressive records compare favorably with those of Green, although the crowds, press coverage, and team competition were all diminished by factors beyond the brothers' control. Lincoln's loss of a Western League club in 1918 and the Beltzers' desire to manage teams in Nebraska led to a change in ownership in the spring of 1918. The sale of the team was announced on April 14, 1918. The Beltzers sold the Nebraska Indians to a group of three Lincoln friends, Charles N. Moon, W.G. Kline, and Mike Allen. Moon was the former secretary of the Lincoln Western League team in 1915 and a business partner of James Beltzer. Moon had also purchased the M Street Park, and the deal with the Beltzers was apparently made to find a home team for the park. Kline, the athletic director of Wesleyan University, and Mike Allen had both traveled with the Nebraska Indians during the 1917 season, with Allen serving as the team's director and spokesman.

So it was Allen who announced that the team would play at M Street Park. Quoted in the *Lincoln Daily Star* (under the triumphant headline "Nebraska Indians Coming Back Home"), Allen said: "The Indians are not a bunch of bushers, but a reall ball clubs. The team we shall have this year will be capable of holding its own with the clubs in the Western league. We are in touch with a dozen or more of the most proficient Indian ball players in America and shall bring the best of the bunch to Lincoln to play on our team."[107]

Figure 9: W.W. Watkins, known as "Big Chief," a star pitcher and third baseman on the Beltzers' teams from 1914 to 1918. *Max Towle Scrapbook. Courtesy of Ian Todd.*

The story went into some detail, listing eight players who had already been signed (including Watkins, Poolaw, Sweetgrass, and Stover), and setting opening day for the team's season on Sunday, May 5. "The success of the venture," it was declared, "is scarcely open to doubt."[108]

Despite the certainty of the *Daily Star*

article, the future of the 1918 team was very much open to doubt. Moon was being urged to reserve the M Street Park for various teams — the Nebraska Indians, the Lincoln Cleaners, and a possible new Lincoln entry in the Western League or Nebraska State League. Apparently, Moon, Kline, and Allen decided not to go ahead with their plans for the Nebraska Indians in Lincoln in 1918, as it was the Lincoln Cleaners who played as home team in the M Street Park later that season. After April 14, the newspapers fell silent about the Nebraska Indians. Sometime later, Bill Watkins resumed semipro and minor league ball in Illinios, Moses Poolaw pursued his minor league career, and the other players went their separate ways. Meanwhile, the Beltzers and Moon made plans for a Nebraska State League team in Lincoln, building Landis Field, named in honor of the major league commissioner.[109] Buck would serve as the Lincoln team manager from 1922 to 1924, and James served as the Nebraska State League president later in the 1920s and early 1930s. Buck would later become president of the Grand Island Trust Company and the Home Federal Savings and Loan Association, contributing generously to University of Nebraska athletics.[110] The Nebraska Indians would re-emerge in 1921, but under unknown ownership [Figure 10].

Nebraska Indians Team Owners

Guy W. Green, 1897–1912
James and oren (Buck) Beltzer, 1912–1918
Charles Moon, W.G. Kline, and Mike Allen, 1918
Unknown, 1921–1923, 1925–1928
Pat Kelsey, Original Nebraska Indians, 1924
Edward Hamman, 1931–1932

Figure 10: Nebraska Indians Team Owners.

The Nebraska Indians of the 1920s

After a lapse of several seasons, the Nebraska Indians reorganized and began play again in 1921 and continued (with a hiatus in 1924) through 1928, with a team of some of Haskell's best athletes. The players on the team were often featured in game stories and box scores, but the ownership of the team went unmentioned [Figure 9]. One article in 1923 refers to a "field captain" named Joe McCarthy, a white outfielder who apparently served as player-manager (and might have been longtime minor leaguer Joseph Vincent McCarthy) but his name does not appear elsewhere.[111] Like Green's best teams, the 1920s team toured in Iowa, Illinois, Indian, Ohio, and ventured east. In the season of 1923, they also played in Michigan, Pennsylvania, New York, New Jersey, Delaware, Rhode Island, Connecticut, Massachusetts, New Hampshire, and as far away as Keene, Maine.[112] A large advertisement in the *Keeene Evening Sentinel* announced the game:

> Best Baseball Attraction of the Season
> Full Blood Indians Coming to Keene
> Saturday Afternoon, 3:15
> Nebraska Indians vs. Keene White Sox
> Emerald Street Grounds will be the scene of the same Indians that are playing all the best semi-pro clubs through New England. The only Indian Team on the road. Don't miss this first class and high priced attraction.[113]

At 50 cents, the admission price in Keene was high for 1923. In addition to steeper admission charges for the Nebraska Indians, the 1920s team sported new uniforms without the old-fashioned collars of Green's uniforms and without the buckskin and fringe of the Beltzers' costumes. The uniforms were very much like those of major leaguers of the day, light in color, with dark knee-length socks, a dark belt. A dark letter *I* was centered stylishly in the middle of a large, dark *N* on the left side of the jersey and on the caps. They also featured a new mode of transportation, as the 1923 team travelled 16,000 miles entirely by automobile, cramming all its players in a Stutz and a Packard.[114] And the players were now lodging in hotels, no longer camping on baseball grounds. Less frequently, but still on occasion, the 1920s team would revive the old ritual of parading through town streets: "Tommy Mee [the local team manager] has made arrangements with the Indian management to have the Indian club parade the important streets of Englewood Sunday afternoon just before the game."[115] Although the papers still advertised the team as "genuine full blooded ... Indians," the 1920s teams attracted more emphasis for the athleticism and less for the exoticism of the players. In a word, the new Nebraska Indians team looked decidedly more modern.

Whoever the owners and promoters of the team in the 1920's, they managed to schedule the Nebraska Indians against some of the best independent teams in the country, including Negro League teams such as the

Homestead Grays (for a doubleheader at Forbes Field in 1925) and the Union Giants of Chicago. In newspapers, the team was billed as "one of the greatest attractions in semipro baseball" and the "best touring team in the U.S."[116] Although the team did not always live up to its billing, the Nebraska Indians of this period were a well-run organization, booking bigger engagements than the Beltzers had been able to, and with better press coverage.

The new management of the team also led to some changes in team personnel. Whereas University of Nebraska players often filled in on the Beltzers' teams, they were nowhere to be found on the teams of the 1920s. Nor did those teams play many games at all in the state of Nebraska. And, strikingly, the team became even more closely allied with Haskell Institute and its best athletes: "The Nebraska Indians have one of the fastest teams in the middle west and formerly were on the Haskell Institute team in Kansas."[117] The elimination of the Carlisle baseball program and the closure of Carlisle Indian School in 1918 had forced the Nebraska Indians, to recruit more heavily from Haskell Institute in Lawrence, Kansas, where they found Tom Thorpe, Sandy Timothy, Willie Wishkeno, Anthony Wapp, Leo Wapp, Lee Daney, and a player known as "Dixon" (possibly Joseph Pappio or Elijah Smith).

Thorpe was a relative of the famous Jim Thorpe and played catcher and first base for Haskell and first base for the Nebraska Indians in 1923.[118] Sandy Timothy was a football and track star at Haskell who played catcher for the Nebraska Indians in 1923, 1925, and 1926.[119] Willie "Chok Tock" Wishkeno played steady infield for Haskell, and for the Nebraska Indians in 1923 and 1925, and was described as "a red flash on short."[120] The two Wapp brothers, of the Potawatomi people of Mayetta, Kansas, played first base (Anthony, or "Tony") and second base (Leo) with the Nebraska Indians in 1925 and 1926. Leo, known as "Running Hawk," would also play professional basketball with Jim Thorpe on a team known as "Thorpe's Indians"[121]; Tony (who was 6'5", 210 pounds), a basketball star for Haskell, would go on to play semi-professional basketball with the House of David team and professional baseball in the Western Association from 1931 to 1935.[122] The big Choctaw pitcher Lee Daney would play briefly with the Philadelphia Athletics in 1928, but he played with the Nebraska Indians in 1923 and 1925 under the psuedonym "Chief Whitehorn": "George Whit[e]horn, a 200-pound big handed third base-guardian who is the life of the team in pepper, and is always talking and chattering to his team mates in field play and at the bat.... [A] clever base runner among a team of base runners he is well worth seeing."[123] And another Haskell athlete played outfield on the 1926 Nebraska Indians under the name Dixon and won enthusiastic reviews: "Dixon, the big Indian from the Lawrence, Kansas, Indian school was easily the star of the day.... Dixon was the 'galloping buffalo' with his long easy strides that carried over a wide expanse of the outfield territory, robbing the Oelwein hitters of base knocks by sensational catches that he made look like child's play. Reaching over the barbwire fence in left field he picked off Weyant's long fly. Then coming off in behind short he caught off his shoe strings for one of the nicest catches ever made on the local field." Whoever "Dixon" was — Eli Smith, Pappio, or another player — he was one of the talented Haskell athletes who made the Nebraska Indians of the 1920s a competitive baseball team.

Two other Native players worth noting on these Nebraska Indians teams were not from Haskell but were players of professional ability. Creek pitcher John Wesley, who was known for constantly smiling from the mound at opposing batters, especially in tight moments in a game, pitched for the team and went undefeated for much of the summer of 1923: "Who will be the first team to win a game against John Wesley?" read Zaneville's *Times Recorder*.[124] After leaving the Nebraska Indians, Wesley would continue to play pro and semipro baseball for the rest of the decade. Potawatomi outfielder Eugene (Gene) Wano of Konawa, Oklahoma, played outfield on the 1925 team and was a player of "speed, spectacular fielding, and hitting power" who was a "10-second man on the cinder paths."[125] Wano, who played with James Wilkinson's famous All-Nations team in Kansas City in 1927, would continue playing professional baseball in Oklahoma into the middle of the 1930s.[126] As before, the Nebraska Indians of the decade also sometimes hired white players to fill in, including minor league pitcher Glenn Ropp and semipro pitcher Chinese Brown.[127]

In sum, these Nebraska Indians appear to have had a lower winning percentage (reported at .658 in 1925) than the teams of earlier decades, and worse, they were embarrassed by some of the best Negro League and semipro teams of the day.[128] The strong Fitchberg, Massachusetts, team pummeled them, 17–2, in 1923, and the Massilon, Ohio, Agathons routed them, 20–2, in 1925. The thin roster of the squad and dependence on Haskell athletes were limiting factors. The team nevertheless managed to whip up excitement and sizeable crowds in both big and small towns. "The Nebraska

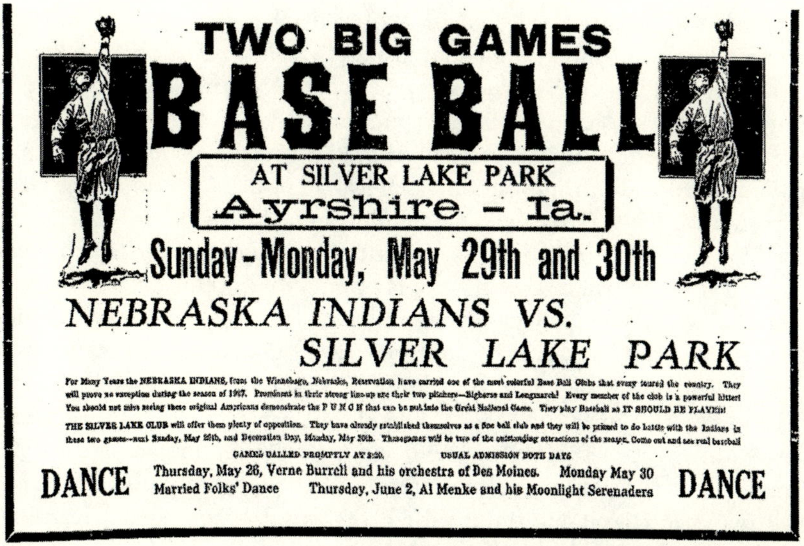

Figure 11: The Nebraska Indians advertised to play in Silver Lake Park, Iowa, early in the 1927 season. *Jeffrey Beck.*

Indians ... one of the most colorful Base Ball clubs that ever toured the country" proclaimed an ad in a 1927 Iowa newspaper [Figure 11]. Although the team seems to have collapsed in Nebraska and South Dakota in the late summer of 1928, the "colorful" claim was still quite true.[129]

Pat Kelsey's Nebraska Indians

The success and notoreity of the Nebraska Indians, starting with Green's teams, kept the baseball team going under new owners for decades and inspired other would-be sports owners to organize their own teams and call them the Nebraska Indians. One such team owner was Pat Kelsey, a talented baseball player from a troubled family of the Winnebago people of Nebraska. Pat Kelsey, along with his brothers Archie and Ben, all played for the Waterloo club in the Mississippi Valley League in 1925, and Pat had signed a contract with Sioux City of the Western League in 1924 only to see the team fold.[130] Off the field, the brothers sometimes ran afoul of the law, as when the *Palo Alto Reporter* reported in 1923 that Charles, Ben, and Pat were arrested for public intoxication and disorderly conduct: "All have the reputation of being bad characters, it was said. Charles Kelsey is an ex-convict."[131] But whatever the Kelsey brothers' reputation, Pat knew that he had a good part of an American Indian baseball team in his family alone; he could play both outfield and infield positions, Ben was an outfielder, and Archie was a lefthanded pitcher. After the Sioux City team went bust in 1924, he advertised for more players for his own American Indian team: "Kelsey's original Nebraska Indian ball club wants to play games in central Kansas from September 11 to 21. After playing here the manager wants to collect some Indian players from the Southwestern and journey to the coast. Anyone wishing games write Pat Kelsey, manager, Kelsey's Nebraska Indians baseball club, Millard Hotel, Omaha, Nebr."[132] The idea of a native baseball team with native ownership was an exciting one, but few American Indians of the 1920s had the capital to support such a venture. Although it appears that Pat Kelsey was unable to recruit and travel with a Nebraska Indians baseball team late in 1924, his brother Archie Kelsey did recruit and briefly play with a basketball team of Winnebago players known as the Nebraska Indians in the winter of 1925–1926.[133] Sadly, all the Kelsey brothers' plans for Nebraska Indians athletic teams ended — when in 1927 Archie was arrested for robbing a gas station and when in 1928 Pat was arrested for stealing and stripping an automobile — along with "three Indians, all baseball stars."[134]

Ed Hamman's Nebraska Indians

The last of the Nebraska Indians touring teams was organized in 1931 and was not centered in Nebraska at all, but in Van Wert, Ohio, by baseball comedian and clown Ed Hamman. Hamman was a vivacious, 5'5" infielder who broke into semipro ball during his teens in Van Wert and would thrive in baseball for the rest of his life. In 1925, Hamman had been making $60 a month playing minor league baseball, but he received an offer in 1926 of $200 a month to join the bearded House of David barnstorming team from Benton Harbor, Michigan. He promply grew a beard and began his life's work as a baseball vaudevillian.[135] In 1931, with the Nebraska Indians now defunct, Hamman saw an opportunity to resurrect the team, and he did so in barnstorming circus style. He managed to hire a number of

Haskell's athletes, including the most famous native athlete in the country, John Levi, for a short stint, and he filled out the team with the kind of baseball circus performers that had made the House of David famous. Hamman played third base and other infield positions for the team, but he was instrumental in managing the team's business and in directing the team's antics. Like the House of David, Hamman's Nebraska Indians now specialized in lightning games of pepper before the baseball started, in shadowball (slow motion baseball plays without a baseball), in circus-style juggling, and in clowning of all kinds. As the *Saint Vincent College Journal* reported, "The visitors were the best novelty attraction of the year with their pepper game and novelty acts between innings."[136]

Alongside Levi, who was an All-American full-back at Haskell and a baseball player of major league ability, Hamman's biggest attraction was the white center fielder Dick McKay, a juggler formerly with Ringling Brothers who worked to "enthuse young and old with his marvelous showmanship."[137] And the team's smallest attraction was "Kewpie" Taylor, "a midget southpaw pitcher standing 4 feet 7 inches, in his moccasins, [who] might be mistaken by many fans for a papoose. However, this young Taylor of the Chippewa tribe, is a hurler of note and the many fans who have watched him perform through the country wonder where the dwarf obtains his speedy fast ball."[138] The comic atmosphere was augmented by Hamman's coaching staff, dressed "in full regalia on the coaching lines."[139] Hamman, known as "Circus Ed," was an inveterate jokester and entertainer who became one of baseball's best-known clowns in the 1940s and 1950s, appearing in clownface with an oversized bat and a trained duck named Susie and throwing the ball backhanded for long distances.[140] Under Hamman, the team played more than 130 games in 1931, on a westward tour, and started the 1932 season early on Hamman's home diamond in Van Wert, donating the proceeds of the first game to the town team for its baseball uniforms.[141] The team played a total of 157 games in 1932, touring in 27 states and Canada.[142] Like Green, Hamman was a capable business man, and he adapted to the difficult conditions of the Depression with innovation. One such innovation was the use of portable lighting equipment to play at night on the road, enabling the team to play more games. However, he admitted that in one series in 1932, his Nebraska Indians team "played before eight paid admissions [i.e., eight paying fans] on a Sunday afternoon in Berks County, Penn."[143]

Hamman organized a basketball team called the Nebraska Indians during the winter of 1932–1933, but just as suddenly began a new business venture with business partner Syd Pollock in the spring of 1933. With Pollock, a promoter and booking agent from New York, he organized another baseball team known as the Canadian Clowns, which toured across the country. He would later work as a clown with the Canadian House of David, Havana's La Paloma baseball club, and the Indianapolis Clowns of the Negro Leagues, which he eventually owned. He was the inspiration of Bill Heward's book *Some Are Called Clowns*, and he served as an advisor for the movie *Bingo Long's Traveling All-Stars* in 1976.[144] Although Hamman's ownership of the Nebraska Indians was only a short two seasons in the midst of the Depression, it seems fitting that Green's team, one of the first successful barnstorming teams, would eventually be owned by the last great barnstormer.

Green's Later Life and Career

After his sale of the Nebraska Indians in 1912 and ownership of the Native Haiwaiians in 1913, Guy Green ended his career as a baseball barnstormer. He went on to form a real estate partnership with a Kansas City businessman named Sam Hawthorne, selling land in the Rio Grande Valley. He also dabbled in photography and early film technology, attempting to found a "motion picture film exchange" in Lincoln.[145] In the early 1920s, he joined the staff of the *American Hereford Journal* (a livestock trade publication) as a photographer and editor, and he began to refer to himself as a journalist: "The way newspaper men are kicked around," he wrote, "I am convinced that most of the world does not regard them as human."[146] Hereford Publications was based in Kansas City, Missouri, and Green relocated his family there. His son Guy Green, Jr., would eventually follow his father into law and become a well-known Kansas City attorney.

Above all, Green's later life in Missouri was dominated by his work as a Presbyterian evangelist. Well known as a speaker, Green began giving talks (less formal than sermons or lectures) first to Sunday school classes, then to churches, and then to all manner of civic clubs and organizations. Dressed in tie and suspenders, with round spectacles and a wide grin, Green joked with audiences and delivered messages with titles such as "We Do Not Well," "Men of Your Size," "A Long Look Ahead," and "Trying Anything Once."

Chillicothe, Ohio's *Constitution Tribune* described Green as "an unusual type of evangelist or revivalist": "A varied career as baseball magnate, newspaperman, farm paper writer and perhaps even more occupations has increased the speaker's knowledge of human nature and given him an insight into many walks of life. This coupled with his ability to express himself clearly and interestingly has been responsible for the crowded auditoriums during his stay here."[147] Once again, Green was travelling and drawing large crowds throughout the Midwest and Western states. He was eventually ordained as a Presbyterian minister. Guy W. Green died in Kansas City on February 11, 1947, less than two years after his wife, Wilhelmina.[148] The publication of his baseball writings ensures, however, that the history of Green's Nebraska Indians teams will long survive him.

Notes

1. "Guy W. Green, Sr., Dies," *Kansas City Star,* 11 February 1947, p. 3, and "Stromsburg High School is Reviving Memories of Fifty Years Ago," *Sunday Journal and Star* (Lincoln, Neb.), 16 May 1937, p. 1.
2. Guy Wilder Green, Doane College Records. My thanks to Karen Morris of Doane College for this information.
3. "Doane Great in Athletics," *Nebraska State Journa*l (Lincoln, Neb.), 4 June 1922, p. 8.
4. "Guy W. Green, Sr., Dies," p. 3, and Guy Green, *The Nebraska Indians: A Complete History of The Nebraska Indian Base Ball Team,* 3rd ed. (Lincoln: Woodruff-Collins Printing Co., 1903), 4.
5. "A Liberal Education," *Lincoln (Neb.) Evening News,* 10 June 1897, p. 1.
6. "Law School Banquet," *Nebraska State Journal,* 10 June 1897, p. 8.
7. *The Nebraska Indians*, 4.
8. Ibid., 2.
9. Ibid., 4.
10. Guy W. Green, "Experiences with an Indian Ball Team," *Nebraska State Journal,* 20 December 1908, sec. C, p. 6.
11. *The Nebraska Indians*, 5.
12. *Ibid.*
13. "Experiences with an Indian Ball Team," sec. C, p. 6.
14. "University Team Sadly Scalped," *Nebraska State Journal*, 27 June 1897, p. 8.
15. *The Nebraska Indians*, 5–6.
16. "University Team Sadly Scalped," p. 8; "Sporting Resume," *Freemont Weekly Herald,* 22 June 1897, p. 4. *Evening News* 26 June 1897, p. 1; Guy W. Green, *Fun and Frolic with an Indian Ball Team*, 4th ed., (Lincoln: Woodruff-Collins Printing, 1907), 79.
17. "University Team Sadly Scalped," 8.
18. "Experiences with an Indian Ball Team," sec. C, p. 6.
19. *The Nebraska Indians*, 12.
20. "University Athletics," *Daily Iowa State Press* (Iowa City, Iowa), 23 April 1900, p. 5.
21. "Experiences with an Indian Ball Team," sec. C, p. 6.
22. Jeffrey P. Beck, *The American Indian Integration of Baseball* (Lincoln, Neb.: University of Nebraska Press, 2004), 209.

23. "Went Down to Defeat," *Weekly Arbor State* (Waymore, Neb.), 17 June 1898, p. 1.
24. *The Nebraska Indians*, 16–17.
25. *American Indian Integration*, 209–212.
26. "Indian Players in Demand," *Daily Review* (Decatur, Il.), 18 October 1904, p. 3.
27. *The American Indian Integration of Baseball*, 126.
28. "Notes of the Local Team," *Des Moines Daily News*, 22 September 1902, p. 8.
29. John Bentley, "May Be Wrong," *Nebraska State Journal*, 4 August 1939, p. 10.
30. "Notes of the Local Team," p. 54.
31. "Other Locals," *Headlight* (Stromsberg, Neb.), 25 April 1901, p. 4.
32. "Tecumseh vs. Indians," *Tecumseh (Neb.) Chieftain*, 4 May 1901, p. 4.
33. "Madison Practice," *La Crosse (Wisc.) Tribune*, 7 April 1908, p. 2.
34. *Fun and Frolic*, 38.
35. Ibid., 70.
36. "Sues Organized Baseball," *Fort Wayne (Ind.) Sentinel*, 13 January 1912, p. 8.
37. *The Nebraska Indians*, 3.
38. Ibid., 25.
39. Ibid., 31.
40. Ibid., 13.
41. Ibid., 48.
42. Ibid., 77.
43. Ibid., 3.
44. *Fun and Frolic*, 13.
45. Ibid., 37.
46. Ibid., 49.
47. Ibid., 9.
48. Ibid., 34.
49. "Western League," *Sporting Life*, 18 January 1908, p. 10.
50. *Fun and Frolic*, 55.
51. Ibid., 32.
52. "Raps Bleacher Jokesters," *Sioux City (Iowa) Journal*, 3 June 1909, p. 9.
53. *Fun and Frolic*, 20–21.
54. Ibid., 21–25.
55. Ibid., 20.
56. Mark Twain, *The Adventures of Huckleberry Finn* (New York: Random House, 1996), 197.
57. Vera V. Hirt, "In the Pictures," *Greensburg (Ind.) Daily News*, 26 June 1935, p. 5.
58. "Experiences with an Indian Ball Team," sec. C, p. 6.
59. *Fun and Frolic*, 66–68.
60. Ibid., 64.
61. "Experiences With an Indian Ball Team," sec. C, p. 6.
62. Guy W. Green, "My New Foe," *Lippincott's Monthly Magazine*, 68, no. 406 (October 1901): 471.
63. "Japanese Baseball Club to Assemble at Lincoln," *Lincoln Evening News*, 28 March 1906, p. 6.
64. Fred Merrifield, "Baseball in Japan," *Sporting Life*, 6 May 1905, p. 15.
65. "*Japan Times* Gone By: Baseball, Brothels and Unwelcome Photograph," *Japan Times*, 15 Sept. 1908. Online. *Japan Times Online* http://search.japantimes.co.jp/cgi-bin/fl20080921ec.html.
66. "Japanese Baseball Club to Assemble at Lincoln," p. 6.
67. Ibid., 6.
68. "*Japan Times Gone By*."
69. Serge Lescouarnec, "11 Rules of Mikado Baseball Team in 1908 Japan (via *Japan Times*),"

25 Sept. 1908. Online. *Serge the Concierge.* http://www.sergetheconcierge.com/2008/09/11-rules-of-mik.html.

70. "Mikado baseball team with Northwest Japanese Baseball Tournament trophy, Seattle, 1911," photograph and caption. Online. Washington University Libraries Digital Collections, http://content.lib.washington.edu/cdm4/item_viewer.php?CISOROOT=/social&CISOPTR=655 (accessed 19 February 2009).

71. "Chinese Nine Coming Again," *Mansfield (Ohio) News*, 20 February 1913, p. 10.

72. *Lincoln Daily News*, 21 June 1913, p. 6.

73. "Speedy Hawaiin [*sic*] Islanders Battle Limaites Wednesday," *Lima (Ohio) Gazette*, 25 August 1913, p. 1.

74. "Where Will 'Ducky' Go?" *Waterloo (Iowa) Daily Courier*, 29 October 1907, p. 9.

75. "Scrap for Pennant Soon to Commence," *Nebraska State Journal*, 13 April 1908, Part 2, p. 11.

76. "Is Not Fault of Guy Green," *Nebraska State Journal*, 25 March 1909, p. 7.

77. "Gossip of the Western League," *Nebraska State Journal*, 7 June 1908, Part 2, p. 11.

78. "Give Lincolns Close Rub," *Nebraska State Journal*, 12 September 1908, p. 2.

79. "Franchise Has Been Sold," *Nebraska State Journal* 8 July 1909, p. 3.

80. *American Indian Integration of Baseball*, 47–48.

81. Bruce Esser, "Nebraska Minor League Baseball By League," Online. http://marian.creighton.edu/~besser/baseball/byleague.html (accessed 20 February 2009).

82. *Lincoln Evening News*, 13 April 1910, p. 8.

83. "Sues Organized Baseball," *Fort Wayne Sentinel*, 13 January 1912, p. 8; "National Board Sued," *Washington Post*, 31 January 1912, p. 8.

84. "Sues Organized Baseball," p. 8.

85. "The Western League," *Sporting Life*, 20 April 1912, p. 13.

86. "The Nebraska Indians," *Nebraska State Journal*, 18 January 1912, p. 3.

87. "Indian Ball Team Formed," *Nebraska State Journal*, 20 May 1908, p. 5.

88. "Oxford Indians, 1908." Photograph. Nebraska Historical Society, Lincoln, Nebraska.

89. "Spectators Break Up Game," *Nebraska State Journal*, 25 May 1908, p. 2.

90. "Hebron 5 Oxford Indians 4," *The Hebron (Neb.) Champion*, 12 June 1908, supplement, p. 1.

91. "The Nebraska Indians," *Nebraska State Journal*, 18 January 1912, p. 3.

92. *Lincoln Evening News*, 22 March 1910, p. 8. "Buck Beltzer '09 Gridder, Dead at 71," *Lincoln Star*, 24 September 1959, p. 21.

93. *Lincoln Daily News*, 21 Sept. 1914, p. 13. "Nebraska Indians Bring Home Bacon," *Lincoln Daily Star*, 21 September 1914, p. 10.

94. "Green's Lincoln, Neb. Indian Team," in *The Reach Official American League Base Ball Guide 1914*. (Philadelphia: A.J. Reach Company, 1914), 458.

95. "Nebraska Indians Here Today for Game With Independents," *Lima (OH) Daily News*, 9 September 1917, p. 8.

96. "Indians Beat A.I.&S. Team," *Lebanon (Penn.) Daily News*, 5 August 1912, p. 8.

97. "Oshkosh Gets Indian Heaver," *Racine (Wisc.) Journal News*, 3 June 1913, p. 21.

98. "Hosek Has Big Bunch of Respect for Alexander," *Lincoln Daily Star*, 13 January 1915, p. 1.

99. *Max G. Towle Scrapbook*, Lincoln, Nebraska, 1915. Courtesy of Ian Todd of Toronto, Canada.

100. *Evening Gazette* (Cedar Rapids, Iowa), 15 May 1913, p. 2.

101. "Watkins Looks Good," *Waterloo (Iowa) Evening Courie*r, 8 April 1915, p. 10.

102. "William Watkins," obituary, *Suburbanite Economist* (Chicago, Ill.), 16 November 1966, p. 34.

103. "Cleaners Easy for Indians," *Nebraska State Journal*, 3 May 1915, p. 3.

104. "Indians 10, Tennille 2," *Atlanta Constitution*, 24 July 1915, p. 8.

105. "Nebraska Indians Coming Back Home," *Lincoln Daily Star*, 14 April 1918, pp. 1, 5–6. "Bush League Bingles," *Pittsburgh Post*, 3 April 1921, sec. 3, p. 2.

106. "More Good Luck," *Janesville (Wisc.) Daily Gazette*, 24 April 1919, p. 12.

107. "Nebraska Indians Coming Back Home," p. 1.

108. Ibid., 6.

109. "Buck Beltzer, '09 Gridder, Dead at 71," *Lincoln Star*, 24 September 1959, p. 21.

110. Ibid.

111. "Nebraska Indians Play Greys at Mark Park This Evening," *Times Recorder* (Zanesville, Oh.), 13 September 1923, p. 9.

112. "Fast Nebraska Indians Expect to Defeat Locals," *Times Recorder* (Zanesville, Oh.), 12 September 1923, p. 10.

113. "Nebraska Indians vs. Keene White Sox," advertisement, *Keene (Maine) Evening Sentinel*, 24 August 1923.

114. "Fast Nebraska Indians," p. 10.

115. Ibid., p. 4.

116. "Nebraska Indians Will Play Normals," *Englewood Economist* (Chicago, Ill.), 22 June 1921, p. 4. "Fast Nebraska Indians," p. 10.

117. "Nebraska Indians Will Play Marion on Bunny Grounds," *Cedar Rapids (Iowa) Republican*, 22 June 1925, p. 11.

118. "Nebraska Indians Play Greys at Mark Park This Evening," p. 9.

119. Ibid., p. 9.

120. Ibid., p. 9.

121. "Senators to Meet Powerful Foe in Thorpe's Indians," *Charleston (W. Va.) Gazette*, 16 January 1927, p. 21.

122. Anthony (Tony) Wapp, The Sporting News Player File, Sporting News Archive, 1931–1935; *The Indian Leader* (Haskell University), 27 April 1934, p. 5.

123. "Nebraska Indians Play Greys at Mark Park This Evening," p. 9.

124. "Undefeated," *Times Recorder* (Zanesville, Ohio), 12 September 1923, p. 10.

125. "Nebraska Indians Play Greys at Mark Park This Evening," p. 9.

126. "Locals Arrange Exhibition Game," *New Castle (Penn.) News*, 16 July 1927, p. 12.

127. "Glenn Ropp Is Sold to Robins," *Lima (Ohio) News*, 23 August 1927, p. 9. "Nebraska Indians Play Greys at Mark Park This Evening," 9.

128. "Nebraska Indians Play Elks This Afternoon," *Morning Herald* (Uniontown, Penn.), 21 July 1925, p. 10.

129. "Semi-pro Baseball: Indians on Roadtrip," *Nebraska State Journal*, 24 July 1928, p. 12.

130. "Hawkeye-Fuls," *Waterloo (Iowa) Evening Courier*, 30 October 1924, p. 12.

131. "Indians Battle With Officers," *Palo Alto Reporter* (Emmetsburg, Iowa), 18 October 1923, p. 6.

132. *Emporia Gazette* (Emporia, Kans.), 19 August 1924, p. 6.

133. "Nebraska Indian Cagers May Play Here Next Month," *Waterloo (Iowa) Evening Courier*, 18 December 1925, p. 17; "Indian Team Wins," *Sioux City (Iowa) Journal*, 14 January 1926, p. 9.

134. "Pat Kelsey Faces Federal Charges on Automobile Theft," *Waterloo (Iowa) Evening Courier*, 3 March 1928, p. 2.

135. Harold Seymour, *Baseball: The People's Game* (Oxford: Oxford University Press, 1990), 275.

136. "St Vincent vs. Nebraska Indians," *St. Vincent College Journal* (La Trobe, Penn.), vol. XLI, no. 9 (June 1932): 2.

137. "Travelling Team Has Made Great Record in Past," *La Crosse (Wisc.) Tribune and Leader-Press*, 22 July 1932, p. 7.

138. Ibid., p. 7.

139. Ibid., p. 7.

140. Gil Gilmore, "Sports Notes," *Tri-City Herald* (Pasco, Wash.), 15 July 1952, p. 9.

141. 142. *Van Wert Daily Bulletin* (Van Wert, Ohio) 30 November 1932, p. 4.

143. "Things You Might Like to Know About Clown Ed Hamman," Kansas City Monarchs and Indianapolis Clowns Program (Indianapolis, 1954), p. 8. Library of Congress, Branch Rickey Papers.

144. Bill Heward, *Some Are Called Clowns: A Season with the Last of the Great Barnstorming Baseball Teams* (New York: Crowell, 1974). James A. Riley, *The Biographical Encyclopedia of the Negro Baseball Leagues* (New York: Carroll & Graf, 1994), 350–351.

145. "Guy W. Green, Sr., Dies," p. 3.

146. "Presbyterians Plan Meetings," *Constitution Tribune* (Chillicothe, Mo.), 21 March 1929, p. 1.

147. "Guy Green," *Constitution Tribune* (Chillicothe, Mo.), 16 April 1929, p. 2.

148. "Guy W. Green, Sr., Dies," p. 3.

The Nebraska Indians:
A Complete History of
the Nebraska Indian
Base Ball Team

Dedication

I dedicate this book (excuse my gall)
    To him whose sporting pulses beat so high
He walks three miles to see a game of ball,
    A bright, expectant glitter in his eye;
To him who unregretful turns away
    From tinkling glasses served in cool retreats,
And uncomplaining fries for half a day
    Upon the torrid bleacher's hottest seats;
To him, who newly shaven, spic and span,
    In silence hears the umpire bellow, "Play,"
Then straightway changes to a crazy man,
    A raging, king-pin rooter come what may.
Yes, he's the man for whom I write this book;
    I know that he will read it, "ads" and all;
Will steal the time required, by hook or crook,
    Attracted by the magic words, "Base Ball."

Introduction

During the years that I have been connected with the "Nebraska Indians" as manager I have frequently felt the need of a book like this one. Everyone seems to be curious concerning the origin of the team, its history and its probable future. Wherever we played I have been assailed with questions of every imaginable character.

"What gave you the idea of organizing an Indian base ball team?" "Where did you get acquainted with your Indians?" "How long have your boys been with you?" "How many games have you played and how many have y you lost?" "Do you ever have any trouble with the Indians?" "What is the history of your players?" "Is this the only Indian team that has ever traveled?" I have listened to these and numerous other inquiries a thousand times if I have heard them once. It is with the intention of answering these questions that this little book has been written.

In penning these chapters I have endeavored to confine myself strictly to the truth. Some of the incidents described may seem improbable — even impossible; I ask you to remember, however, that "truth is stranger than fiction" and that the nomadic life of the base ball wanderer, while it may at time be hard and wearing on constitution and temper, is nevertheless filled with the hurry and change and excitement that make existence worth living.

If you are interested in the Indians as a disappearing race; in the attraction which I have the honor to manage; or in the national game of base ball, I am sure you will find something in these pages to repay you for their perusal. If, on the contrary, you care nothing for the Red Man or for the game which he plays under my direction, I still venture to hope that you will read the book solely for the book's sake. I am sure you can find worse reading, even though, I doubt not, you can find better.

THE AUTHOR.

CHAPTER I

My Own Connection with Base Ball

I cannot remember a time when I was not interested in base ball.

As a boy of tender years I used to gaze with longing eyes from the school-room window to the grounds where the local games were played. Upon the occasion of a match game between my own town and some neighboring village only the fear of the professor's wrath kept me in the school room until the day's work was over. The minute the exercises were finished I flew to the diamond to join the howling mob that was assembled there.

I was captain and first baseman of the first "kid" nine my Nebraska home knew, and I continued to fill this exalted position until I graduated from high school and went to Doane College at Crete, Nebraska. During my Freshman year at college I played first base on the "scrub" team. During the next year I was captain and first baseman of the "scrubs." The following season found me captain of college team and still the guardian of the initial sack. During my last year I acted as captain, managed and caught for the Stromsburg, Nebraska, independent team. I caught, simply because there was no one else to fill the position, and while I was not a howling success as a windpad artist, I succeeded in throwing my arm "out" in an endeavor to head off venturesome base stealers. Ever since 1892 my arm has contained as much glass as the scrap pile of a queensware store.

In 1893 I entered the University of Iowa and for a short time played right field on the Varsity team. I was death on flies, but I had to carry the ball in as I couldn't throw it over fifty feet. I retired in disgust and at the earnest request of the captain after playing a few games.

I went back to Stromsburg, Nebraska, in 1894 and worked in the post-office at that point. I held that position until 1897, when I entered the Law department of the University of Nebraska, Lincoln. During my stay in Stromsburg I managed and captained the local nine and played first base. My arm was as bad as ever and the only way I ever got the ball from one corner of the diamond to the other was by running half way across and pushing the sphere the rest of the way.

I ceased playing base ball altogether in 1897, but have never lost my love for the sport. I consider it the king of athletic amusements. It demands more skill from those who play it successfully than any other outdoor game known to man. It has a hold on the American public that will never loosen. I confidently predict that the game will follow the flag around the world.

I graduated from the University of Nebraska in 1897 and at once organized the Nebraska Indians.

CHAPTER II

How I Became Interested in Indian Base Ball

STROMSBURG, Nebraska, where I was brought up, is situated about 30 miles southeast of Genoa. Genoa is the site of the Genoa Government Indian School. This is one of the foremost institutions for the education of the Red Man in the United States. The Loup river runs close to the grounds, the buildings are large, beautiful and well-kept, and teachers and pupils are happy and contented.

For many years the Genoa school has supported a base ball team. The team was at first very weak. But even then it occasionally contained a star player. Every "fan" in Nebraska has heard of Ed Hedges, the big Sioux, who pitched for the Genoa boys years ago and whose speed was something terrific. Then there was John Baptiste, a full-blood Winnebago, whose services were in demand all over Nebraska. Willie Weaver, the Chippewa, who was with my team last season, is the latest star to arise in the Genoa firmament of slab artists. For three years he has been a terror to neighboring teams.

The Genoa team gradually improved until in 1895 it was a very good one. In that year I was managing the Stromsburg nine. The Indian team and my team were close together, geographically speaking, and they frequently met in hotly contested games. Before the summer was over I knew most of the Genoa boys and

a great many of them knew me. When they played in Stromsburg I tried to make their stay pleasant. When we went to Genoa the Aborigines exerted themselves to show us a good time. I frequently attended their dances. I even played on the team once in a while when they happened to meet some outside aggregation during my visits to their school. I observed that even in Nebraska, where an Indian is not at all a novelty, a base ball organization composed of red men drew everyone who was alive. When the Indians came to Stromsburg, business houses were closed and men, women and children turned out *en. masse* to see the copper-colored performers corral the festive fly and chase the elusive grounder. I reasoned that if an Indian base ball team was a good drawing card in Nebraska, it ought to do wanders further east if properly managed. I accordingly determined to organize "The Nebraska Indians."

I went to the boys I knew and laid my scheme before them. They were willing to enlist under my banner but the government officers, under whose control the players lived, were not enthusiastic in their support of the enterprise. They were unwilling to permit their charges to go so far from home. Numerous other Indian teams had stranded on the rocks of adversity and the players had been compelled to walk home. Objections came thick and fast and one at a time I thought seriously of abandoning my scheme altogether.

Finally, however, I succeeded by numerous methods, which I will not tire your patience by describing, in signing a full team of red men, and the "Nebraska Indians" played their first game. We were ingloriously beaten by Wahoo, Nebraska. The score was 10 to 0.

CHAPTER III

Our 1897 Tour in Nebraska

As stated in the foregoing chapter, we open our 1897 season at Wahoo, Nebraska. Wahoo is a town of about 2,000 people situated thirty miles north of Lincoln. Their grounds, which were beautifully arranged and nicely fenced, were located only two blocks from the business center of the town. The crowds that came out to see the games were large and enthusiastic, and strange as it may seem, their sympathies were overwhelmingly in favor of the Indians. Sympathies availed nothing, however, and after being shut out the first day we were beaten the second. Score: Wahoo 10; Indians 5.

The manager of the University of Nebraska team, who had heard we were to be in Wahoo for two games, was present to see the second contest. He decided that the red men were strong enough to put up a good contest against Nebraska's chief educational institution, and accordingly booked my aggregation for Lincoln for Friday and Saturday, June 25 and 26.

Our disastrous experience at Wahoo is easily explained. Most of my players had come directly from their reservations to the place of opening. They were stiff from travel, were out of condition and lacking in practice. I was surprised to see them make as good a showing as they did.

From Wahoo we went to Fremont and astonished that city, which contains about 8,000 people, by defeating their crack team the first day 4 to 3. We were vanquished the second day 10 to 7 and left the town with plumage badly disarranged.

We went up against the State University team the day after we played Fremont and walloped the educational representatives 17 to 11. This was not a very good game but it showed that the Indians were comers and we were not at all discouraged when we were taken into camp by the University team in our next game by a score of 15 to 6. We did not win a game in Nebraska after leaving Lincoln, being beaten at Louisville, Springfield and Fort Crook.

Louisville, in '97, had probably the strongest team in Nebraska. B.

Jones, later with the Chicago Unions, was their star twirler, and his work in the box was reinforced by the efforts of two other fine pitchers. The team behind him was a "crackerjack" and it is little wonder that we failed to occupy first place on their score board. It was this same Louisville team that went to Omaha after playing us and defeated the Omaha Universities. The Universities were considered as good as any team in the west and it is said that Tobe Parmele, the Louisville manager, won a pot of money by the victory of his boys.

At the time we played Fort Crook the soldiers claimed to have as good a base ball nine as there was in the army. It was too fast for us at any rate. I shall never forget that game. We played it on a guarantee, and everyone about the fort, who was not bedfast, was present. The grounds were in beautiful shape. An awning for the officers and their wives had been erected on one side of the diamond. On the other side of the field the soldiers were assembled, rising tier upon tier along the entire length of the grounds. When the last man was out and the boys in blue were victorious, their joy was indescribable. It is due the soldiers to say that we never encountered a more gentlemanly lot of fellows. They exerted themselves to the utmost to make our stay pleasant and we remembered our meeting with them for many weeks.

We played at Fort Crook on June 30. The next day we left for Tabor, Iowa, where we were due to play at the Independence Day celebration on July 3rd.

CHAPTER IV

Our 1897 Tour Through Iowa

We crossed the Missouri river at Bellevue on a ferry boat, the "William J. Bryan." We drove all day on July 1st and until late in the afternoon on July 2nd. When we reached Tabor we found the citizens anxiously awaiting our appearance, as the ball game was their principal athletic attraction for the morrow and they did not want it to fail them. We were furnished an inviting spot for a camp ground and the people made us feel thoroughly at home. An immense crowd attended the celebration the next day and they were all at the game. Tabor had a fine team but the Indians were on their metal and won the game by a score of 15 to 9. The ball grounds were surrounded by a grove and the redskins batted ball after ball into the tree tops. During this game the grand stand fell by reason of the enormous weight placed upon it and men, women and children were thrown into a helpless, terrified, screaming mass. Strange to say, no one was seriously injured and after the excitement had subsided the game went on.

From Tabor we went south to Sidney. Sidney defeated us 12 to 11 after an exciting game. The next day we beat Hamburg 28 to 7 in a seven inning contest. We then came back to Sidney and vanquished them 18 to 13. Both teams played very ragged ball.

Tabor was anxious for two more games and she got them. On July 8th she easily disposed of the Indians 17 to 7, and the next day the Indians smothered her by a score of 19 to 7. Thus do the fortunes of base ball change.

We played Carson on July 10th. Carson was loaded for us and won by a score of 9 to 7. This was a beautiful game and one of the largest crowds ever in Carson saw it.

From Carson we drove to Avoca. Avoca had recently beaten Carson, and as Carson had beaten us, everyone reasoned that we ought to fall an easy prey to the "Avocaites." To the intense surprise of the crowd, and of ourselves as well, we almost shut our opponents out. They managed to make one lone run on an error. The final score was Indians 9, Avoca 1. We won from Harlan on July 13 by a score of 18 to 6 and from Earling the next day 22 to 11. Then we went back to Avoca again, and although we had them shut out 5 to 0 up to the fifth inning, they entered on a batting streak and beat us in a Garrison finish 21 to 5. The next day we met Carson in our second game of the season against them and they "walloped" us 12 to 1. Then in quick succession we lost two games to Carroll by scores of 15 to 5 and 8 to 7, and one to Coon Rapids buy the score of 4 to 1. Billy Morrison, who signed with the Louisville team of the National League the next year and was later farmed to one of the teams of the Western Association, pitched for Coon Rapids.

After the series of disastrous defeats just enumerated our luck seemed to change and we defeated Perry 7 to 6 and Boone 13 to 7 and 11 to 3. We buried Dayton 10 t0 8, and, after losing to Lehigh 15 to 17, we beat Stratford 59 to 4 and Jewell Junction 21 to 14. Eldora beat us 7 to 2 and Hampton added to our woes by defeating us 5 to 2 in a very pretty contest. On August 3 we played the New Hampton team at Ackley and added one more to our string of defeats, losing by a score of 1 to 9. We took satisfaction out of Ackley the next day, however, and won from them 10 to 9.

We made a long, tiresome drive from Ackley to Independence and played the latter team on the famous kite-shaped track on August 5. We won in the best game ever seen in Independence by a score of 4 to 1. The next day Manchester beat us 10 to 7 but we won from them on the following afternoon 6 to 1. It was during this last game that George Long, the full-blooded Winnebago fielder of the Indians, made the longest hit ever seen on the Manchester grounds. He drove the ball clear into the river, which surrounded the Manchester park on two sides.

The Indians still retained the impression that they could beat New Hampton if given another chance. They accordingly played the northern Iowa team at Lawler but the Hawkeyes were too much for the Nebraska representatives and defeated them 14 to 7. The next day Central City scalped the Aborigines 23 to 13. The Anamosa beat them 19 to 6 and 9 to 1. The red men rallied from these defeats and triumphed over Oxford Junction by a score of 5 to 4 and over Lost Nation by a score of 11 to 5. Delmar then beat them 17 to 13. This game closed the season.

The team disbanded at Delmar on Aug. 14 and the players went to their respective homes. During the season 47 games were played, of which 21 were won and 26 lost. The season was only moderately successful whether surveyed from an artistic or from a financial standpoint.

My readers naturally wonder why the team disbanded so early in the season. The answer is easy. The boys were literally worn out. It was often necessary to ride all day and all night and then play a game of ball as soon as the end of the drive was reached. This was more than a human flesh and blood could stand and the season was curtailed as a result.

CHAPTER V

Our 1898 Tour East Through Nebraska and Iowa

OUR playing season in 1897 had not opened until July. I determined to begin earlier in 1898, and accordingly played the first game of that year on Friday, June 10th. Our opponents were the University of Nebraska team and the game was played in Lincoln. We defeated the University boys on the 10th by a score of 8 to 5 and again on the 11th by a score of 13 to 1. As the University team had recently won the western intercollegiate championship from the universities of Kansas, Iowa and Missouri, our defeat of the organization was rather noteworthy, especially as the two games played in Lincoln were the first of the season for my boys.

From Lincoln we went to Wymore, Nebraska. Wymore had at that time the best team in southeastern Nebraska, and we were expected some warm contests. We got them. We took the lead in the early stages of the first game and held it up to the last half of the ninth inning. Then a series of inexcusable errors by our second baseman permitted Wymore to us out by a score 11 to 10. The next day Wymore beat us in a very decisive manner, the score being 8 to 2. Sam Crawford, who afterwards went to the Canadian league, then to the Interstate and then to the Cincinnati team of the National league, was in the box for Wymore during this second game. He twirled the "game of his life" and struck out no less than 17 of the Indians. I doubt if he has ever pitched a game to equal his performance that day.

After our Wymore defeat we won thirty-seven games through Iowa, Missouri and Illinois. So it is apparent that Wymore possessed a pretty fast aggregation of ball players. In Nebraska we defeated in rapid succession the following teams by the score appended: Crete, 3–0; Exeter, 13–1; York, 17–0;

Seward, 11–4; Staplehurst, 18–0; Surprise, 24–6; Schuyler, 12–3; Ashland, 17–1; Louisville, 7–1; 7–3 and 12–7. Our defeat of Louisville in three straight games filled us with satisfaction because, as will be remembered, the Louisville team had buried us very deeply in 1897.

We entered Iowa on June 27th at Tabor and defeated that team by scores of 24 to 12 and 26 to 7. We had been scheduled for three games there but after two days experience with the savages the Hawkeye people decided they had enough and cancelled the third game despite our protests. As fast as we could get to them we beat Villisca 17–1; Clarinda 21–10; Creston 6–1, 22–3 and 14–8; Corning 12–4, 35–4 and 35–8; Osceola 10–0 and 13–3; Leon 15–3 and 21–0; Humeston 13–1 and 14–4; Corydon 38–10; Allerton 16–9 and Seymour 41–6.

Our tour east in Iowa took us through only the southern part of the state. We passed out of Iowa at Seymour, a coal-mining town and one of the most cordial and friendly communities that it has ever been our pleasure to play in. After dropping from Seymour down into Missouri we played only one more game in Iowa for several weeks. That was with the Fort Madison team and it will be referred to in the story of our trip east through Illinois.

CHAPTER VI

Our 1898 Games in Missouri

Our first game after leaving Seymour, Iowa, was played in Unionville, Missouri. On account of lack of a railway connecting the two points we were compelled to drive from Seymour to Unionville. We left Seymour about six o'clock on the morning of July 20th and expected to reach Unionville in ample time to get dinner and play in the afternoon. But the country was one of the hilliest that God ever permitted out of doors and we did not reach the Missouri city until about one o'clock in the afternoon. Everyone was out of sorts and ready to fight at the slightest provocation. The baggage had not yet arrived when we reached our destination but we expected it almost any minute, and as the camp apparatus was with the baggage we ate our dinner at a restaurant. By the time dinner was concluded the citizens were lined up on the streets waiting for the parade and still no baggage was in sight. Consequently the Indians had to go into the parade in their citizens' clothes.

I sent a livery rig back over the road to find the baggage if possible and bring at least the uniforms into town. The baggage wagon was discovered "stuck" a few miles out of Unionville and the liveryman hurriedly loaded the uniform trunk into his buggy and brought it to the ball park. So we finally started the game although the hour was a little late. We won it by a score of 16 to 3. The baggage finally arrived and both the poor devil who drove the wagon and the man he was working for were treated to an assortment of the most picturesque language they had ever listened to. The next day we again defeated Unionville, this time by a score of 20 to 2. That night we left for Kahoka.

There was no direct line of railroad between Unionville and Kahoka and so, in order to fill the dates we had in the latter place, we were compelled to drive from Unionville to Glenwood Junction, a distance of about forty miles, and catch an early train to Kahoka. The good citizens of Unionville told us that the roads from Unionville to Glenwood were much rougher than the roads from Seymour to Unionville and so we determined to leave the baggage to come around by way of train, which would take something less than a week, and take only the men on our long night journey.

We hired a 'bus* and four horses and a driver, who was said to know the country thoroughly, and started on a drive which I would not repeat for fifty dollars. Luckily for us our driver was on speaking acquaintance with every boulder and stump along the entire forty miles of misery. We left Unionville at six o'clock in the evening and never reached the Junction until seven the next morning. Our driver was sending his horses along every minute of the time too. Perhaps my readers can realize something of the tortures we went through.

On one occasion one of the leaders dropped down into a washed-out culvert over his head and we all climbed out of the 'bus and helped drag the animal from his embarrassing position. At another time we mired in two feet of mud and water and were compelled to lighten the vehicle before we could proceed. Such hardships couldn't last forever, and we finally reached Glenwood Junction in time to eat a hasty breakfast and take the train for Kahoka.

Kahoka was a beautiful little town. The ball park was a very fine one and the team was said to be the best in that section. A big crowd was out to see the first game and we smothered the Missourians by the score of 20 to 5. Some college pitcher twirled the game for them. Their star box artist had been saved for the concluding engagement which took place the next day. "Coke" was the name of the victim that they offered up for a second sacrifice. During the morning of the day on which the second game was to be played the Kahoka manager chalked all over the sidewalks of his burg the words, "Coke will pitch." The effect was magical. Everyone who could raise the money was out to see Coke perform. He was an old professional and was said to be invincible.

Kahoka went to the field and Coke stepped into the box. Ogee, the Indian shortstop, went to bat. The grand stand was packed to suffocation and as Coke rubbed his hands over the ball to get the lay of the seams, some enthusiast on the seats sang out, "Don't waste a one, Jimmy." Jimmy smiled confidently and said, "I won't." Then he turned his first ball loose. Ogee caught it on the end of his bat and the horsehide is supposed to be going yet. At any rate none of the fielders went after it when it disappeared over

*Editor's note: *'bus* is a contraction for *omnibus*, indicating an extended horse-drawn coach.

the fence. Twice more in the first inning did the Indians "lambast" the Missouri "phenom" for home runs. At the conclusion of the game the score was 34 to 7 in favor of the red men, and several precincts had not yet been heard from.

The Kahoka cataclysm occurred on Saturday. We left the next morning for Fort Madison, Iowa. A few days later we heard that the Kahoka magnates had begun to tear down their fence and were going to turn their ball park into a cow pasture.

CHAPTER VII

Our 1898 Tour East Through Illinois

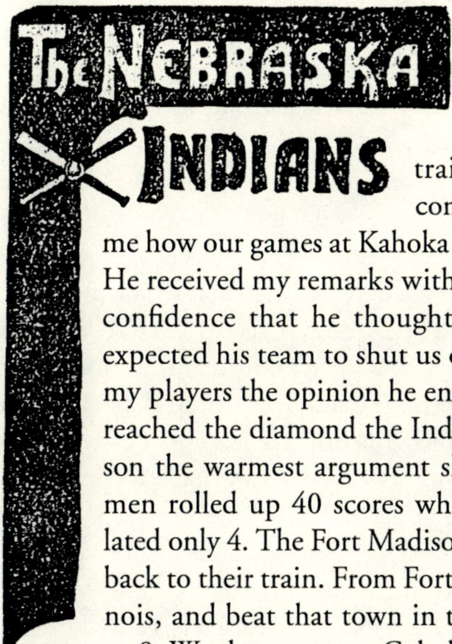

PLAYED Fort Madison on July 24th at West Point. Big preparations had been made for the game and we went out to the grounds on an excursion train. On the way to the scene of the conflict the Fort Madison manager asked me how our games at Kahoka had resulted, and I told him the scores. He received my remarks with great incredulity and informed me in confidence that he thought I was "stringing" him and that he expected his team to shut us out. I took the first opportunity to tell my players the opinion he entertained of them and when we finally reached the diamond the Indians were prepared to give Fort Madison the warmest argument she ever had. In seven innings the red men rolled up 40 scores while the Iowa contingent had accumulated only 4. The Fort Madison representatives had enough and went back to their train. From Fort Madison we went to Stronghurst, Illinois, and beat that town in two games by scores of 20 to 2 and 16 to 8. We then went to Galesburg. We had expected a big crowd at Galesburg as we understood it was a good town and that the team was very fair. The manager, however, proved to be a loafer whose principal possessions were his thirst for liquor and an abiding love for cigarettes. He had not even advertised the game and the paper which I had sent to him was reposing under the counter of a saloon. The gross receipts of the game were $7.80. That amount by no means represented the attendance, however, as deadbeats swarmed through every hole in the fence and the Galesburg management did not have energy enough to provide policemen to keep them back. The Galesburg team was very mediocre but the Indians were thoroughly disgusted with the treatment accorded them and they merely went through the motions of playing. Galesburg won 13 to 2.

Oneida was our next stand after Galesburg. Although the place is a small one we had a "large and enthusiastic crowd," as political speakers would say, and we played a fine game, which we won by the score of 7 to 4. We then went to Gilchrist, a small mining hamlet, but one of the craziest base ball towns I have ever seen. The Gilchrist team was considered the best in western Illinois and eastern Iowa, and had defeated professional aggregations without number. They won both games from us, the first by a score of 13 to 9 and the second by the score of 7 to 5. This last game was a "hair-raising" contest. It lasted eleven innings and was won by a home run hit by one of the Gilchrist players after two men were out. Before leaving Gilchrist we made arrangements to come back and play them on our way west from Chicago.

We went from Gilchrist to Orion. We defeated Orion 6–3, Cable 16–6, Kewanee 7–6, Sheffield 14–5. Sheffield then beat us 17 to 16. We went to Princeville to play the Maroons. This was a very good team, and while it was composed of all home talent, it had defeated everything it had played that season. We evidently scared the Princeville boys to death as we beat them by a score of 20 to 3. In rapid succession we then "trimmed" Wyoming 13 to 2, and 14 to 2, Lacon 11 to 9, Varna 22 to 4 and Toluca 9–3. Before we succeeded in overcoming Toluca however, they lowered our colors by a score of 4 to 3 in the first game we played them. The Morris Reds defeated us 11 to 8 in a ten inning game but the next day we took revenge by beating them 19 to 2. We then won two games from Wilmington by scores of 10 to 8 and 7 to 6. Mike Millette, who afterwards made a great record in the Texas and Atlantic leagues, pitched both games for the Morris Reds, and Donahue, who later shone so brightly on the Notre Dame University team, played infield on the Wilmington nine against us. We went directly from Wilmington to Chicago. We played the Auburn Park team there on August 21.

About two thousand people were out to see the Auburn Park team meet us a it was one of the fastest semi-professional teams in the city, and had many admirers, especially on the south side where the grounds were located. Gertenrich, who afterwards joined the Joliet Standards, was in the box for the Chicago team and he was batted very freely. The red men made five runs in the first inning and the Windy City never caught them. The final score was 8–5. This game was a surprise to people who had imagined that the Indians could not play the game, and it gave the copper colored boys a great reputation throughout Illinois and adjoining states.

CHAPTER VIII

Our 1898 Tour West Through Illinois

FOR several days after leaving Chicago the team seemed to be thoroughly demoralized. The excitement of the city had evidently proven too much for the boys from the plains and they lost several games as fast as they could play them. Joliet beat them 15 to 6; El Paso won two games from them by scores of 8 to 3 and 12 to 9. Willis, who afterwards joined the Wabash team of the Illinois-Indiana league, was in the box for El Paso both days and was largely responsible for the defeats sustained by the Indians.

We went from El Paso to Varna for a return game and broke the "hoo-doo" which seemed to have pursued us, by beating Varna by 5–2. This was a very interesting game. The Varna battery was Gregory and Kane, both of whom were well known in professional ball circles for several years. This pair afterwards went to the Bloomington team of the Western Association. Gregory pitched a magnificent game, but his support was ragged at one or two critical times and all his efforts went for naught. The next day Toluca went down before us by a score of 11 to 4, and Henry was defeated on the day following a score of 20 to 5. Blatz, who was fresh from some disbanded league team, pitched the game for Henry, and the Indian put him out of the box in the fifth inning. His place was taken by a young Thornton of the University of Illinois, who did very nice work.

From Henry we went to Princeville for a second game with the Maroons. It will be remembered that we had overwhelmingly defeated them on our way to Chicago, and we expected another victory easy victory. The Indians made three scores in the first inning, and never gathered another run.

Princeville won 5–3, and yet this was the same team which we had defeated a few weeks before by a score of 20 to 3.

We then defeated Bradford 10–2, Sheffield 5–3, Neponset 20–2, Kewanee 24–3, and Geneseo 12–7. Many of these contests were return games played at the request of citizens who had seen the team on its way east and had defeated and were anxious to see the boys in action again.

From Geneseo we went to Cambridge, where we were defeated in two close games by scores of 5–3 and 4–2. We then defeated Woodhull 10 to 1. From Woodhull we went to Gilchrist for our series of three games, two of which were to be played at Gilchrist and one in Alexus. The attendance at the first game was only fair. The game was uninteresting and Gilchrist won by a score of 12–5. We rather expected to lose the first game but we were determined to win the second. Since playing in Gilchrist before I had secured a left-handed pitcher, who had been with me during the preceding season, and I was confident that he would prove a stumbling block to the heavy hitters of the Gilchrist aggregation. An immense crowd came to see the second game. People drove a distance of fifty miles. Gilchrist had never been beaten on her home grounds and it was rumored that we were going to try to do the trick. When the gates were opened the crowd almost swamped the ticket sellers and swept the ticket takers off their feet.

Routzong went into the box for the Indians and he had Gilchrist at his mercy throughout the game. He shut them out 5–0. The town went broke on its favorites and the Indians will be remembered as long as base ball is talked of in Gilchrist's vicinity. The next day we played eight innings at Alexus and we were compelled to call the game to catch a train. The score when the game was called was 9 to 8 in favor of Gilchrist.

Our last game in Illinois was played at Keithsburg. Keithsburg should have been "easy picking" but from some unaccountable reason we lost the game, the score being 3–2.

CHAPTER IX

Our 1898 Tour West Through Iowa

After playing the Keithsburg, Illinois, game we laid over in that city two days. I am afraid that some of the wiseacres of the place became alarmed for fear we were financially embarrassed and unable to get out of their community without walking. As a matter of fact two or three of our dates had been cancelled on such short notice that we were unable to fill them in, and hence we were compelled to take a short vacation.

On the evening of Thursday, September 15th, we took a boat up the Mississippi river for Davenport. We reached Davenport the next noon. We then caught a train for De Witt, where we laid over long enough to attend the county fair. We reached Calamus on the evening of the sixteenth, and prepared for our games there on September seventeenth and eighteenth.

The first game at Calamus was a beauty. Routzong pitched for the Indians and shut his opponents out by the score of 2–0. The only scores the Indians made were on a home run by Ogee with one man on the base. They frequently hit the ball and hit it "a mile" but the Calamus fielders were playing over in the next township and gathered in everything that went anywhere near them. The second game was won by the Indians by a score of 20–2.

After leaving Calamus we defeated Mechanicsville 20–4, Lisbon 25–2 and Center Point, in our first contest, 8–7. Center Point had a very strong team. The club carried six salaried men and had such good ones as Hupp, who afterwards went to the Interstate League and had been in the Western Association previous to going to Center Point; the Myer brothers, who had been with the strong Anamosa team the year previous; and several other stars whose names I do not now recall. Our second game with them was played in the rain and we lost by a score of 10 to 7.

We defeated Walker in two games by scores of 9–1, 14–4. Jamieson, an old Nebraska boy, who had played against us in numerous engagements in the west the year previous, took part in the Walker games. We went from Walker to New Hampton for two games, one of which was played in Boyd, a small town about ten miles from New Hampton. New Hampton had just defeated the Detroit team of the Western League and the Indians were badly scared before they went on the field. Hart, who joined the Rock Island team of the Western Association the next year, and went from Rockford to Duluth upon the break up of the Association, was pitching for New Hampton. Shafer, who later played for the Ottumwa team of the Western under Pat Flaherty, was catching. The entire New Hampton team was made up of players fully as fast in their respective positions as the two mentioned. We lost both games with New Hampton, one by a score or 9–2 and the other by a score of 6–1. We then lost to Charles City by a score of 11–10. But we immediately won the two succeeding games from Charles City by scores of 12–4 and 24–3. The two last mentioned games were played at Osage and Waverly respectively. We defeated Mason City 20–3 in seven innings.

We played at Forest City in a cold rain storm. A remarkably clever pitcher, Isaacs by name, was in the box for Forest City and we lost by a score of 6–3. Isaacs was a bank cashier and an amateur in every sense of the word but he could certainly pitch. We played Forest City a second game at Boyd and we defeated them 18–5. We then defeated Lake Mills 9–3. This last game was played in a snow storm. As Lake Mills is right on the Minnesota line my readers can imagine that the temperature was not the balmiest in the world.

We dropped from Lake Mills to Slater and began a series of games through central Iowa which concluded our season's tour and that resulted in an unbroken string of victories for us. We defeated Slater 11–6, Woodard 23–8, Jamaica 22–11, Bayard 6–2 and 22–9. The second game with Bayard was played at Coon Rapids.

We were billed for games at Glidden, Carroll and several other towns close to the ones named, but a cold rain began which continued uninterruptedly for two days and nights and we disbanded on Monday, October 10th. A few days later the country in which we had expected to play experienced a severe blizzard. I congratulated myself on the fact that I had not endeavored to prolong the playing season.

Our season lasted four months embracing two days over seventeen weeks. We played 103 games of which we won 81. We traveled by rail and lived in tents and found this the most desirable mode of travel and existence while on the road. The Indians were nervous and ill-at-ease while cooped up in hotels. But the minute they were furnished with tents they felt at home and gave me their best efforts.

CHAPTER X

Our 1899 Tour Through Nebraska and Iowa

OUR playing season in 1899 began on May 10th. This was a month earlier that we began in 1898. We wished, however, to meet several of the college teams and it was necessary to reach them before the school season ended. Then, also, we desired to play as much as possible in the east and it was incumbent upon to get an early start in order to remain any-length of time east of Chicago.

The team for 1899 was made up of many of the same men who had played with me the year previous. Several of them were late in getting into Lincoln, however, and our first game was played under many disadvantages. The University of Nebraska defeated us very badly, the score being 18 to 5. We were to have played the University on both the 9th and 10th but the wind was so strong on the 9th that it was an impossibility to keep the canvas, with which the University fenced its campus during athletic events, in place.

Our second game of the season was played with Havelock, a suburb of Lincoln and the site of the B. & M. Shops. The shop team was composed of a big, husky lot of fellows, but we defeated them rather easily by the score of 13 to 8. My team had been changed considerably since the day before and the boys were working together in better shape.

We jumped from Havelock to Avoca, Iowa. We had not visited Avoca for two years, but we found many old friends there and a big crowd was out to see the game. Scully, of Omaha, had been imported to pitch, but the Indians "drove him to the woods" in short order and Beymer, a local player, finished the game for him. The Indians won by a score of 20 to 2. We defeated Audubon 34–5 and then went to Indianola for a series of two games against the Simpson College and incidentally to open their new athletic park.

The first game with the college boys resulted 13–2 in our favor. The second game was a much closer contest and we won only after considerable trouble by a score of 5–1. Middleton pitched very effectively for Simpson and the Indians found a great deal of difficulty in connecting with his curves. We bore many pleasant recollection of Simpson away from the college with us and the Indians were unanimous in their desire to return if an opportunity presented itself.

After leaving Indianola we defeated Perry in two games by scores 17–8 and 16–7, and won from Gowrie 7–4. In the forenoon of May 22 Gowrie defeated us 11–5 and in the afternoon of the same day we won from Dayton by a score of 8–4. We then defeated in rapid succession the following teams, by the scores indicated: Eagle Grove, 21–2 and 11–1; Iowa Falls 22–2 and 6–2; Belmond 8–1.

On May 29th we began a series of three games with Upper Iowa University. The first game was played at Hampton and it was a beautiful contest. Weaver pitched for the Indians and Shook for the University, and there was not much difference between the work of the two men. The Indians, however, were lucky enough to bunch their hits in one inning and won by a score of 3–0. The second game was played at Clarksville on Decoration Day. Clarksville was the home of one or two of the University players and an immense crowd was out to see the contest. The Indians won this game rather easily by the score of 11 to 3. We played the third game with the Iowa school on the campus of the institution at Fayette and this time the tables were turned. The college boys won by a score of 9 to 7. This series with Upper Iowa University was one of the best we have ever played, and the two teams parted with the best of feeling and with a desire to meet again in the future.

We next won from Janesville by a score of 16 to 1 and then from Waverly by a score of 8 to 1. We then defeated the Iowa State Normal School at Cedar Falls by a score of 20 to 11. We shut Fairbanks out 9–0, defeated Lenox College at Hopkinton 12–2 and won two games from Manchester by scores of 16–4 and 9–4.

We closed our Iowa tour by playing a series of three games with "Kennedy's Kolts" at Dubuque. Had we known the base ball conditions of the city we never would have gone there. For several weeks Dubuque had been endeavoring to support a tail end team in the Western Association. Their team never won a game except by accident and the citizens were thoroughly disgusted with it. It had been turned loose on the cold world the day before we reached Dubuque and base ball interest could not be discovered within the limits of the municipality with a microscope.

Dubuque had good reason for her poor opinion of her representative in the Association. I will give you some idea of its strength. A few days after I entered Illinois I hired one of the pitchers of the defunct Dubuque team. One of my Indians had been hurt while performing in the box and I found it necessary to secure someone else at once. Hence I secured the late Dubuque star. While with the Dubuque team the man I hired had been played in the field when he did not pitch, as the Iowa manager had been anxious to avail himself of this particular player's batting ability. I naturally supposed I was getting a phenomenal "sticker." Imagine my surprise when I discovered that he was the weakest man with the bat I had and that his proper place was at he foot of my list. It is needless to say that I did not put him in the game at all when he did not pitch. If the player I have described was one of the strong batters of the Dubuque team I leave my readers to conjecture what the ordinary batters must have been.

Our crowds at Dubuque on the first two days were very poor. We won both games by scores of 12–5 and 7–6 respectively. On the third day of our stay in the city we drew a good attendance and won by a score of 7–1. We left Dubuque with few regrets. I lost money by visiting the place, and the manager, J.E. Skemp, was the most thoroughly disagreeable man I have ever met.

CHAPTER XI

Our 1899 Tour East Through Illinois

BEFORE entering Illinois on our tour east we played one game in Wisconsin. This game was at Plattsville, the site of the Wisconsin State Normal School. We had no trouble in winning from the disciples of learning, the score being 13 to 2. We then won two games from Apple River, Illinois, one by a score of 13–3, and the other by a score of 15–0. From Apple River we went to Freeport for a series of seven games with the Freeport team.

The Freeport aggregation was managed by H.B. Smith, one of the leading citizens of the town, and the superintendent of the northern Illinois branch of the Standard Oil Company. Smith had the strongest independent team in Illinois outside of Chicago, and there were people who affirmed that it was even superior to the best Chicago teams. According to our arrangements the first, the fourth and the last game of our series of seven were to be played on the Freeport grounds. The remaining games of the series were to be played on the Freeport grounds. The remaining games of the series were to be played in Illinois and Wisconsin cities near Freeport.

The first of the series of contests was played in Freeport on Thursday, June 15th. Salene was in the box for the Indians and Woodyat, a Dixon man, for Freeport. Freeport made four hits and as many errors. The Indians made three hits and no errors and shut the Freeporters out by a score of 4 to 0. One of the Freeport dailies said the next evening that "a great many people thought the Indians were simply traveling on their shape and their war paint, but they soon showed the spectators at the park differently."

The next day both teams went to Warren, Illinois, where a pretty game was won by Freeport, the score being 8–2. The day following Dodgeville,

Wisconsin was the scene of a very ragged contest, Freeport winning by a score of 15 to 9. The grounds at Dodgeville were largely responsible for this awful score as they were in very bad condition and the local management had made no effort to better them.

When the team lined up for the fourth struggle of the series, which was to be played on the Freeport grounds, Freeport was one point to the good of the red men, having won two games out of the three played. With Salene in the box the Indians were invincible, however, and easily defeated their opponents by a score of 6 to 1. This evened up the series, and both teams prepared for a close game at Mt. Carroll, Illinois, on June 19th.

This mount Carroll game was one of the most remarkable the team has ever played. When the Indians went to bat in the last half of the ninth inning the score was 11 to 7 in favor of Freeport. The Indians had been almost universal favorites with the crowd, and gloom a foot thick had settled over the park. Ten minutes later the Indians had won the game and the noise made by the rooters could have been heard a mile. This is the way the five runs happened: Old Buckheart, the first Indian to bat, singled. Green, the Sac and Fox fielder, smashed the ball for two bases and scored Buckheart. Barber singled, and so did Fulmer, and those two hits scored Green and put two Indians on bases. Jonas came to bat and caught the first ball pitched him on the nose for a home run. Barber, Fulmer and Jonas came home, five runs had been registered, the game was won and as yet nobody was out. Mount Carroll will remember this game for years to come.

The next game of the series was played at Sharon, Wisconsin, and Freeport won it by a score of 3 to 2. Freeport also won the last game of the series by a score of 12 to 2. Thus Freeport won four games out of the seven played. The series was a very good one and gave universal satisfaction to the patrons of America's national sport in northern Illinois.

It may be of interest to the followers of base ball to know that this entire series of games was umpired by Harry Dooms, the one-time great pitcher of the Newark club. Dooms was employed by Manager Smith to umpire all the games played by the Freeport team and he drew the same salary that was given to the players. Dooms died this winter (1899) in St. Louis. He was one of the most gentlemanly ball players I have ever met, and I heard of his death with genuine regret. We went from Freeport to Rochelle, where we won by a score of 11 to 4. Bubser, who was fresh from the disbanded Western Association, pitched for Rochelle, and he was hit very freely. Our next game was with Paw Paw. This was a genuine slugging match, and when the smoke of battle cleared away Paw Paw had won by the altitudinous score of 17 to 16. The next day we won easily from the same team by a score of 17 to 5.

Our last game with Paw Paw was played on June 24th. On the 25th we went into Chicago to play the Auburn Park team. The less said about this game the better for me. The Auburn Park team had been especially strengthened for the occasion and my team was so badly "off" that any high school organization in the country could have beaten them. Barber, my high-priced Western Association acquisition, attempted to pitch for the Indians. He was treated so badly that Salene relieved him in the fifth inning. Salene did fine work but the damage had been done before he entered the box and the team behind him played like a lot of automatons. The red men made no fewer than eight errors in the in-field. Auburn Park won by a score of 10 to 1.

We went from Chicago to Sterling to play two games and open a new ball park in the thriving little Illinois city. Sterling was base ball crazy and our games attracted big crowds. Both contests were fine exhibitions. We won the first by a score of 10 to 9 in ten innings, and the second by a score of 5 to 3. Haberle, a young left handed pitcher, who twirled the last game for Sterling, showed exceptional promise. We next won two games from Dixon, the scores being 4–2 and 3–2, and defeated Hinckley twice, the scores being 13–6 and 23–9.

From Hinckley we went into Chicago to play the famous colored Unions. On account of rain we played only six innings, the Unions winning by a score of 3–2. For five innings we shut the Unions out. The rain began to fall and despite our protest Fred Pfeffer, the

Union's umpire, compelled my team to go into the field and play in a driving storm until the colored boys had made three runs. Then the obliging Pfeffer decided the grounds were too wet for play and called the teams from the field. W.S. Peters, the manager of the Union's, not content with robbing us of the game, refused to pay me within $70 of the amount he had guaranteed me, and this amount is still due to me from him. I have not the space here to enter into a discussion of the crookedness of this colored aggregation. Suffice it to say that I have cut them off my visiting list and I have talked with numerous other managers who have done the same.

After the game just described we left Illinois and did not again visit the state until October.

CHAPTER XII

Our 1899 Tour East Through Indiana and Ohio

WE entered Indiana on our way east on July 3rd. A reunion in honor of "Studebaker's Tigers," who had recently returned from the Spanish-American war, was in progress at Plymouth. Two games of ball were played there on the afternoon of the third. The first one was between Rochester and Logansport and the second, between the Bremen Blacks and the Indians. The first game was very ragged and our game, which immediately followed it, came like balm to a wounded spirit. The Indians won by a score of 11 to 3. During this game one of the spectators, who was somewhat the worse for liquor, became very demonstrative and in the fifth inning, when the Indian left-fielder, Hopinkah, ran down to first base, the intoxicated gentleman hurried out to the line and kicked him. Quick as a flash the burly redskin whirled, knocked his tormentor down by a well directed left hand blow, then went back to his base as if nothing had happened. The crowd rose *en masse* and cheered the Indian.

We went from Plymouth to South Bend, where we were to play three games with the Green Stockings, two on the fourth and one on the fifth. The morning Fourth-of-July game resulted 6 to 3 in favor of South Bend. About noon it began to rain and the heavens were still weeping copiously at three o'clock. I had given up all idea of playing, when one of the boys, who had been out to the grand stand, reported that it was full of people. I went out and found the amphitheatre literally packed with fans who were clamorous for a game. The South Bend manager and myself cleared the stand, sold and collected tickets and finally got the game started. The Indians won by a score of 7 to 5. The game on the fifth was won by the Green Stockings by a score of 5 to 1. During this last game Okey, one of the best men on the Indian team broke his finger, and he was added to my hospital list, which was already so large that my team looked like a collection of cripples. We determined to fill our dates, however, and went up to Michigan City for two games, the first of which we won by a score of 5–3. We lost the second contest 13 to 6. We then lost to the Rochester Red Fellows 14 to 6 but won the second game from them by a score of 8 to 4.

Winamac defeated us 9–8 in ten innings and we then defeated La Fountaine 15–4 and 14–3, but lost the third game of the series — 7–6. The game last mentioned was played at Wabash and more people climbed over the fence than paid admission at the gate. We defeated Alexandria 7–4 and Matthews 3–2. The Alexandria grounds were two or three miles in the country and we drew about $30. In the light of my experience there I am sometime amused to read long letters in the sporting papers dwelling on Alexandria's merits as a ball town. We drew well at Matthews, a small town which had been but recently reached by the railroad. The park was jammed despite the rain, which had set in during the morning and continued all day. The game was one of the best we ever played. My team was the only one which bested Matthews during the entire season of '99.

Fortville defeated us 4–3 in ten innings but we evened up by beating the same team 24–11 the next day. We went from Fortville to Portland, where we played at a street fair on July 19. I was guaranteed $50 for playing there and this was assured me by the street fair committee and several of the leading business men of the town. After the game, which we won 7–1, the committee paid me $40 and explained that they were short of money and could not liquidate the rest of my claim. So I still have $10 due me at Portland, Indiana. This account can be purchased cheap. Shepard, who had just returned from one of the teams of the Illinois Indiana league, pitched in the Portland game.

We went from Portland to Union City where we won 20 to 8. We then opened the new base ball park at Marion in two games, both of which we won, the first by a score of 8–5 and the second by a score of 27 to 11. In rapid succession we defeated Warren 36–15, Bluffton, 8–3, 12–6 and 9–6, and Payne, Ohio, 8–3. The Bluffton games were all very fine contests and they were largely attended. Manager John Hartle, of the Bluffton team, was a straightforward gentleman and had advertised the games thoroughly and had a team which was first class in every respect.

The game at Payne, Ohio, was a remarkable contest. Payne did not play her own team but imported the Decatur, Indiana, nine. This was considered the fastest aggregation in that section and they certainly played the game from start to finish. When the Indians went to bat in the first half of the ninth inning the score was five to four in favor of Payne. In the first half of that eventful inning the bases were filled by a combination of base hits on the part of the Indians and errors by their opponents. With three men on the bases Buckheart came to bat. Buck is over six feet tall and has the strength of an ox. He let one strike go by and then lifted the ball squarely over the center field fence. Four men paced around the diamond and registered at the fourth station amid the shouts of the frenzied crowd. Payne never recovered from the shock and failed to score in her last half.

We dropped one game to Paulding 8 to 7 but almost shut her out the second day by a score of 22 to 3. We then defeated Celina 8–3, Fort Recovery 18–3 and 14–6, Versailles 8–1 and 8–6, Degraff 14–3 and Mount Victory 10–2. Both of the Versailles games were pitched by Schwormstedt who was signed by Indianapolis a few days later. The Indians batted the man with the unpronounceable name hard in both games.

Findlay robbed us of a game by a score of 10–6 and we then won from her 6–4. We defeated Carey 11–4, Plymouth 12–3, Medina 18–13, Akron 8–1 and 18–2, Canton 6–5, Salem 11–9 and New Waterford 8–6. The game at New Waterford closed our eastern trip through Ohio.

CHAPTER XIII

Our 1899 Tour Through Pennsylvania and New York

A drunken drayman and a mixture of sun time, standard time, eastern time and ten or twelve other brands of time were responsible for our missing the train which should have taken us out of New Waterford, Ohio, to Sharpsville , Pennsylvania. As a result we reached Sharpsville very late for our game on August 16th and the park was overrun with people before we appeared on the grounds. About half the population seemed to have passes to the park, which had been issued to them in prehistoric times for manual labor performed in improving an alleged race track. We went ahead, however, and played against a team recruited from Warren, Pittsburg, and several other burgs. The Indians made eleven safe hits off of the first thirteen balls thrown by the Sharpsville pitcher, and nine runs in the first inning. This was a surprise that the Pennsylvania people had not counted on, and before they came to their senses we won the game by a score of 21 to 6.

We then went to Mercer to play the Mercer Grays. We beat them 20 to 4. In the last half of the ninth inning with Mercer at the bat and two men out, the batsman was hit by the third strike. The umpire called him out and we supposed the game was over and started up town. After we were well out of the grounds the umpire, yielding to the persuasion of the frantic Mercerites, concluded that his former decision had been wrong and insisted that we come back and finish the game. It is needless to say that this logic did not appeal to us. The Mercer management did considerable bellyaching through the columns of the Pittsburg and other papers and the good people of the little Pennsylvania burg are probably still mourning over the reprehensible conduct of the Indians who were so savage that they would not tamely submit to robbery.

Greenville, which at this time had one of the strongest independent

teams in Pennsylvania, was then defeated by us by a score of 3–2. This was the best game ever played in Greenville and it was pitched for Greenville by Johnson, who had recently been imported from Buffalo. Salene pitched for the Indians. The red men won this game in the last half of the ninth inning. Greenville defeated us the second day by a score of 10 to 4. We drew large crowds to these games and the people were unanimous in their desire to have us return.

We were to have played at Tidioute on August 21st, but rain prevented the contest. We played in Warren on the 22nd against the Y. M. C. A. team of that city. We shout our opponents out 17 to 0. This result was due largely to the excellent work of the Indian battery, Salene and Corbet. We jumped from Warren to Randolph, N.Y, where we were billed to play the K. O. T. M. team, but in reality played the Salamanca team. We won easily by a score of 5–1, and then defeated Jamestown in a pretty game at Celeron by a score of 5–2. Here our luck seemed to desert us and we lost several games right off the reel.

Salamanca beat us 9–6 and my boys lost a large amount of their wages on the result. Jimeson, the famous Indian pitcher, twirled this game for Salamanca. The day after our Salamanca disaster Erie, Pennsylvania, defeated us 5 to 2. On the following, Erie again beat us 9–8 in eleven innings. B. Taylor pitched this game for the Indians and would have won out for a rotten decision in the last inning which gave Erie a three base hit out of a ball which was foul by fifty feet. A loser's apologies are always received with bad grace, however, and so I shall not dwell upon the painful scene which ensued when we realized that we had been euchered out of a hard contest.

These games at Erie concluded our campaign in Pennsylvania and New York, and then went back into Ohio.

CHAPTER XIV

Our 1899 Tour West Through Ohio

WE opened a series of two games at Ashtabula, Ohio, on August 28th. The Ashtabula team was very strong, having defeated several Interstate league teams, and my team was in poor condition. It is not surprising, therefore, that we lost both games, the scores being 5–1 and 8–4. During the second game Pitcher McCann, of the Ashtabula team, broke his arm while in the act of throwing a ball in the third inning. The arm snapped so that it could be plainly heard in the grand stand and the arm fell helpless to the pitcher's side. The break was located between the shoulder and the elbow. I had often heard of accidents of this kind but had never seen one before.

We went from Ashtabula to Painesville, where we lost two more games. The score were 5–1 and 17–12. Painesville had a team which was stronger even than Ashtabula's. The second game at Painesville was a slugging match pure and simple. Salene, who began the game for the Indians, was knocked out of the box and Corbet finished the contest for him. The Painesville twirler, Whisner, was "hammered all over the lot" but he managed to pull out a victory.

Our next game was a Warren, where the team was managed by Mr. R.W. Elliott, who also ran the opera house, and was thoroughly conversant with the amusement business. Despite a disagreeable rain we played the game as arranged before a large crowd and lost again by a score of 6–3. We were beginning to think that we were "hoodooed" and were fated never to win. We managed to defeat Lisbon by a score of 17 to 6, but our success was only temporary as we quickly lost two games, to Canton, the scores being 10–9 and 7–8. We had no license to lose the first Canton game. We had it won and the greater part of the crowd had left the grounds when a lucky home run by Canton in the last half of the ninth inning with two men on bases gave her a victory. If there was ever a disgusted lot of ball players they were to be found in the tents of the Indians after this game was concluded.

We had seen our darkest hours, however, as we began to win immediately after our Canton experience and added five successive victories to our list. We won from Wadsworth 11–7, Elyria 16–3, Crestline 12–10 and 13–0 and Nevada 8–6. The second Crestline game was a "hummer with horns." Ninham pitched for the Indians and allowed the opposition only two safe hits. They never had a shadow of a chance to score at any time. The Nevada game was a fine contest. It lasted for twelve innings and at no time did either side dare take a breathing spell. Nevada had the pick of the Oberlin college team including the famous Fauvers. Salene pitched for the Indians and for inning after inning the struggle remained even. Finally the first half of the twelfth the red men made two score and Nevada expired without registering. The next day, however, Nevada avenged herself by defeating us rather easily by a score of 13 to 6.

We played the Mount Victory team at Idlewild park near Kenton and defeated them 13 to 6. Mr. A.V. Salisbury, who ran the park, was a nephew of Salisbury of "Buffalo bill" fame and he made our visit at his resort a very pleasant one. The next day we played Mount Victory again, this time on their home grounds, and we won 17 to 6.

We went out of Ohio on our way west in a blaze of glory. We defeated Bellefontaine 16–6, Urbana 17–12, Milford Center 17–5 and 10–3, Woodstock, 18–5 and 10–4, New Madison 7–4 and 10–8 and Camden 4–0.

Woodstock, which is a very small village, is the best ball town of the size we have ever played in without single exception. We were there in the latter part of September and the weather was bitterly cold. Yet for two days good crowds drove in from the surrounding country to see the games and the people sat through the contests wrapped in furs and overcoats.

Both of our games at New Madison were pitched by Billy Damman, late of the Cincinnati national league team and more recently of Indianapolis. The Indians batted him hard both days. The last game was won by my team in the ninth inning. When my boys went to bat for the last time they were three runs behind. They "lambasted" Mr. Damman for five hits in succession and won the game right there.

The game at Camden was worth any man's money. Camden had imported most of the Krebs team of Hamilton and when the Indians shut them out 4–0 surprise was very noticeable in the western section of Ohio.

CHAPTER XV

Our 1899 Tour Through West Indiana and Illinois

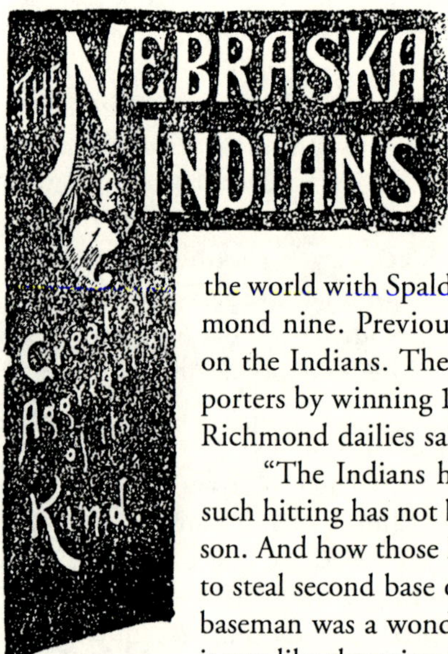

PLAYED the Entre Nous team at Richmond, Indiana, on September 24th. This team was entirely salaried and contained a number of first class men. Billy Earle, who was formerly with the Chicago national league team, and who made the tour around the world with Spalding, caught for and captained the Richmond nine. Previous to the contest betting was 100 to 50 on the Indians. They justified the confidence of their supporters by winning 11–5. The day after the game one of the Richmond dailies said:

"The Indians hit everything that came their way and such hitting has not been seen on the local diamond this season. And how those Indians did run. It was no trouble at all to steal second base or to beat a bunt out at first. Their first baseman was a wonder and when a ball was thrown to him it was like throwing it into a box car or into a barn door."

Richmond was not to be beaten the second day and after a stubborn struggle they won 5 to 2.

We defeated Redkey 17 to 3 and lost to Ridgeville 7 to 6. This Ridgeville game furnished another illustration of the stranger being robbed within the gates of a foreign city. We took our medicine, however, and said nothing. We went from Ridgeville to Kendallville for two games during their county fair. We lost the first game 13–11, but won the second 10–7. The second game was interrupted several times by a snow storm.

We next won two games from the Bremen Blacks, the scores being 12–1 and 8–0. Ninham pitched the shut-out game for the Indians. We then shut Winamac out 8–0 but could not win from them again and lost 8–7. It will be remembered that we played one game with Winamac on our way east and we lost it. So Winamac won two of the three games played with my team during the season. Yet I am convinced that I have the stronger team and that the result of our series was simply one of the accidents of baseball.

We went from Winamac to Morris, Illinois, for two games against the Morris Reds. We were anxious to win these games as we had broken even with the Reds the year previous and had been up against their crack pitcher, Glendon, earlier in the season. We had given Glendon an unmerciful beating at Hinckley and he had boasted of the things he would do to us when we came to Morris. Well, we went to Morris. We hammered Mr. Glendon freely both days, batting him out of the box during the second engagement. We won both games. The score were 7–4 and 15–13. We finished our season by defeating Wyanet 15–5 and Sheffield 14–7.

We disbanded at Sheffield, Illinois, on Friday, October 13. We played 143 games during the season, of which we won 108. We covered over two thousand miles of territory and played in eight different states. During 1899 we traveled entirely by rail and lived in tents as we had done during the previous year.

CHAPTER XVI

In Nebraska and Iowa in 1900

I began my 1900 season earlier than I shall ever begin another one unless I go crazy. We played our first game on Friday, April 13th. The place was Lincoln and the opposing ream with the University of Nebraska aggregation. We won the game by a score of 10 to 9. Then we went to Omaha to open the new Western League park in that city and our bad luck commenced.

The Indians and Omaha were booked for two games and the city had had been billed for them as if a circus were about to blight the community. The park was a new one and in most of it the green clay was a foot deep. On Saturday the weather was cold, damp, gloomy and generally disagreeable. A handful of faithful fans risked pneumonia and quick consumption in order to see the game. Newmeyer pitched for Omaha and won a pretty game by a score of 6 to 2. The league men worked for all they got too. Everyone was pleased with the game and Bill Rourke and I went to bed with pleasant expectations of a "killing" the next day, as we knew that everyone who could move, including old men and cripples, would come out to see the contest. We figured on an attendance of 4,000 people and with decent weather we should have had it.

But the next day it rained and we stood under the grand stand like a couple of disconsolate orphans and saw the gentle drops beat us out of a thousand dollars. That was a mighty nice beginning for my season. No wonder people say the number, 13, is unlucky. I had begun my season on the 13th of the month.

The next morning we slopped down to the Rock Island and caught a train for Iowa. The rain accompanied us. It had evidently resolved to be my close companion and it started in Omaha and stayed with me the rest of the season. Every once in a while some fair female or giddy youth rubs up against me and says "it must be a lot of fun to run a ball team and travel over the country." When this happens, I sigh softly to myself, look around to see if any officers are in sight and then kill my sapient friend with the weapon that is handiest. Had some of my envious acquaintances been with me in 1900 they would soon have gone back home disgruntled and discouraged.

Our first game in Iowa was with Adel. We won 14 to 5 and it rained. We beat Simpson College at Indianola 14–2 and it rained. We won from Cleveland 18–17. It had rained so much in Cleveland that adventurous boys were navigating the grounds in boats and we were compelled to play the game in Lucas where the mud was a little shallower. As it was, I understood that an old man and a blind boy fell into a pond out by first base and were drowned in the excitement, their bodies being found the next July when the ground finally dried. I have always been inclined to doubt this story but the occurrence was not at all impossible.

We defeated Marengo 9 to 3 and then lost to her 5 to 7. The Des Moines Western League team "trimmed" us at Cedar Rapids by a score of 14 to 2. Had this score been any larger I would so state here. Jake Weimer twirled for Des Moines and was largely responsible for our discomforture. From Cedar Rapids we went to Iowa City where we played a series of three games with the University of Iowa. Green pitched the first of these games for the Indians and won it by a score of 5 to 4. We had a large crowd and everyone was out to see another good contest the second day. Mr. Graham presided in the box for the Indians and what happened to him would fill several harrowing chapters of a "James Brothers Weekly." The college boys hit every ball high and far away. A small river bounds one side of the Iowa City outfield and once in a while some ambitious student would drop the ball in the stream and our players would be compelled to swim after it. My ticket taker retreated from the gate on account of the bombardment of the fence around him by university batsmen. He was afraid that flying splinters would ruin his eyesight.

My outfielders ran flies until they were exhausted and then I brought them to the diamond and sent a fresh set of men to the outer garden. The university team made 20 scores. The Indians didn't get any. In fact, had we played until now I doubt very much if we should have had a single mark to our credit. At the conclusion of this engagement the Indian tents were swathed in crepe and visitors were not welcome to the wigwams.

About seven people came out to see the third game. Salene pitched for the Indians and won his game by a score of 4 to 2. What do you think of that in the light of the experience of the day before?

We defeated Washington by score of 18 to 8 and 32 to 9. These scores might have been higher but I give here all that were turned in to me at the close of the festivities.

CHAPTER XVII

In Illinois in 1900

Our first games in Illinois were with Rock Island against the newly organized independent team that represented that city. We won the first engagement 10 to 5 and the second 16 to 4. Lidders, who afterwards went to the Three I league, pitched the second game for Rock Island and the Indians made so many runs off him that the crowd, which was a big one, telephoned for the city fire department to put us out.

We played Cambridge, Illinois, on April 30th. We were defeated 18–17. This is the third game we have played in Cambridge and we have lost all of them. The town is certainly a "hoodoo" to me. This 1900 Cambridge game was a lurid exhibition. In fact it was one of the most remarkable we have ever played. Ole Kranz, who pitched for Rock Island in 1901, was in the box for Cambridge. Graham pitched for me. The Cambridge boys massacred Graham so badly that Ninham relieved him, while Colonel Kranz held the Indians just where he wanted them up to the ninth inning. When the Indians went to bat in the ninth the score stood 18 to 6 against them. Then Kranz climbed into his balloon and ascended amid a shower of two-baggers, three-sackers and home runs. The red men actually made 11 runs on good hard hits and were finally beaten by only one score.

We played two games with the Monmouth College team. The first was won by the college boys 9 to 8. They were so rejoiced that they celebrated the victory hilariously in the evening by getting out their band and giving a shirt tail parade. The next day, by way of variety, the Indians, with Green pitching, shut out the seekers for an education 10–0. After this carnage we looked carefully and long for shirt tail parades but we saw none.

We beat Kewanee 25–13 and 23–10 and Toluca 22–3. At Wenona the everlasting rain prevented the game and it did likewise the next day at Eureka, where we were scheduled to play the college team. We finally played Eureka on the forenoon of May 9 and won 22 to 11. In the afternoon of the same day we beat Fairbury 28 to 3 and we buried them again in the next afternoon 19 to 1. We won from Saybrook 34–10 and from Hoopeston 24–5. Newman imported a team to play us and thought they stood a mighty good chance of winning. When the smoke of battle lifted from the corpse-bestrewn field the results indicated victory for the savages by a count of 24–0.

We bested Oakland 17–4 and 13–3. We added a victory Sidell 11–2. Just here I want to say a word about Sidell. This is a small town of about 700 people. They had less than a week to advertise and yet they turned out one of the largest crowds we had in that region. Sidell will certainly receive another visit from us if we are in her vicinity again. Our game with Sidell was the last one we played in Illinois during the season of 1900.

CHAPTER XVIII

Our 1900 Games in Indiana

We opened our 1900 tour in Indiana very auspiciously. We defeated the Indianapolis Reserves at Rockville by a score of 8 to 3. The Indianapolis Reserves are considered the flower of all the semi-professional teams of their region. The good people of Rockville secured them to play against us and advertised the game thoroughly. The prospects were good for the largest crowd ever known at a ball game in that community when the rain began. It fell steadily all the forenoon and continued manfully into the afternoon. Finally the moisture stopped long enough for the game to be played and between waterspouts we pulled it off before a good crowd which braved the elements rather than miss the contest. Graham pitched for my team and scared most of the Indianapolis men to death with his speed. We made so good an impression in this game that we have been requested to return to Rockville several times since, but we have never been able to arrange our schedule so that we could get back there.

We were billed to play Wabash College at Crawfordsville the day after we beat the Reserves, but the gentle reader is probably able to guess what happened if he has read the account of my 1900 tour carefully up to this point. It rained and we laid over in Crawfordsville Saturday and Sunday and played the college team Monday forenoon. We won 16 to 4. In the afternoon we went to Greencastle to play DePauw University.

A good many times during my connection with base ball I have seen my team robbed by incompetent, dishonest and rotten umpires, but I think I never witnessed as disgusting an exhibition as the DePauw official gave us. Even then, we were beaten with the greatest difficulty only after an 11-inning game. The score was 9 to 5. Previous to our games with DePauw the team there had been losing money steadily and was deep in the hole when we visited them. We drew the largest crowd of the season and went out of town leaving our opponents with enough cash to pay their debts and look the world in the face again. Yet notwithstanding this, some cheap reporter, who was probably working for $3.oo per week and carrying his dinner in a tin bucket, stated in a local paper that the Indians drew a very small crowd and played a poor article of ball. Think of it, my friends, who maintain that justice still lives in Greencastle.

We played the Indiana State University at Bloomington and defeated them 21 to 7. During the game I was an unwilling witness of a very peculiar and painful accident. A prominent lawyer of Bloomington was in attendance at the game. He had driven out and was watching the contest from his buggy in the outfield. Suddenly his horse was became frightened and ran away. In some unaccountable manner the lawyer fell over the dashboard and hung for a few moments suspended between that and the horse. Then his hold loosened and he fell behind the animal, which ran the length of the field battering the unfortunate victim's head with his rear leaving a trail of blood behind. Finally the man was jarred loose from his terrible position and friends picked him up for dead. During all the time this was occurring a crowd of probably a thousand people watched it, unable to lend a helping hand. The people were in a little valley. The runaway occurred on higher ground and it was as if the awful spectacle had been provided especially for them. I understood the attorney subsequently recovered, although if he did it must have been a miracle.

We defeated Spiceland at Newcastle 14 to 6 and then played two games with the Entre Nous team at Richmond. We lost both of these, the scores being 4–2 and 6–3. Ingalls beat us 10–9 but we "walloped" them the second day 5 to 1. Our game at Pendleton was postponed on account of the ever-present rain. We played two games in Cicero on Decoration Day. Cicero is one of the best towns of the size we have ever played. Bud Taylor pitched the morning game for the Indians and shut Cicero out 5 to 0. In the afternoon Salene pitched and we won 5 to 2. At Cicero I was smiled upon by good fortune for the first, last and only time in the season. The rain prevented games all around me but we played without interferences from the elements. The next day, however, we were soaked at Flora so accounts were evened up to a certain extent.

The South Bend Green Stockings beat us 6 to 3 and the Notre Dame team "took a fall out of us" by a score of 16 to 13. Norwood Gibson, who later went to Kansas City and did such brilliant work for the Western Leaguers there, pitched for Notre Dame. Taylor pitched for me and the game was a slugging match *par excellence*. We secured 16 safe hits off Gibson while the University men made 14 hits off Taylor. But the red men succeeded in accumulating more errors than the other fellows and so we lost. We have met a good many college teams at different times but I must state without any reservation that the Notre Dame people treated us with more kindness and consideration than any institution we have ever played and both students and professors were shining examples of what true gentlemen should be. They resembled the De Pauw crowd about as much as an assemblage of U.S. senators does a gang of hoodlums. Soon after our game at De Pauw the Kentucky State University players quit the Greencastle ground in disgust on account of the ruffianly treatment accorded them. I guarantee that no one will ever have occasion to walk out of the Notre Dame park for any reason of that kind.

CHAPTER XIX

Our 1900 Tour East Through Wisconsin and Michigan

JUNE 3 marked the beginning of a dark page in the history of the Nebraska Indians. On that eventful day we started a series of thirteen games against a chocolate colored aggregation from Chicago known as the Columbian Giants. The Colombian Giants were a little bit the fastest lot of ball players we ever encountered and for almost two weeks we played them every day in Illinois, Wisconsin, and Michigan without winning a game. Several time we came so close to winning that the hair of the spectators stood on end and once or twice we played extra inning contests but our hands always slipped just as we were about to grab victory. We were mighty glad when we finally severed the ties that bound us to the colored boys. We had nothing but kindly feeling for them, but they played too good a game to suit us. Colonel Johnson, the road manager, was a nice, companionable fellow who had commanded an Illinois colored regiment during the Spanish-American war, and I was sorry to lose him so far as he was personally concerned, but I did not regret for a minute the departure of his players. It is not the most agreeable thing in the world to lose game after game for 13 days. The places and scores of our matches with the Columbian Giants are as follows: All the games, as before stated, resulted in favor of the Giants. Chicago, 4–3; Janesville, Wisc., 11–3; Broadhead,

Wisc., 4–3; Janesville, Wis., 17–5; Watertown, Wis., 11–5; Evansville, Wis., 7–0; Albany, Wis., 9–8 (ten innings); Chicago 8–6; Sturgis, Mich., 11–5; Burr Oak, Mich., 1–0; Colon, Mich., 11–5; Hastings, Mich., 8–1; Three Rivers, Mich., 8–4.

After we had breathed a sigh of satisfaction at being rid of Chicago's colored experts we began to win again and defeated Sturgis 13–9. Ream, who afterwards went to Colorado Springs in the Western League and who had previously been with Fort Wayne, pitched for Sturgis. From Sturgis we went to South Bend, Indiana, for another game against the Greens. Mullen was in the box for the Greens. He had just finished with the Indiana State League and pitched good ball against us but somehow the Indians hit him hard and literally tore the boards off the fence with their long drives. Mullen subsequently went to Fort Wayne team of the Western Association and this year (1902) he has signed with the Detroit team of the American League. He should be able to make good in the fastest company as he is a first class twirler and a heavy hitter and handles himself like a ball player in whatever position he is placed. The second day we played the Greens we lost 15 to 6.

Immediately after our South Bend games we started on a series through Michigan. Burr Oak beat us 5–2 with Ream in the box. We won from Coldwater 7–1 and 9–0; Homer, 16–1; Clinton, 10–3. This last game concluded our trip east through Michigan in 1900.

CHAPTER XX

In Ohio in 1900

In the northern part of Ohio, nestled on the shore of Lake Erie, are two towns of about equal size. One is Oak Harbor, the other Port Clinton. In 1900 both towns had ball teams. Previous to our dates with them they had played several games against each other and the rivalry was very intense. Each team had won its share of games and old citizens told us the two organizations were about evenly matched. Old citizens ought to know, because if there is any subject they do not think themselves infallible in I have never yet discovered it. Oak Harbor was the first town we played in Ohio. We beat them 19 to 8 and had to travel slow all the way for fear we were going to lose our opponents. Then we went down the lake to Port Clinton expecting another easy thing. To our surprise Port Clinton fought us like a wildcat and finally in the 10th inning beat us out 6–5. After this, when old citizens come around telling me about the comparative strength of different teams, I feed them strychnine and look on with dry eyes while their remains are hauled away.

We beat Wakeman 7–4 and Bellevue 16–4. We then went to Medina. We had played in Medina before and the people gave us a hearty welcome. They knew that the Indian aggregation was a pretty fast one and rather than trust a local team against us, they sent up to Cleveland for the Cleveland Wheel Club. Graham went into the box for the Indians and we walked up and down the spines of the pilgrims from the oil city, beating them 11 to 4. This pleased the Medina people immensely, and they informed us that the next time we came through their region they expected to import a team to beat us if they sent to the ends of the earth for it.

We won from Wadsworth 12–3 and from the North End Athletic Club of Akron, 10–2. We were to have played at Akron on Sunday, July 1st, but a dark blue, dangerous looking cloud prevented us. This cloud appeared in the shape of a trolley car loaded with policemen to the number of 25 or more, who came out to the park under the leadership of the gallant chief, Harrison and forbade the game. When we saw this warlike demonstration we tearfully informed the chief that we had not thought of playing and that marbles was the most exciting sport we ever indulged in on the Sabbath. So the chief and his minions spent the afternoon telling stories in the shade of the trees. We watched the crap games in the grove, the fakirs who operated cane and knife boards, and various interesting amusement of a gambling nature which were not forbidden on Sunday because they were conducive to the moral welfare of the community, while base ball was prohibited on account of its sinful tendency.

Kent next claimed out attention and we played two games there. We lost the first one 4–3 and won the second 11–6. Kent has a newspaper which is the best base ball sheet I have ever seen in a town of that size and it was due largely to the efforts of the hustling editor of this paper that we drew good crowds two days in succession in opposition to a "fake" street fair which was pestering the people. We went back to Akron for two games on the 4th of July. We lost the forenoon game 6–4 and won in the afternoon 12–5. The day was intensely hot and one or two of my players were prostrated before the contests were finished.

We defeated New Philadelphia 12–7 with a crippled team and were in such bad shape the second day that I picked up a couple of local men to do my battery work. We lost the contest the local stars took part in 12–3. We next played the Morgan Engineering Works team at Alliance. Pawnee Bill's show was in town the same afternoon and we were afraid we should have no crowd at all. The factory shut down work, however, and the hands came to the game in preference to going to the show. We had about as many people as Pawnee Bill drew and we won the game by a score of 11 to 1. I cannot be too enthusiastic in my praise of the treatment accorded me by the Alliance organization.

Canton beat us 11–4. We won from Warren 9–6. The day we played in Warren was cold and chilly and for a long time we thought we should be unable to pull the contest off at all. A good crowd gathered, however, and they were all pleased by a nice game. Young McNeil, who subsequently pitched for Cleveland in the American League was in the box for Warren. This game would have been very close bur for a lucky home run made by Haley of my team with three men on bases.

We shut Lisbon out 23–0 and concluded our 1900 trip through Ohio by winning three games from East Palestine, the scores being 19–5, 13–7 and 11–7. We enjoyed our stay in East Palestine very much. The town is the site of two potteries and the employees were a jolly set. We became acquainted with many of them and most of my boys too souvenirs away with them in the shape of fancy china which they had seen made.

CHAPTER XXI

In Pennsylvania in 1900

We began our Pennsylvania tour with a game at Beaver Falls against the strong Athletics of that city. Gumbert, who used to be with the Chicago National League in prehistoric times, pitched for Beaver Falls and did not strike out a man and had no curves or speed to speak of. He won his game by a score of 9 to 3, however, and I suppose that the result ought to silence all criticism of his methods. We had a big crowd at this game and the next day being Sunday and a day of idleness with us, we stayed in camp on the grounds. We were visited by several thousand people. In fact I have never seen so much interest show in my team as was exhibited after our game with Beaver Falls.

The Etna team beat us by robbery at Millvale by a score of 8–7. We were scheduled to play Etna the next day also on the same grounds but a nonentity named Neff who managed the Etna team and had about as much business honor in his composition as a snake, attempted to make a deal that would deprive me of my full share of the receipts. I refused to submit any bulldozing tactics and so the game was called off. The people of Etna regretted this action very much and many of them openly denounced the nincompoop who had deprived them of a good contest. We arranged a game with the Millvale team to take the place of the Etna engagement and we won 6 to 1.

The following day we went up against Homestead Library and Athletic Club team to our sorrow. We were sound trounced by a score of 14 to 4. We were to have played Homestead again but the rain, which had been following me all the season, got in its work and prevented the contest.

Natrona beat us 6–5 and Millvale "trimmed" us 11–1 in a return engagement with them. The game with Millvale ended our stay in the vicinity of Pittsburg and we went south to Uniontown where we played two games and won them, the score in each instance being 8–7. During all the time we have been playing ball I have never seen a crowd of spectators more anxious for their team to win than were the Uniontown people. We won both our games there in the 9th inning when it seemed to me that everyone on the grounds was right up on the lines pawing dirt, beating tin cans, throwing sticks and yelling like an insane rabble. Luckily for us our men were not easily rattled.

The rain (note this, please) prevented the game at Johnstown. The Altona Monarchs beat us 4–3 and we then disposed of Huntingdon by scores of 19–3 and 6–3. We drew only fair crowds at Huntingdon, but this was not the fault of the manager there. He advertised our visit as well as I have ever seen a job of the kind done anywhere and he literally worked day and night for the success of the games. But the people seemed to take no interest in base ball. After we left Huntingdon I discovered one reason for this. The editor of the leading Huntingdon paper told me he was going to give us a nice write-up of the games and so I arranged to have him send me a copy of his mental illuminant. It contained just four lines. He called that a nice write-up. Are you surprised that we had small crowds in Huntingdon?

We beat Lewiston 8–2 and 7–4, lost to Middletown 12–8 and won from York twice in the same afternoon by scores of 8–4 and 17–11. Manheim defeated us 11–6. Manheim is an old fashioned German town that it is a pleasure to visit. In the evenings the young men and women gather on the village green and play "kissing ring" before the admiring gaze of the older members of the community and life proceeds on its way very happily indeed. I tried to break into this game of "kissing ring" because some very nice girls were taking part in it, but strangers were barred and so I was disappointed.

We defeated the Lancaster Actives 11–10 in a ten-inning game. This so pleased a dog fancier of the city that he presented us with the thoroughbred fox terrier that has been our mascot ever since. A billposter by the name of Tom Goodhart was the manager of the Actives. During the game he lost a fielder's glove that probably cost 75 cents when new. In someway his infinitesimal brain became possessed of the idea that my left fielder had stolen his glove, although I have always been at a loss to discover what use we could have made of it. While we were at the depot preparing to leave the city a pot-bellied constable, who smelled like a distillery and talked like a bowery tough, came to the train with a warrant that Mr. Goodhart had sworn out. As I could not afford to stay in Lancaster two or three days to prove that we had not stolen a 75-cent glove, I gave the microcephalous miscarriage of the law some beer money and we went on our way. This is but a sample of the treatment a stranger sometimes receives in a strange land.

We lost to Downingtown 6–2 and 3–1 and went up to Burlington, N.J., to play two games with the Burlington, New Jersey League team. Burlington was at that time the leader of the league but notwithstanding that, she sent around to the other cities composing the organization for their best men. We won both games, the results being 8–5 (ten innings) and 5–3. We then played two games with the Athletics of Chester, Pa. The Athletics were, at that time, the best independent team in Pennsylvania. We won the first game 12–9 in ten innings and the second we lost 13–4. Curt Wiegand, who managed Athletics, was an old league player and as straightforward a gentleman as one will ever meet. The admirable Mr. Goodhart, of Lancaster, could take a few lessons from Wiegand very advantageously.

We played a series of three games against North Philadelphia, a suburb of Philadelphia, which had an elegant ball park and a very good team. We lost the first game 7–4 and won the next two 14–3 and 6–0. We beat Germantown 8–4 and 9–5, thus ending our tour in Pennsylvania.

CHAPTER XXII

Our 1900 Tour West Through New York, Canada and Michigan

We went direct from Philadelphia to Brooklyn, N.Y., where we played the Skelly team on August 18 and 19. The Skellys claimed to be the semiprofessional champions of Brooklyn but we defeated them in our first engagement 8 to 6. The second day, however, they sharpened their little hatchets and went after us, "skinning" us 13–4. Mt. Vernon, the fashionable suburb of New York City, next claimed our attention. The manager of the Mt. Vernon team, as soon as we reached the grounds, took me back of the grand stand for a confidential chat. He lowered his voice to a hoarse whisper and addressed me something in this manner:

"Now I have a very strong team here and they have been playing good ball. In fact our people have been used to seeing close contests and I hope you will put in your very best team and at least try to give my boys a run for their money. Of course I realize that you can't win but I don't want your boys to get discouraged and it is my desire that they play for all that is in them. Put in your very best pitcher because I have a team of sluggers."

The game resulted 15–0 in favor of the Indians. Salene pitched for me and gave the Mt. Vernon men just one little, measly hit. The next morning the Mt. Vernon paper said: "The Indians could hit the ball at will and place a hit within a two foot space every time they tried. Nothing has ever been seen to equal it on the home grounds. The big first baseman gave many an exhibition of nervy batting when he would smilingly watch the first strike come sizzling across the plate and allow it to be called up him. He would disdainfully turn his back to the home plate for the second strike to go by and then turn around and slam the third good one into any part of the field he wished. Such was the playing of the Indians all the way through.

We defeated Brewster 21–5, Hudson 8–0, Chatham 11–3, Waterford

6–3 and St. Johnsville 3–0. We were to have played at Ilion on August 27th but the rain fell and so we postponed the game until the 28th. Ilion beat us by a score of 4–3. At that time Ilion had a very fast team composed of such men as Malarkey, the pitcher, and others equally as good. Weedsport triumphed over us 4–2 but we shut them out at Auburn the next day 8–0. Then we beat Seneca Falls 24–6 and Clifton Springs 3–2. Clifton Springs had as good an amateur team as we have ever played and we enjoyed our stay with them. After the game there, George Green, who had pitched the contest for me, was persuaded to run 100 yards with a professional foot racer who was spoiling for a heat. George lost his man before the finish line was reached. After this trial of speed the Clifton Springs people told me we had done about everything possible to them and that we were at liberty to leave town almost any time.

We played two games at Waverly on Labor Day and lost both of them. The score were 9–4 and 6–5. The last game was one of the closest and most exciting we have ever participated in. The right fielder of the Waverly team pulled down a long fly in the 9th inning that looked good for a home run and so saved the game for his boys. Accorsini was catching for the Waverly team at the time we played them and the remainder of the nine was composed of men from the disbanded Atlantic league.

Corning won from us 7–6 and we then defeated them 9–3. We beat Avoca 7–3, Hammondsport 9–6, Livonia 20–8 and the Tonawanda Indian team at Akron 9–3. Our game with the Tonawanda Indians was a peculiar one. The redskins had been playing all the best teams in their region for several years and had never lost a contest. Their method of procedure was a very simple one. The moment their opponents appeared on the grounds the entire tribe gathered on the side lines and began a series of blood-curdling yells and whoops. They would threaten to cut the hearts out of their pale-faced adversaries and do various other unpleasant things. By this method the Tonawanda braves produced a reign of terror that took all the courage out of the teams which opposed them and the dusky sons of the forest were invariably returned winners. They tried these tactics with us but my men had been there before and laughed at the efforts of their Tonawanda brethren. We took the lead in the very first inning and were never headed. I remember that before the game began one little, fat Indian sat up on top of the water keg like a Chinese idol on a pillar and tore the atmosphere into shreds with his vociferations and savage yells. After the first round of the battle he wilted like a sensitive plant in the breath of a simoon and didn't utter another word. In fact the whole tribe subsided and became the most docile lot of Aborigines I ever saw. They had arranged to hold their annual green corn dance the evening of the day we played them but we were compelled to leave in order to make connections for Dunnville, Canada, and so we missed this terpsichorean festival. Our redskin opponents were a jolly lot of fellows notwithstanding the bluff they put up to visiting teams and we were sorry that we could not take part in the celebration that evening.

Our first game in Canada was played at Dunnville, Ontario. It resulted in a score 1 to 1 in thirteen innings. This was pronounced by everyone the best game ever played in eastern Ontario. It was finally called on account of darkness. Every man on both teams did phenomenal work and it is altogether probable that those who were at the game will never see so good a contest again. The next day we beat Dunnville 9 to 8 and we won from them the third day 11 to 10. Dunnville was a good ball town and had a nice park. This was the first time we had ever appeared on other than United States soil and we were first surprised to see the British flags at the corners of the grounds instead of Uncle Sam's and to hear games called "matches" and see them so advertised everywhere.

We defeated Aylmer 13–0 and Leamington 27–8 and then we jumped clear to Tecumseh, Michigan. Tecumseh beat us in a cold rain 11–4. Robb, who went to the Southern League in 1901, pitched the game for Tecumseh. On September 19th we played two games at Hudson during the street fair. We lost both of these contests. The scores were 8–2 and 6–3. At this time the Interstate League had disbanded and we played against most of the pennant winning Toledo team at Hudson. These games at Hudson closed our season and we at once left for Chicago from which point the boys scattered for home.

During the season we played 144 games. We won 90, lost 53 and tied 1.

CHAPTER XXIII

Our 1901 Tour in Nebraska and Kansas

Our 1901 tour began on Monday, April 22, at Wahoo, Nebraska. It will be remembered that the first game the Indians ever played took place in Wahoo and so we felt somewhat at home when we got back on the old grounds. We lost our first game by a score of 12 to 8. This was largely the result of luck, however, and we were by no means cast down. We had played the University of Nebraska a practice game a few days before and beaten them by a score of 12 to 8, so we knew that ordinarily Wahoo had no license to beat us. We won our second game at Wahoo 13 to 3 and felt that this contest was a fair criterion of the merits of our team. Subsequent events proved our opinion was correct, as during the season of 1901 we made the best record we had ever attained. We played 163 games. Of these we won 136, lost 26, and tied 1.

As I have stated above, we opened our 1901 season at Wahoo, where we broke even in a series of two games. We then went to Genoa to play two games with the Genoa Indian School team of that place. We won both these games and so established beyond a doubt that my team was better than any Indian team in Nebraska, as the Genoa Indians were universally conceded to be the best aggregation of red ball players within the state outside, of course, of the Nebraska Indians. The scores of the Genoa games were 10–6 and 7–6. White Boy and Mitchell, who did the battery work for Genoa, were fine players and the men behind them also did excellent work. We beat Ulysses 11–9 and lost to them 6–5. The last game at Ulysses was played in the strongest wind storm that we had ever battled against. The Ulysses diamond was laid out in the midst of a converted corn field and the breeze blew clods of dirt as big as marbles into the players' faces. A fly that looked good for two bases would go up into the air and be blown back into the diamond.

The wind was really responsible for the loss of the second game but then losers always have some excuse and I am no exception.

We beat Stromsburg 27 to 16 and the wind was still so strong (but this time with, instead of against the batters) that eight or nine home runs were made. From Stromsburg we went to Exeter, where we won the first day 11–2 and lost the second 11–4. We beat Belvidere 27–9 and 21–3 and then went into bleeding Kansas, where we proceeded to eat up Belleville, the first enemy we encountered, by a score of 21–1. The next day it rained and we loafed. We won from Hanover by a score of 11–3 and from Hiawatha 24–4. The weather was bitter cold the day we played Hiawatha, the grounds were a mile and a half from town and the gate receipts were exactly $8.90. Enough said.

From Hiawatha we went back into Nebraska, where we played four more games before entering Iowa. We lost to Tecumseh 14–5 and won from the same team 13–10. Nebraska City beat us 17–14 and 10–2. Nebraska City has a peculiar and original method of winning games. Her grounds adjoin the Missouri river and every ordinarily hard hit ball to right field goes into the purling waters of that limpid stream. The Nebraska City Manager keeps colored youth in scant raiment on the banks of the river to fish out the balls. While the visiting team is in the field the wet balls are given to the pitcher for use and he is compelled to lob up a sphere which is so slippery that it is absolutely impossible to get either speed or curves on it. When the Nebraska City cohorts go into the field the astute local manager digs up dry balls for the pitcher to use and all goes merry as a marriage bell. It takes a good many balls but the Nebraska City team wins its games and that is what they are after.

CHAPTER XXIV

East Through Iowa in 1901

Our opening game in Iowa was at Essex. We won 27–0 in a game in which we did not make an error. We then defeated College Springs 27–13 and 27–4. College Springs is an inland town of about 900 people. It is the seat of Amity College and from that institution it derives its name. But railroad or no railroad, its people turn out to ball games and we drew very large crowds there for two days in succession. These games were caught for College Springs by Bodwell, the well known University of Chicago athlete. Bedford beat us 1–0 in a five-inning game, which was called on account of rain, but the next day we beat the same team 12–2. We then "trimmed" Kent 20–0. Beckwith, Robert Lincoln's famous son-in-law, pitched this game for Kent and the Indians pounded him pretty hard. We lost to Cleveland 1–0 and won from them 2–1. We drew fair crowds to these Cleveland games but they would have been larger had it not been for the fact that Cleveland had been beating everyone so badly that the people had lost interest in the games they played.

We won from Hiteman 13–5, Hynes 16–8, Centerville 11–6, Lancaster, Mo., 19–6, Bloomfield, Ia., 24–5, Pulaski 27–7. Mr. J.C. Harvey, who managed the Centerville team, had advertised his game thoroughly and had out one of the largest crowds ever known to a ball game in his region. He treated me finely in every way and so I was surprised at his conduct subsequently, which I shall touch upon in the proper time.

We lost to Bonaparte 22–19. Bonaparte is a good ball town and had a nice team and a gentlemanly manager in the person of Mr. E. D. Brunk. From Bonaparte we went to Keokuk where we lost two games, the scores being 12–10 and 18–6. The umpire robbed us of the first game. The second day we were fairly beaten. If I were called upon to offer a word of advice to the ball team contemplating a visit to Keokuk it would be this: "Don't." Keokuk attempted to rob and bulldoze me from the moment I struck the town until I left it. Before I had alighted from the cars I was approached by a drayman, who told me he had been sent down by the local manager, and who wanted $12.00 for a $4.00 job. In settling after the first game a leading railway official, who is connected with the Keokuk base ball organization, attempted to "do" me out of $6.00 and when I caught him at it he laughed and said he trusted there was no harm done; that he figured he would be ahead if his scheme worked and nothing out if it failed. Nice idea of business honesty wasn't it? During our first game at Keokuk, the official scorer, who was a pimple-headed newspaper reporter, deliberately refused to credit us with one run we had made. I remonstrated in good forcible language and the next day my friend of the quill said: "A disagreeable feature of the contest was the constant and unremitting objections of the Indian manager. He acted as though he had the hydrophobia and spewed out more rhodomontade than has been witnessed on the diamond here for a long time. The Indians were gentlemen compared with this noisy unknown."

When I read the foregoing extract I laughed, cut out the effort for preservation in my scrap book and bought an extra copy of the paper to send home to Nebraska so my people could see what the embryo Greeleys of the Hawkeye state were doing to me. We were robed so badly in our first game by the Mississippi river town that I absolutely refused to play the second game there unless I was permitted to use two umpires, one of whom was to be furnished by me. Mr. Harry L. Miller, who manages the Keokuk team, waited until a big crowd had assembled and then he came to me as said he would not play and would refund the money taken in unless I consented to one umpire and that one to be furnished by him. I looked Mr. Miller over a minute. He is a hotel clerk and I suppose is lucky to own a suit of clothes. Then I asked the swelled gentleman if he really imagined I was in his city broke and depending on his wealth to get out of town. I told my boys to remove their uniforms at once. Miller changed his tune so quickly that he threw the orchestra off the pitch and the game went ahead with two umpires. He had tried to "run a bluff" and it didn't go. After we left Keokuk a team from Ottumwa played there and was forced to collect its guarantee by process of law. So you see Keokuk is a good town to stay away from.

We defeated Burlington 15–6 and lost to them 10–7. We beat Wapello 13–6 and Muscatine 6–5 and 9–6. The grass in the outfield at Muscatine was rather long and the first day we played there it was responsible for our winning the game. The Muscatine players lost a ball at critical time and the

Indians ran around the bases with "none to harm or make afraid." The second day my fielders lost track of a ball and Muscatine scored a couple of runs as a result but not enough to win. Mr. L. M. Neyens, who managed the Muscatine team, is an honor to the baseball business and one whose word is as good as his bond. It was a pleasure to deal with him. We defeated Atalissa 10–5, Port Byron, Ill., 17–6 and 11–3, Hopkinton, Ia., 28–11, Greeley 25–1 and Strawberry Point 15–5.

Dyersville won from us 11–4. The next day we played Earlville. Dyersville and Earlville are bitter rivals and most of the Dyersville people went down to Earlville with us. They won a large wad of Earlville money when we took the game 9–8. A funny thing happened during this game. Shirk, my shortstop, was arrested by the Earlville city marshal on the charge of "tagging" one of the Earlville players a little bit too hard. Shirk was soon released, however, and allowed to finish the game.

Manchester beat us 5–4 in ten innings. We won from Maynard 25–2, Clermont 17–2, West Union 30–1 and Volga 14–5. Elkader beat us 12–8. Everyone expected us to win this game and so strong was the sentiment in our favor that a professional gambler of the town tried to buy the game from me the day before it was played. Augusta pitched for us and the Elkader boys pounded him in a manner that was fit to procure the intervention of the society for the prevention of cruelty to animals. Not a cent was bet on the game, and this was a conclusive proof that it was played on its merits.

We won from Waukon 13–9 and 12–8, Nashua 19–9, Nora Springs 30–6 and 29–3 and from Northwood 11–4. We then left Iowa and did not enter the state again until the 15th of September.

CHAPTER XXV

In Minnesota in 1901

Previous to this season we had never played in Minnesota and I so arranged a good schedule of games in that state. The first one was played at Albert Lea on June 23rd. Albert Lea won without trouble by a score of 15–4. The next day we drove to Hartland along as beautiful a road as I have ever seen. Hartland is populated mostly by Swedes. She had a brand new ball park with grand stand and every convenience. This grand stand was filled with people of Swedish extraction. All the members of the ball team were Scandinavians. Every time a Hartland player came to bat such encouraging ejaculations as these were numerous. "Put it vere you did yesterday, Ola." "Smak dat von dere, Yohnnie." "You vas a dandy, Anders." But despite all this we won 18–2.

We defeated Winnebago City 10–8 and 12–8. Winnebago City sent to Minneapolis for a pitcher to twirl the first game and for a time he did nicely and the contest was very close. Then suddenly, in one more inning, we made three home runs, two two-baggers and a single and won the game. The next day the local pitcher went in and did better work than the imported player had been able to show. The second game was a ten-inning affair.

We beat Vernon Center 16–5 and then began a series of three games against Weseca, one of which was played at Owatonna and the other two at Waseca. Waseca won the first game 4–2 but ought not to have done so. The grounds were new and a heavy rain had fallen the night before. A two-horse scraper was working in left field and with two men on bases one of the Waseca players hit a long fly which dropped between the horses. Our fielder was compelled to stand idly by while Waseca scored three runs and won the game. The next day we beat Waseca 5–4 in ten innings. This was the first game the Waseca people had lost on their home grounds and the second they had lost anywhere during the season up to that time. Waseca won the third game from us 14–0. We stood no chance of scoring at any time and in fact made only one safe hit.

We defeated New Prague 8 to 1. New Prague is a Bohemian town and half the village is in one county and half in another. The two sides of the main street have different city marshals and they pay their taxes in different places. A man who visits New Prague is kept busy figuring out the county he is in.

We beat Farmington 20–7, Rosemount 14–0, Waverly 10–1 and 34–2 and Delano 14–5. Our first game at Waverly was played on the Fourth of July and on account of rain it did not begin until about 5 o'clock. Yet we played a full nine-inning game.

Our next engagement was an interesting one of 11 innings. It was played with the White Bear Lake team and the score, and when we were compelled to stop to catch a train, was 1–1. Mr. Al. Weidenborner sells wall paper half the year and manages the White Bear Lake ball team the other half. During our game he sat on the bench and was out in the middle of the diamond half the time delaying the game by trivial kicks. Had he adorned the grand stand continuously during the contest the results would have been better all around. The White Bear umpire was also a peculiar individual. When not rendering decisions he was coaching the local team. It was rather a novel experience to me to see on man trying to fill two arduous positions simultaneously. I suppose that both Al., the manager, and Bill, the umpire, are naturally nice boys but one of these days they will get too miscellaneous during a game and a weeping contingent will follow their remains to their last resting place.

We beat Anoka 9–1 and 15–6. During the first game the Indians made ten two-base hits, which is something very unusual. Our last game in Minnesota was played in Elk River. We won it 26–3.

CHAPTER XXVI

Our 1901 Tour in Wisconsin

We opened our campaign in Wisconsin at River Falls. We were dated for two games there. We played and won the first contest 34–5. The grounds in River Falls are on the campus of the state normal school. A stub branch of the public road runs along one side of the park and this was filled with deadheads and deadbeats who looked at the game we played without paying a cent. I said nothing the first day, but that evening the local manager and I saw the city council and secured permission to close the road along the side of the grounds for the second day, hoping in this manner to prevent the riffraff of the community from sponging the game. The mayor was out of town when we made our arrangement. The next day we closed the road and were collecting from everyone who went into the grounds without any trouble, when suddenly the city marshal appeared on the scene, and acting under orders of the mayor, threw open the road and advised the gang of bums and loafers who had gathered, that the chief executive and himself desired them to go in and crowd as close up to the grounds as is possible without paying a cent. He counseled them to get all they could for nothing. I waited until a nice crowd of the deadbeats had gathered. Then I refunded the money to those who had paid and we went down town and took off our uniforms. It was so comical to see the disappointment of the small-souled people who had waited in the sun for a couple of hours in the expectation of seeing a game without money and without price. It did me good to fool the "cheap skates" for once at least. In all my experience I have never before seen city officials deliberately go out of their way in order to encourage a lot of "cheap screws" to beat both a visiting team and the local base ball boys out of admission fees. The name of the burg where this happened is River Falls, Wis. Note the name.

From River Falls we went to Ellsworth. After coming in contact with the officials of both River Falls and Ellsworth I knew how the angel from

Hell felt when he woke up one morning and found himself in Heaven. The Ellsworth people went out of their way to make our stay among them pleasant. We beat them two games, the scores being 15–3 and 9–6. In the forenoon of July 15 we beat New Richmond 14–2 and in the afternoon we won from the Hammond high school team 12–7. Hammond had the best high school team I have ever seen. They have won the championship of their high school league three years in succession and the league embraces a number of big towns like Eau Claire.

We beat Menomonie 13–8, Durand 6–1 and 4–2, Mondovi 17–8, Chippewa Falls 23–0, Merrillan 24–6, Black River Falls 29–5 and 24–7, New Lisbon 15–7 and 18–2, Elroy 18–0, Portage 9–7, Westfield 18–0, Waupaca 5–4, Stevens Point 12–6, Grand Rapids 17–5 and 6–4. It will be seen from the foregoing record that we won 32 games without losing one. We played some unusually good teams in this bunch, too. At Grand Rapids, for instance, we met most of the Marshfield state league team. At Waupaca we played the state league team of that city.

After winning 32 games without skip we fell down badly at Kaukauna, where we met the state leaguers, and we were beaten by a score of 24 to 8. This result was attributed to the poor work of Augusta, who pitched for me, as he had absolutely nothing, neither speed, curves nor control and the Wisconsin men batted him for 27 safe hits. My boys game him gilt-edged support but no one could win handicapped by a pitcher who could not pitch.

We won from Two Rivers 18–2 and 13–1. The one run that Two Rivers made in the second game was a gift to them from my umpire, Chief Eagle, and it beat his pardner, White Eyes, who was pitching, out of a nice shutout. We defeated Plymouth 21–10, Port Washington 8–1, West Bend 18–4, South Milwaukee 20–4, Cedarsburg 18–6, Kenosha 7–6 and 14–1. Foulkes, of the Milwaukee Sentinels, pitched for Port Washington against us and lead his team to defeat.

Our first game at Kenosha was an exciting one of 12 innings in which we tied the score in the ninth inning after an uphill fight and then won out in the twelfth. The second day we buried the Kenosha people beyond hope of resurrection and knocked two pitchers out of the box for them. An individual by the name of W. J. Swift managed the Kenosha team. So far as I am able to judge he is absolutely devoid of every principle of business honesty and has no more regard for his word than the Corsican who smiles to your face then stabs you in the back. He lied to me when there was no occasion for it and lied about my team without the semblance of an excuse. Swift is a rather undersized little gentleman who works in one of the Kenosha factories. He wears a dinky cap to show his head and a pair of dinky golf trousers to show his legs. Before our first game he told me that his people had no faith in my team and that he hoped I would give them the very best I had in stock as he didn't want to disappoint his supporters by booking a fake. He said his boys had been beating everyone, as indeed they had, and that he wanted the first game close so the crowd would be large the second day. As I have said, the first game was a "corker" and we won it strictly on its merits, making more hits and fewer errors than the Kenosha boys. But in the face of this, the Kenosha correspondents affirmed in the daily papers that they outplayed us and that we robbed them of the game.

We "laid" for them the second day and certainly took sweet revenge. The crowd was enormous. We jumped in from the start and ran the Kenosha team to death. We battered and biffed and banged them until good Brother Swift's crowd grew disgusted and began to leave in the sixth inning. When the game was over I asked the local correspondents if they were contemplating sending any more dispatches to the papers to the effect that the Indians were outplayed. They said nothing. Colonel Swift took his little cap and his little golf panties and his little legs sadly home.

We won from Burlington 25–10 and 21–5 and from East Troy 25–11. East Troy was an inland town but it furnished us a good crowd and the people were a pleasant class to meet.

Clinton "spiked up" with most of the Beloit College team and won from us 15–11. The next day we played practically the same aggregation at Sharon and were victors by a score of 7 to 1. Herman Kath, a big, good-natured German who managed the Clinton team is probably smiling yet because he beat us, while Sharon was unable to turn the trick.

And so endeth the account of our numerous engagements in Wisconsin in 1901.

CHAPTER XXVII

In Illinois in 1901

We descended on Illinois like a wolf on the fold, beating Hebron our first day in the Sucker state by a score of 49 to 4 in seven innings. Elgin then took a fall out of us. She won by a score of 2 to 1 in the prettiest game ever seen on the grounds of the watch-making city. In rapid succession we beat Plainfield 34–11, Manhattan 26–5, Peotone 24–5, Manteno 9–1, Bourbonnais 6–3, Momence 18–4 and 11–5, Gardner 15–5, Dwight 16–6, Ohio 11–5, Sublette 23–4 and Mendota 13–4. Our second game at Momence was an interesting contest. Momence expected to win and we were rather half afraid that she would. The game was very close up to the eighth inning. In that fatal inning the Indians accumulated three men on the bases and Ed Davis, the full-blooded left fielder, came to bat. He lost the ball in the next county somewhere and four runs came in, which clinched the game.

Paw Paw checked our victorious career by defeating us 14–13. This result was sure to the misdirected efforts of new shortstop I was trying out in this game. He garnered as juicy a bunch of errors as I have seen for a good many moons and Paw Paw scratched out ahead of us.

Somonauk was disposed of by a score of 15–11, but it was only after the hardest kind of work in which the Indians won out in the ninth inning.

We played two games with Ottawa. We won the first 11–2 and lost the next 24–8. In the second game Green, who was pitching for the Indians, was spiked by an Ottawa man and put out of the game for a month. His foot was badly cut and it recovered only after careful and prolonged treatment. Such are the risks of base ball.

We defeated Earlville 28–13, Oregon 14–2 and 26–2, Leaf River 17–8. At Earlville we encountered the Merrifields of the University of Chicago and at Oregon we ran up against "Tub" Myers and "Johnnie" Johnson, both from Northwestern University and the latter of whom is the famous football player. Monroe Center, with Bubser of the Western League in the box, beat us 10–6.

We next went to Savanna to play the famous Maroons of that city. We had heard a great deal about the Maroons. They were considered the best team in western Illinois and had played 25 games of which they had won 24. We were a little bit troubled with stage fright and Joe Barthololmew, who went in to pitch against the terror-spreading sluggers, looked as though he would rather be at home with his father, cleaning out the barn. A big crowd was out to see the game and all of them were hoping the Indians would win, as they had seen Savanna triumph so often that they were anxious for a change. The first Savanna man to bat made a three-bagger off the first ball pitched. Joe looked over to me with a mute appeal in his eyes to take him out but I told him to stay in and the very next hitter lined out a clean single over second base and Savannah had scored her first run. It was also her last one, as she did not tally again during the game, while we were a bit more fortunate and made twenty-seven (count 'em) twenty-seven runs. We knocked three pitchers out of the box. The next day Savannah beat the Rockford Three I league team 10 to 6.

Our next stand was at Morrison. Morrison had made up a team from the Three I league, with Ashton, of Cedar Rapids, pitching. We won the game 22–1 and C. A. Booth, who was managing the Morrison aggregation, refused to play the second day of our stay on account of the big score of the first engagement. He did not notify me of his determination until about noon and so he left me no time to fill in the date. It is bad enough to cancel a game, but it ought at least to be done in season and not at the last minute.

We were to have played at Milledgeville at a sailors' and soldiers' reunion but rain prevented. We then went to Sterling where we played practically the same team we had met at Morrison and they shut us out 15–0. We then beat Moline 24–8 and Gilchrist 5–1. It will be remembered that Gilchrist was the town where we had played several warm engagements in '98 and we met many old friends there. Sandy McCullum, who has been catching for several years, still holds his old position; Heinz Miller still cavorts around second base although he is close to 90 years old, and Shuler plays brilliantly as ever. Shuler is the man who made such a name for himself as a base ball and foot ball player at the University of Illinois.

Our game with Gilchrist ended our visit to Illinois and we kissed the state good bye and told her to be good until we returned.

CHAPTER XXVIII

West Through Iowa in 1901

Winfield claimed us for its own for our first game in the Hawkeye state on our way home. The day was very cold, the grounds were out in the country so far that it took half a day to walk to them and the Winfield team was just a trifle *passé*. We won the game 50 to 5. The receipts were $11.75.

We then won from Mediapolis 13–6 and from Richland 23–4. We were to have played at Batavia on the 19th but we cut out the contest on account of President McKinley's funeral. We were at Centerville on September 20, 21 and 22. We won the first of these games 12–6, lost the second 9–6 and won the third 4–3. Before I left Centerville this time I arranged with J.C. Harvey, the manager, to come back and play him again on the 27th. I had numerous offers for this date but gave it to Harvey at his earnest solicitation. We went south from Centerville to Seymour where we won 24–5 and 29–8. We also beat Sewal 6–3 and 4–2. In Seymour I met many old friends whom I had became acquainted with four years previous. Among them were H. E. Gaddis and W. B. Perkins, both of whom have helped me in many ways whenever an opportunity presented itself.

We went to Centerville on the 27th ready to play but found that Harvey had done absolutely nothing. In fact he had gone into the country, leaving us to shift for ourselves as best we could. I sent my team on to Beacon to fill their next date while I stayed in Centerville for the express purpose of seeing Mr. Harvey and telling him what I thought of him. I finally found him late in the evening, sitting close to a newly tapped beer keg back of a joint in the lower part of town. I outlined my impressions of him in words that scintillated and then took the train for Beacon. Harvey's conduct is easily explained. Mystic was anxious to secure a date with me. Harvey hated Mystic and knew that if he made me a good offer for my only open date I could not go to Mystic. After he had closed a deal with me, thus insuring my staying away from Mystic, he paid no more attention to the matter and deliberately let me down.

Beacon is a coal mining town near Oskaloosa. We won two games there and never wish to meet a nicer lot of boys. The score of the first game was 6–4 and the second 28–1. Through the misunderstanding we did not play at Knoxville and our next game was with Pleasantville. We won 12–1. We then beat Collins 19–5. We were booked for Maxwell on the 3rd of October but on reaching that town we found no enclosed grounds and a crowd of several hundred people outside the wire fence patiently waiting for a free exhibition. As soon as I grasped the situation I sent up town for the livery rigs we had used in coming over from Collins and we drover merrily away after I had made the people a little speech on he error of their ways. For several years the people of Maxwell have been getting their base ball for nothing. I gave them a jolt that surprised them.

We defeated Madrid 22–0. The Madrid players are a nice set of boys but they have some rooters that are the most vulgar, profane and disagreeable hoodlums that I have ever listened to. In the two hours that we played in Madrid we were forced to take more abuse than we ever received in any town before. For this reason I told my players to shut the local team out if they could, just to show the creatures on the side lines what we were capable of doing. Hence the score. The people of Madrid in general do no approve of the conduct of the undesirable coterie I have referred to but that does not help a visiting team any.

We defeated Woodward 18 to 4, Boone 23–4, Bayard 8–7 in ten innings and Jamaica 5–4. This Jamaica game was a peculiar one. It was the last contest of our season and so, in order to have a little amusement, each member of my team pitched one inning. Jamaica was strengthened from all over central Iowa and we expected to lose by a good big score, especially as Gilmore the crack twirler from Mason City, was opposing us. To our surprise and the surprise of everyone else we won the game 5–4. The change of pitchers was a puzzler to Jamaica and worked like a charm.

So saying, we bade farewell to the season of 1901, this taking place on October 9th.

CHAPTER XXIX

A Few Incidents

During an experience of many years in base ball I have seen several amusing things. Were I to tell half of them they would more than fill a little book like this one. In this concluding chapter* I shall detail only a few of them.

A Player's Bench

One day in Randolph, N.Y., the manager of the local team came to me just before the game commenced and entered into a conversation on the amount of baggage we carried. Finally he took me aside and asked me if we carried our own player's bench. He wanted to be sure about the matter as he was about to have one hauled down to the park. I told him we had quit carrying a players' bench and he went away satisfied.

The Result of the Foot Race

It was in the same town of Randolph that this same manager conceived the idea of pulling off a foot race before the game in order to created a little excitement and attract a crowd to the contest on the diamond. We arranged a race between one of the Indians and a local sprinter. Randolph is located close to one of the five civilized tribes and numerous local Indians were in town to see the game between people of their own color and the whites. When they discovered that a foot race was to be run they became much excited and bet all the money they had on my player. The white man proved to be a fast runner and he beat the Indian about a foot. The New York boys, who had lost their money, were much disappointed but said noth-

*Editor's note: This chapter was the final one of the 1900 edition of the book. For the second and third editions, Green added further chapters without amending this comment.

ing at the time. They went to the game and saw my team win and after the contest was over they celebrated by getting tipsy on liquor which they obtained in some unaccountable manner. That evening a party of them discovered the white runner in the suburbs and they started after him, their blood curdling whoops splitting the atmosphere. The sprinter ran as he had never run before but at an unfortunate moment he stubbed his toe and the representatives of the civilized (?) tribe caught him. They were handling him with unnecessary roughness when a deputy sheriff happened to drive up and tried to quell the disturbance. The Indians attacked the officer and his hopes of seeing home and friends again were rapidly fading away when a crowd of white men, who had heard his cries, came to his rescue and succeeded in placing the Indians under arrest. When we left Randolph the local bastile was full of red men but my boys were too busy to learn what penalty was inflicted on them.

A Night in Iowa

During our first season, while we were yet traveling in wagons, we were overtaken one night by a rain storm and slept in a school house between Boone and Jewell Junction. The Indians were in good spirits and decided that the surroundings were favorable to a few festivities. So they stripped, each participant improvised a breech clout,* and for three hours they made the walls rattle with their savage songs and dances. There was no light in the room save the illumination which came from an occasional lightning flash and the contorting savages made a weird picture. As I looked from the schoolhouse window I could see a light appear occasionally in some neighboring house, but I afterwards learned that the citizens were afraid to approach the seat of the disturbance. It happened that a short time previous an old acquaintance of my baggage man had asked permission to join my people and he had been traveling with us for several days. He had never enjoyed a very close acquaintance with the idiosyncrasies of the red men and during their midnight demonstration his terror was pitiable. He was seemingly expecting every minute to cross the divide into the next world. Morning finally came and with the first flush of dawn our friend departed never to return. He had experienced one night of savage life and that was enough.

*Editor's Note: i.e., cloth.

The Surprise of the Game

Everyone knows that pitchers are notoriously weak hitters. In 1901 we were playing a game at Manchester, Ia. They contest was very close and was tied 4 and 4 up to the tenth inning. We failed to score in our half and retired two of the Manchester men in their half without trouble. Then Brown, the Manchester pitcher, came up. He had not made a hit in two years, and we began to plan on winning out in the eleventh. Suddenly something broke and Brown for the first time in his life connected for four sacks and won the game.

A Bad Accident

As bad an accident as I have ever seen befall players in a contest occurred at Nora Springs, Ia., during a game we played there in June, 1901. A player by the name of Wiley was on first base for Nora Springs and a man named Dexter was catching. A high foul rose between home plate and first base and both players went after it. They came together with a crash and the two men dropped to the earth senseless. When they were picked up they were covered with blood and Dexter had his jaw broken, five teeth knocked out and his forehead so badly cut that several stitches were necessary to draw the gash together. Wiley's face was also badly cut. The strangest part of the whole matter was that Dexter caught the ball and hung onto it through all the trouble, thus securing a put-out.

Two Putouts Were Enough

We were playing a game in Northwood, Iowa, one time against the local team of that place. Some of the Northwood players were kickers *par excellence*. I was scoring the game and our opponents looked on my count with a very suspicious eye. Finally, in the seventh inning, we began to tally runs and made several scores after one man was out and before anyone else was retired. Northwood then disposed of another man and their right fielder came running in from his position in the high grass, bellowing like an ox, swearing that three men were out and that there would be a riot unless I agreed with his contention. He looked like he actually wanted to fight and we were so far in the lead that the matter was not a serious one to us. Besides, my accident insurance had lapsed. So I looked at the score sheet again, told my belligerent friend he was wrong but that we sometimes played under the new rules that prescribed only two put-outs for the Indians and three for the other fellows, and my men trotted out to the field.

The New Prague Police Force

One morning we rose at an unholy hour in New Prague, Minnesota, and strolled down to the depot to catch a train. We had no breakfast and no prospect of getting any and felt generally gloomy, disagreeable and ready for war. At this unpropitious time the local drayman approached me and said he had not been paid enough for the job of hauling he had done for me and that he would have to be given more money. I knew my baggageman had overpaid him and I felt righteously indignant. The drayman was a small individual and I thought I could whip him. So I jumped at him like a hungry trout for a fly and told him I was going to start a massacre right on the platform in front of the passenger station. The native backed off and precipitately retreated up town. In a few moments he returned with an officer at his heels. The officer had a policeman's club in one hand, a small billy in the other and a huge revolver conspicuously protruding from his hip pocket. Up to the time the train left my drayman friend walked up and down the platform with the policeman following close behind him as sort of a bodyguard. I think they were anticipating bloodshed at any minute. Nothing happened, however, and as we pulled out of town I saw them going back to the principal saloon to take a drink of congratulations on their escape with their lives.

When Smith and Sandy Joined the Procession

Everyone has heard the expression, "Keep up with the procession." I never realized its full significance until after a little incident that occurred in New York City during our 1900 tour. When we jumped from Philadelphia to Brooklyn the cook table was left behind to come on a following train as there was no room for it in the baggage car which accompanied us. When the table finally reached New York we made arrangements with a transfer company to haul it over to Brooklyn but the company neglected its duty and we were forced to do without the piece of furniture during our stay in

Brooklyn. We were still without it when we went north to Mt. Vernon. I left my handsome and accomplished partner, Mr. John De Y. Smith, and the courteous and efficient baggageman, S. Tennyson Leach, in New York City to find the table and bring it on. The rest of us went ahead to play the afternoon game.

John and Sandy finally found the table in Brooklyn, where it had been taken after we left. As there was no transfer office within a mile they persuaded the driver of a pickling works wagon to haul the table and themselves to the Grand Central station on the other side of the river. The wagon bore in big gilt letters on its sides the inscription, "Pickled Pigs Feet, Tongues, and Ox Mouths." When the table and several half barrels of preserved dainties were loaded into the bed of this chariot, and the driver, Smith and Leach occupied the seat, the vehicle was just about full. It had iron tires and every time it crossed a car track the rattling could be heard a mile.

Every thing went swimmingly until New York was entered. Then the pilot drove squarely into a long funeral procession which was crawling across his pathway at right angles to the direction he chanced to be going at the time. The driver, however, was a wise lad, always ready to take advantage of every opportunity and he figured that if he joined the procession he would be free from interruption and danger and would be able to take a nice, even gait which would not tire his horse. So he turned in *directly behind the hearse* and just ahead of the mourner's carriage. In this manner the procession went through New York's crowded streets. First the hearse, then the tripe wagon with Smith and Leach perched upon the seat with the driver and all of them smoking cob pipes, and then the mourners. All the vehicles in the procession with the exception of the tripe wagon, were rubber tired and this wagon alone made enough noise to have wakened the corpse had there been any possibility of doing so. Finally the animal Smith and Leach were driving cast a shoe and they bade good bye to the procession. They are still returning thanks because they encountered no one who knew them.

When We Were All Arrested

As I have said elsewhere in this volume, our game at White Bear Lake, Minn., was finished in a hurry. We had so short a time to catch the train back to St. Paul that I sent two of my men up to the room where the team had dressed with instructions to gather up all the citizens' clothes and bring them to the train. The boys followed instructions and reached the train with the apparel just in time to jump on the cars. My men changed clothes in a room in the St. Paul union depot and after they were dressed they discovered an extra suit. It appeared that unbeknown to us, one of the White Bear players had changed in our room, hung his clothes up with ours, and they had been brought to St. Paul in the hurry. We turned the suit, which would have been dear at $5.00, over to the station authorities with a request that they hold it until it was called for. A few minutes after we had done this, a squad of policemen from the central station swept into the depot with a crowd at their heels and three of my boys in tow, whom they had picked up on their way down. They announced that they had received a telegram from the White Bear management requesting them to arrest the entire team on the charge of purloining a valuable suit of clothes. The station authorities told the officers what had happened and the officers explained to the White Bear magnate that he was evidently mistaken in the assumption that the Indians had stolen his clothes. Then the police force went on its way in peace and so did we.

Fourth of July in 1901

I enjoyed the novel experience of celebrating the nation's birthday on three different dates in 1901. We celebrated on the 4th at Waverly, Minn. The rain spoiled this celebration to a certain extent and so we celebrated there again on the 5th. Then we went to Ellsworth, Wis., where we played on the 13th. We again celebrated there. The rain had poured down on the 4th in that town and they had awaited our coming before indulging in their pyrotechnics, fireworks, foot races, etc. For once, at least, we enjoyed enough 4th of July.

CHAPTER XXX

A Resume of Our 1902 Tour

THE Nebraska Indians began their 1902 tour on Friday, April 18th at Havelock, Nebraska. They were beaten 11 to 7. They closed the season at Cedar Falls, Iowa, on Thursday, October 2nd. They won the last game of the season 14 to 0. In their concluding contest each of the Indian players pitched one innings as had been done at the close of the campaign of 1901.

During the season the team played through Nebraska, Iowa, Illinois, Indiana, Missouri, Kentucky and Tennessee. They took part in 152 games of which they won 136. They lost fifteen and tied one. The drawn engagement occurred at Fairfield, Illinois on Saturday, July 19th. This game was played in a heavy downpour of rain which made good work impossible. The mud was knee deep in some places and every time the ball hit the ground it disappeared in the water.

We played only one extra inning game during 1902. This lasted twelve innings at Galena, Illinois, on Thursday, September 25th., and it was won by the red men by a score of two to one. The contest was a pitchers' battle throughout, in which Day officiated for the Indians and Smith, of Dubuque, for Galena.

During 1902 we invaded the south for the first time, playing sixteen games in Kentucky and Tennessee. The tour of Dixie was very successful as we won thirteen of the battles in which we engaged.

The following table gives a complete list of the games played in 1902 together with the scores. It will be seen that the Nebraska boys shut our their opponents 29 times, while they themselves were shut out but once. The

Chickasaws, of Memphis, Tennessee, were the gentlemen who made the Indians taste the bitterness of scoreless defeat. We lost only one game out of the last forty-three played.

Teams Defeated by the Nebraska Indians During 1902

Alexis, Ill. 14–2.
Anna, Ill. 13–4.
Arcola, Ill. 10–5.
Ashkum, Ill. 7–1.
Ashmore, Ill. 24–5.
Aurora, Nebr. 15–7.
Beacon, Ia. 19–0.
Bedford, Ia. 10–6; 13–1.
Bedford, Ind. 14–5
Bellevue, Ia. 14–5.
Bloomfield, Ia. 24–14.
Bonaparte, Ia. 17–5; 10–9.
Braceville, Ill. 6–0.
Brazil, Ind. 16–2.
Brownville, Tenn. 4–1.
Cadiz, Ky. 19–5.
Cairo, Ill. 11–2.
Cape Girardeau, Mo. 4–0.
Carlisle, Ind. 17–3
Carmi, Ill. 22–1.
Cedar Falls, Ia. 14–0.
Centerville, Ia. 17–2; 4–0.
Cicero, Ind. 7–0.
Clarksville, Tenn. 23–8.
Clay City, Ill. 9–8.
Cleveland, Ia. 6–0.
Coin, Ia. 15–0.
College Springs, Ia. 11–6.
Collinsville, Ill. 13–4.
Covington, Tenn. 8–0.
Darlington, Ind. 9–5.
Delphi, Ind. 14–6; 3–1.
Donnellson, Ia. 14–3
Dwight, Ill. 10–6; 23–8.
Dyerville, Ia. 15–3.
Earlville, Ill. 17–4.
Eddyville, Ky. 14–4.
Earlville, Ia. 6–0.
Eureka, Ill. 11–5.
Evansville, Ill. 25–4.
Exeter, Nebr. 13–5.
Flanagan, Ill. 15–0.
Frankfort, Ind. 10–5.
Flora, Ill. 9–5.
Friend, Nebr. 12–10.
Galena, Ill 2–1 (12 innings.)
Galva, Ill. 22–2.
Galveston, Ind. 20–2.
Giltner, Nebr. 12–5.
Girard, Ill. 12–0.
Greenup, Ill. 19–3.
Gresham, Nebr. 14–0.
Hartford, Ky. 9–4.
Harrisburg, Ill. 6–0.
Hazelton, Ind. 9–0.
Herrick, Ill. 30–2.
Hillsboro, Ia. 10–1.
Hopkinsville, Ky. 13–7.

Huntington, Tenn. 14–1.
Iowa Wesleyan University, Mt. Pleasant, Ia. 6–0.
Jerome, Ia. 25–6.
Kent, Ia. 68–8.
Keokuk, Ia. 4–3.
Kewanee, Ill. Regulars 12–6.
Knox Coll., Galesburg, Ill. 8–3.
Ladoga, Ind. 8–1.
Manchester, Ia. 15–3.
Manteno, Ill. 20–10.
Marion, Ill. 11–9.
Marion, Ky. 18–1.
Marshall, Ill. 22–1.
Martin, Tenn. 10–3.
Mascoutah, Ill. 21–7.
Mediapolis, Ia. 16–1.
Momence, Ill. 5–3.
Mt. Vernon, Ill. 12–0.
Mt. Vernon, Ind. 7–6.
Moweaqua, Ill. 11–3.
Murphysboro, Ill. 23–6.
Nashville, Ill. 12–0.
Oakland, Ind. 23–2.
Oakville, Ia. 23–2.
Odell, Ill. 22–1.
Odon, Ind. 20–3.
Oskaloosa, Ia. 12–6.
Otley, Ia. 24–5.
Owensboro, Ky. 7–0; 19–1.
Pesotum, Ill. 13–2.
Pontiac, Ill. 17–5.
Poseyville, Ind. 19–5.
Prairie City, Ia. 14–10.
Princeton, Ind. 7–1.
Pulaski, Ia. 17–0; 8–0.
Ramsey, Ill. 13–6.
Reddick, Ill 15–10.
Ripley, Tenn. 18–7.
Robinson, Ill. 4–3.
Roseville, Ill. 15–0.
Salem, Ill. 15–2.
Sandoval, Ill. 24–0.
Saybrook, Ill. 17–3.
Seatonville, Ill. 16–1.
Sorento, Ill. 8–2.
Sparta, Ill. 19–9; 7–3
Streator, Ill. Reds 9–5.
Sullivan, Ill. 11–2; 5–0.
Sullivan, Ind. 15–0.
Thorntown, Ind. 27–5.
Tipton, Ind. 29–0.
Tiskilwa, Ill. 23–2.
Tolono, Ill 15–2.
Toluca, Ill. 11–2.
Tuscola, Ill. 18–5.
Ulysses, Nebr. 6–4.
Valley, Nebr. 34–12.

Veedersburg, Ind. 4–0.
Vincennes, Ind.,
Idaho Stars 6–4; 3–1.
Wahoo, Nebr. 5–3; 19–14.
Westfield, Ill. 8–0; 29–5.
West Lebanon, Ind. 17–3.
Williamsport, Ind. 9–3.
Winterset, Ia. 12–0.
Winthrop, Ia. 14–0.
Wyanet, Ill. 13–4.

Teams Which Defeated the Nebraska Indians During 1902

Benton, Ill. 10–4.
Collinsville, Ill. 5–4.
Creighton University Omaha, Nebr. 22–15.
Dyersburg, Tenn. 9–8.
Harvard, Nebr. 16–15.
Havelock, Nebr. 11–7.
Linton, Ind. 6–3.
Loda, Ill. 2–1.
Memphis, Tenn. Chickasaws 8–1; 7–0.
Saybrook, Ill. 6–4.
Staplehurst, Nebr. 10–5.
Trenton, Ill. 8–7.
University of Nebraska, Lincoln, Nebr. 13–5.

Tie game

Fairfield, Ill. 15–15.

CHAPTER XXXI

Murphysboro, Illinois

A well known citizen of Murphysboro, once visited St. Louis. His name wasn't Jenkins but I shall call him Jenkins because it is a nice, common name at which no one can take offense. Jenkins was a sport of the broad gauge pattern. When he "saw the town" he saw it right. And if the particular burg he was investigating refused to show up as well as expected he rammed his hand down its throat and turned it inside out.

Jenkins took two large drinks at his hotel before he started out to see St. Louis. The mixer who compounded his varnish, leaned over the bar confidentially and asked him if he wasn't from Murphysboro. Jenkins replied in the affirmative. Then the white-aproned impresario told his newly-discovered friend that he used to live in Murphysboro himself and "worked in Johnnie's place just across from the court house." Jenkins remembered the budge slinger and felt a bit gratified that he had found an old acquaintance so early in the evening.

Out into the night went Jenkins and ten minutes later he was buying a stack in a guilded lair of chance. The chalky-faced individual who took his money, looked at his customer uncertainly a moment, then grabbed him by the arm and cried, "Have you forgotten me? I used to deal in Joe's rooms in Murphysboro. I ain't been back to the old town for some time but if she's as good as she used to be, she's a peach."

Then Jenkins remembered that he had seen this "gent" before and shaking him cordially by the hand he said, "You're the second man from Murphysboro I've seen tonight. St. Louis must be full of 'em."

"Full? That's no name for it," replied the man who bossed the check rack, and with this remark ringing in his ears, Jenkins moved over to the other side of the room and lost his chips.

Jenkins visited in rapid succession the biggest gambling houses in the city and he met men everywhere who acknowledged Murphysboro as their home and were loud in their praise of "the hottest town in the state." Murphysboro evidently produced professional gamblers faster than St. Louis could assimilate them.

Weary of shuffling cards and clicking ball, Jenkins turned toward the palaces of vice where the social evil thrusts out its tentacles for the feet of the unwary. He no sooner seated himself in the parlor of the first house he entered then there was a swish of silken shirts and a high keyed titter of recognition. When Jenkins untangled a pair of bare arms from around his neck and brushed the cigarette fumes out of his eyes he recognized a siren whom he had seen less than a month before in Murphysboro.

"Yes," she said in answer to her townsman's question, "I'm from Murphysboro and I wish to God I was back there. Folks may talk about St. Louis being a big burg and a good burg but I had rather stay in Murphysboro a week than live here two."

Jenkins rubbed his eyes. Evidently he had not appreciated Murphysboro. Then he handed the girl a dollar, told her to buy a bottle of beer and sought another house a trifle lower down in the scale of infamy.

The landlady did not wear so many rings and the girls were fatter than the inmates of the bagnio he had just left. They graded about 2. One of them called him, "sweetheart" and asked him for a half a dollar for beer. Then she read his name and address in his hat.

"No wonder I knew your face," she said, "I used to wait table at your hotel in Murphysboro. That's where I got my start in this business. Belle's house there is the first one I was ever in."

Jenkins handed his old waitress the fifty cents she craved and went on down the line.

In a little place which boasted only one room and an attic that was reached by a ladder, he found an aged hag whose face was seamed and scarred by sin. A blackened pipe hung from between her ragged teeth and her skinny hand trembled as she thrust back the scanty grey hair which hung disconsolately about her temples.

"Auntie," said Jenkins, "I presume you are from Murphysboro," The decrepit old lady straightened up, a strange fire kindled in her eye, and she answered in a queer, cracked voice, "Right you are, sir, and if I can drag my old bones back in time I'm going to be laid away there when I die. It's the sportiest town that ever grew."

Jenkins went back to his hotel. The next day he went home. Then he called "the boys" about him. He told them that Murphysboro was furnishing disreputables for all of southern Illinois and eastern Missouri and that it was useless for them to go outside their own town for "sport." "What's the use," said he, "of going to St. Louis when everything you find there has been grown right here?"

"The boys" applauded this sentiment vigorously and resolved to waste no energy browsing in big cities.

At the entrance of a public park in Murphysboro is this sign in big letters:

> No one allowed in this park after
> six o'clock p.m. except on
> occasions of public gatherings.

I asked a policeman why this legend adorned the gateway. He told me virtue was so rare in Murphysboro that the only way to preserve the respectability of the park was to keep everyone out of it after six o'clock. This was a sad commentary on Murphysboro but I was soon convinced that it was justified.

We played in Murphysboro on July 11th and won the game 23 to 6. The most remarkable thing about this game was the crowd. I stood at the gate of the ball park and watched the people come in. They streamed up to the entrance like the spewings of Hell. There were bagnio beauties, with the paint yet damp on their faces, accompanied by their society-shunned satellites; low browed bullies from whose pockets protruded sling shots and brass knuckles; pendant-lipped loafers who fumbled with cigarette stained fingers for the admission price; toggle-jointed old men, who furtively devoured with lecherous eyes the shameless women that jostled them; young boys with tobacco stained lips who uttered oaths that would have staggered a Sykes.

I rarely saw a respectable face; I seldom heard a decent word. Criminals most of them were in looks, words, desire and deed. Nervous hands reached unconsciously for murderous knives if a tone rose to an unusual pitch; dirty fingers strayed to revolver-layden hips at every evidence of excitement. As the game progressed the women became louder, the men less regardful of appearances and part of the contest was played in the midst of a scene that one would scarce suppose could exist in public in enlightened America.

I was in Murphysboro two days. God being kind to me, I shall never be there again.

A stranger who asks for a drink of water receives the kindly reply, "Go buy beer if you're dry." Request a bit of information from a public official and he turns drowsily in his den, stretches his corpulent limbs lazily and then growls like an aged cur who has outlived his usefulness and is looking pessimistically forward to a boneless future.

Near the postoffice is a saloon with a house-of-ill-fame attachment. Little children who go for mail, run a gauntlet of drunken loafers rushing tin growlers and tired-eyed harlots who lounge about open windows in frowsy red wrappers and ogle the passers-by.

Murphysboro has two daily papers. If you are ever forced to read a copy, lock yourself in a padded cell before you begin the ordeal. They are fearfully and wonderfully made. They are constructed with reference to everything but the English language.

"Your reporter's grammar is a little shaky in places," I said to one of the editors of the town.

"Yes, maybe it is," replied the genius who ornamented the tripod, "but he's doin' pretty well. I took him off turnin' the press a couple of weeks ago and now I'll be darned if he ain't doin' pretty good at reportin'."

And has Murphysboro no advantages you ask? Well, none that I discovered. Her only art galleries consist of discouraged patent medicine advertisements that flutter from the rear ends of attenuated livery stables. The results of her library advantages are seen in weazened, pimply-faced boys who read lurid literature by the light of gasoline torches. Her orators are the chuck luck of her drinking places who utter such words as, "ace, deuce and a lovely trey." Murphysboro is certainly far gone and, like the garbage box into which every kitchen virago tosses her refuse, the town grows rottener with age. It is difficult to see why this should be. Murphysboro sits in the midst of a pleasant, prosperous country like a cancer on a fair woman's face. All about her are bustling, little cities that it is a pleasure to visit. But, like a perverse and wicked child in an otherwise respectable family, Murphysboro is an object of wonder and commiseration for all the region round about.

Have I made this picture too lurid? Have I shown Murphysboro's sins in too strong a light? Ask any traveling man who makes southern Illinois, for the name of the most putrescent town in that part of the state and he will name Murphysboro. Read a St. Louis daily paper for a month and you will notice that day after day accounts of robberies, burglaries, ravishings and murders come out of Murphysboro. Too strong! I haven't told the half.

CHAPTER XXXII

A Few Remarks on Umpires

During the time I have managed my baseball organization I have seen a great many different varieties of umpires. Almost every town has a man to preside over the destinies of its games who is considered a king pin in his particular department and most of these diamond autocrats are perfectly competent. But occasionally I run across gentlemen who are very peculiarly constituted. Sometimes they are ignorant; sometimes willfully unfair; and sometimes so inflated with ideas of their own importance that the spectator in the grand stand is treated to an exhibition that would cost him a dollar in any first class theatre in the country.

I always use two umpires, one of whom I furnish myself. I am thus sure of a square deal at least half the time. For this reason I look upon the umpiratical exhibitions with a great deal of complacency and see only the amusing features of them.

The season of 1902 was exceptionally prolific of unusual umpires. At Covington, Tennessee, the home umpire was a brother of the local pitcher. It was necessary for Romulus to make a good record on the slab and so Remus helped him out as much as possible. No matter where Romulus threw the ball, Remus called it a strike. Some of the pitches plowed up the dirt in front of the home plate; some of them were so wide the catchers could not connect with them; some of them were so high that they sailed over the backstop like balloons. But brother Remus called them all strikes, and so well did he do his work that it was only by the most extraordinary efforts we kept Covington from scoring.

Hopkinsville, Kentucky, had another remarkable autocrat. My second baseman made a wild throw during a little warm-up while we were waiting for a local man to get up to bat. The ball went far over the first baseman and into the crowd. The second baseman ran after the ball instead of waiting for the first baseman to get it. To our surprise the local judge of play immediately waved my first baseman off the diamond and ordered him out of the game.

"Why is that?" everyone asked. "Because," proudly said the umpire as he looked wisely about him, "every player must chase his own passed balls. That ball went over the first baseman's head and the first baseman's duty was to get it. Because he didn't do it I must put him out of the game. That's the rule as given in the last guide."

My captain went out to remonstrate. The umpire produced a knife about a foot long and threatened to cut somebody's "innards" out while the crowd yelled, "Stick 'im. Stick 'im. We'll stand by you." It is needless to say that Captain Roberts very precipitately retreated. Finally, however, the local solon consented to modify his decision and the game proceeded on its tranquil course.

But it remained for Bellevue, Iowa, to produce the rarest bird of the entire aviary of umpires. He was a barber, Bragg by name. Bragg took a small dose of stimulant before he marched on to the diamond and as he looked about him he felt much as Alexander the Great did when he surveyed a conquered world. We had a large crowd and there was no place for my battery to warm up except in front of the grand stand. Bragg told them to go back of the stand but nothing was there except a wilderness of unhusked corn. So the boys moved over toward the crowd as far out of the way as they could get.

"You are fined five dollars apiece," shouted Bragg. "What's that?" asked the battery. "Five dollars more," answered Bragg.

At this point I "chipped in." I inquired how the fines were going to be collected. "Hold em out of the gate receipts," was the reply. I cried, "Whoa!" and hunted up the local manager. I was afraid that when the contest was over my share of the proceeds would be devoured by fines and I would discover myself in debt to the Bellevue Baseball Association. The local manager assured me that everything was all right and the battle began.

Mr. Bragg was pretty yellow on balls and strikes but one can't object seriously to errors of judgment and nobody said a word. Then occurred a remarkable decision. I had a man on second and a man at bat. The batsman hit a sharp grounder to the shortstop and as he did so, the base runner on second started to third. The runner did not interfere with the ball in any way — in fact he did not come within three feet of it but Bragg called him out.

"What's that decision for?" we queried. "The base runner didn't touch the ball."

"No, but he might have touched it from where he was," was the swift response, "and so I'll call him out for that. The place for your runner was behind the shortstop, not in front of him."

As the Bellevue shortstop was playing very deep, I have often wondered how far out in left field Bragg's interpretation of the rules would have required the base runner to go.

Speaking of umpires, we had another funny experience in Ripley, Tennessee. Olson was umpiring for me. We had the bases full when my batter hit a sharp grounder two or three feet inside the third sack. Olson called the hit fair and two runs came in. An uproar at once arose. Olson walked over to the crowd assembled around third base and said the decision would have to stand as made. Then he saw several enthusiastic individuals begin to drag out long, keen, shiny knives.

"Ole" held up his hand for silence and said, "Wait a minute, gentlemen. There is always a possibility of an umpire being mistaken." Then he squinted carefully along the foul line and remarked, "Upon investigation I think perhaps that ball was foul and I shall call it so. Back to the bases, you runners."

The owners of the cutlery exhibition sighted regretfully as they realized they could have no fresh Indian meat for supper and the game went on. But at intervals throughout the afternoon the Swede umpire from Wahoo shed enough perspiration to float half the battle ships in the navies of the world.

CHAPTER XXXIII

Miscellaneous Observations

I

They say that when a man sticks his hand in an inoffensive prairie dog's hole and pulls out a quart of rattlesnakes he is a pretty much surprised community. I have never seen a wild, western incident of this kind but one day I observed a youth who appeared as much astonished as the investigating naturalist who picks up a mess of serpents.

During the progress of a game in Ottawa, Illinois, a dapper young rooter occupied a nice, sunny spot in front of the grand stand. In fact, he stood down by the players' bench, leaning against the wooden backstop. Suddenly a line foul winged its way to interested, little Willie. As he dodged and uttered a girlish, little squeal the ball struck him in the side of the coat, hammering the cloth up against the boards with a resounding whack.

Willie continued to smoke his cigarette and, as he did so, the people who watched him noticed a wisp of smoke curling up from his coat pocket almost exactly matching the one which was rising from his mouth. This phenomenon excited considerable interest and this interest developed very rapidly when the coat suddenly burst into a blaze that glowed like a miniature Vesuvius.

Willie hurriedly removed his coat and stamped it into quiescence. Then he explained the mystery to a curious populace. He carried a box of matches in his pocket and the concussion of the foul ball against his coat and the boards of the backstop had ignited the firesticks. When Willie discovered the trouble his coat was ruined beyond redemption and one more peril had been added to the list that accompanies cigarette smoking.

II

"What is the biggest piece of brute luck you ever saw in a base ball game?"

This question is sometimes asked me. I think that one of the luckiest accidents I ever observed on a ball field occurred at Sewal, Iowa, a little town in the southern part of Hawkeye state. We were playing a very close game and every run was valuable. Finally, however, we succeeded in getting the bases full with two men out and a hard hitter at bat. The batsman lined out an unusually fast ground ball which travelled toward the Sewal first baseman. The husky guardian of the initial sack saw the ball coming and with visions of sudden death before him, turned his back to it. In imagination I saw two runs coming across the pan. Then the horsehide struck the doughty first baseman in a very expansive Grecian bend and actually stuck in his hip pocket, snuggling down into its newly found nest like a bird coming back to its home shelter. The Sewal warrior leisurely reached his hand around behind him, removed the ball from his clothes, and retired the runner and the side while the crowd jarred the welkin with applause of the great play.

I don't know, though, that this play was any luckier than a streak of pay dirt into which the Marion, Illinois, team ran while we were playing them. The Marion field is marred by a lone tree which stands some distance back of first base. At a crisis in the game when runs were a mighty scarce commodity with my team, one of my batters lined a nice hit over first base that looked good for two sacks. But the drive struck the tree, bounced accurately back into the first baseman's hands and one little runner was out. My next hitter reached first safely and immediately started to steal second. He had the task easily accomplished when he twisted his ankle, snapped a tendon and fell in his tracks unable to move. He was easily touched out, as the accident happened just before he reached second base. I am still waiting for some member of the congregation to rise in his place and tell the waiting brethren a tale of consecutive bad luck equal to the story of these two putouts.

III

Old Buck Adams told me this story one day when we were playing in Plattsmouth, Nebraska. Buck is an old timer who has "hit the grit" many a time and oft in journeying from one part of the country to another. His language would not grace a drawing room but he makes his meaning perfectly plain.

"You see it was dis way," said Buck to me as we were sitting in the shade discussing baseball before the game commenced. "We was playin' a game one Sunday in a little town in Oklahoma. All de geeks an' spivies in de country was dere an' dey all had dough bet on de game.

"We was one run to de good in de last half o' de nint innin' an' de oder team was battin' wid two men out an' a man on first. De runner started to swipe de secon' sack but w'en he was half way down he dropt out o' sight like de eart had eat 'im. Dere was notin' but a hole to show where de guy had bin. We gedered roun' an' sent fer shovels an' ropes to get de jay outer de hole. De trouble was, dere had bin an ol' well in de path between de two sacks an de boards wot had covered it had all rotted trew. So wen de man stepped on 'em dere was Hell to pay.

"Dis accident happened about four o'clock in de afternoon an' long about six we pulled de player outer de well. Jes as his head come above de ground our secon' baseman, wot had de ball all de time, put it on 'im an' yelled, 'How's dat?' De umpire said, 'Out,' an' de game was over.

"You see de umpire hadn't called time wen we begun to dig fer dis feller an' nacherly dere was notin' ter prevent puttin' 'im out wen he come in reach.

"Of course de oder side roared dere heads off, but wot was de use? We had de game an' we drawed de spon wot was bet on it."

IV

The subject of glass arms is an interesting one. They result from various causes but often the disability comes as suddenly as a bolt from a clear sky.

I remember a game in which we participated in Gilchrist, Illinois. A man by the name of Alvorsen, who had a great reputation in northern Illinois, was pitching for Gilchrist. The ground was a little damp as there had been rain in the morning. Alvorsen used a side step in his delivery and when the game was almost over he slipped slightly in making his side step. The ball went wild and Alvorsen rubbed his arm in a puzzled manner. From that day to this he has been unable to pitch.

I had a pitcher with me one season who was what the natives call a "whirlwind." He had remarkable speed and a fine drop ball. I put him into a game and he twisted his elbow in delivering the second ball. His pitching days ended right there.

I knew another pitcher who was getting into condition in the spring by punching the bag. He misjudged his distance a little, struck the bag a glancing blow and his shoulder went out of joint. Ever since then he has enjoyed baseball as a spectator. His throwing arm was irretrievable ruined.

I could multiply these instances indefinitely. A little twist, a sudden jerk of the arm while it is cold, and the salary wing often disappears so suddenly that the player cannot realize how the accident has happened.

CHAPTER XXXIV

Some Disadvantages of Travel

People never entirely rid themselves of the feeling, which, in ancient times, impelled them, at the approach of a stranger, to raise the drawbridge and flood the moat. We naturally think our friends are a little bit better than the rest of creation and that our daily companions are more to be trusted than the stranger who tarries within the gate for only a short time. In Auburn, New York, the hotel man told me the following incident: A prominent citizen visited the Auburn penitentiary and attended a religious gathering in which all the prisoners participated. During the exercises a light-fingered convict annexed the visitor's watch. The loss was soon discovered and the victim of the theft complained to the warden. The warden was surprised and grieved and said, "You must have lost that watch somewhere else. I don't think any of *my* boys would take it."

Every town in the country thinks "its boys" are all right and that everyone else is all wrong. That's the reason I dislike to hear of a violation of law in a city while we are visiting it. The chances are strongly in favor of the local sleuths convening in solemn conclave and deciding that "them darned injuns" are the guilty parties.

After a visit we made to Indianola, Iowa, a prominent taxpayer missed a slab of bacon from his smoke house. He telephoned to the city marshal at Lucas, whither we had gone, describing his bacon accurately, telling which end of the chunk was worm eaten, and giving the age of the hog which furnished the succulent breakfast dish. The anxious meat curer ended by asking the Lucas officer to go through the Indian cook's grip, as he thought the meat was secreted in that roomy receptacle and we were only awaiting a favorable opportunity to permanently destroy its commercial value in the culinary frying pan. The Lucas officer declined this bit of work as the reward offered for the return of the goods was not large enough.

In another town a young child strayed from home into the woods while we were unfortunate enough to be filling an engagement in the vicinity. The frantic mother, who had filled her brain with weird Indian tales, at once jumped to the conclusion that the savage red men had kidnapped her "cheild." A fat "copper" came to camp to investigate but after he had looked through a couple of trunks and stuck his face in the third baseman's dirty clothes bag, news was brought from the parents of the lost cherub that "Little Precious" had come back to them full of sand burrs and huckleberry stains. If the distracted mother had only known how many small boys I dissuade from a traveling life of adventure with the Nebraska Indians every season, she would have had no fears that we had taken her offspring.

In Center Point, Iowa, the mayor appointed a large force of special police before we arrived in the town and these brave minions guarded the sleeping citizens through the perilous night, while an occasional voter put in the lone hours with a trusty gun across his knee waiting for an uprising. The funny part of all this was that we did not learn of it until we were at the depot ready to leave town. We had been in the midst of all these alarms profoundly ignorant of them.

At Collinsville, Illinois, we camped a long way from town in a little grove. Collinsville is not a large town but our camp was so located that is was hard for one unacquainted with the locality to find it. One of my players started for the tents late in the evening and after walking several blocks he decided he was out of the way and turned his steps toward a convenient residence with the object of making inquiries to set himself right. He no sooner entered the gate than the door of the house was thrown open and he found himself looking into the muzzle of a revolver, while a stern voice said, "Don't stir or say a word." In vain the Indian tried to explain but his captor would not permit it. The householder left his wife guarding the player while he ran for the police, his tongue hanging out of his mouth so far that he stepped on it at every jump. At the station he told a strange story of a big burglary and came prancing back to the scene of war with a lot of officers panting at his heels. Then the Indian, who had sat dumb with amazement, through all the excitement, was dragged away to the bastile. In the morning the whole proceeding assumed such a ridiculous aspect and some of the better people of the town were so incensed that my player was released without even the formality of a hearing.

The Indian who went through this experience was a nice appearing, well-educated young half-breed, a graduate of one of the leading Indian schools, and he never had trouble with anyone in his life. He would think of burglary about as soon as he would think of committing suicide. But he was a stranger and strangers are always safe objects of suspicion.

A most remarkable instance happened in Kokomo, Indiana, the comic opera town of the hiccough name. During the season of 1902 we stopped all night in Kokomo on our way from Tipton to Galveston. I was writing letters in the hotel office all that evening and personally saw that all the members of the team went to bed at an early hour. The next day I read in an Indianapolis paper, a long and glowing account of an attempted holdup at Kokomo the night before. The dispatch said that Nebraska Indians were the bold criminals who tried to accomplish the crime but that they escaped the officers. This story was so absurd that I wrote the Chief of Police at Kokomo in regard to it and this is the reply I received *verbatim et literatim.*

OFFICE OF
Metropolitan Police Department.
R. M. TAYLOR, Superintendent.

COMMISSIONERS:
GEO. P. WOODS,
V. D. ELLIS,
JOS. T. TARKINGTON.

Kokomo, Ind., Sept 3-1902
Guy. W. Green

Dear Sir
in reply to yours of the -Ith, inst?
will say thair was none fo your Men arrested in our city, some of them should have binn, tha did try to hold a party up, but tha run and got a way. i think in justes to your self and all corlserned, your red Men should be called down, and called proper.

Yery Resp,t Yours
R.M.Taylor
Supt.of.Police

I have always suspected that some roysterer was unsteadily taking his jag home with him the night we stayed in Kokomo, and among other things, imagined he saw an attempted Indian hold-up, which he reported to the police. I cannot understand how Chief Taylor got his information otherwise.

Fun and Frolic with an Indian Ball Team

PART I*

Of Interest, I Hope

NAKOMAS

Nakomas

One of the most peculiar players I ever had was Nakomas, a Wyandotte from Indian Territory. Nakomas, who is still in the game, is the oldest red-skin ball player alive today. When he was with me in 1906, he was fifty-five years old, but played first-class ball. Nakomas was the scrappiest player I ever had; he had been a fighter all his life, and when he came to me he was a mass of scars of various shapes, ages and varieties. He had been chipped so often about the mouth that his lips were fluted like the sides of a fancy salt-cellar. In the hotels he was compelled to eat with a sugar spoon because the ordinary article would not fit his face. Very frequently when cooks around the places where we stopped were in a hurry, they grated nutmeg and horseradish on old Nakomas' countenance, to the intense delight of the hardy aborigine. My ball players, instead of cleaning their shoes with paddles like ordinary diamond-artists, often cracked Nakomas over the "nut" with their spikes in order to jar the mud loose from the soles of their foot-gear; the rugged old red-skin would come up smiling through the shower of dirt and dust, and enjoyed the procedure very much indeed.

For years before he joined me Nakomas had been the living meat sup-

*Editor's note: Guy Green prefaced *Fun and Frolic* with the same dedicatory poem and introduction he used in *The Nebraska Indians: A Complete History*. In this edition, the repetition of these pieces has been omitted.

ply of Indian Territory. During a severe winter any aborigine who became hard up for family supplies, went to town and hunted up Nakomas; then he engaged the old boy in an altercation, and before the battle was over managed to carve off enough sirloin to replenish the family larder for weeks to come. Nakomas simply went home and grew more meat. In a short time he would come out of his tepee as plump, bright and fresh as ever, barring of course the scars.

Nakomas learned this trick of reproducing himself from a harness-maker in Muskogee by the name of Peters. Peters made a specialty of what he called the rattle-snake whip. Back behind his harness shop, he kept a large colony of vicious rattlers; he cut the tails off these serpents every two weeks and used them for crackers on the special brand of whip which he manufactured. The snakes, after each surgical operation simply looked around, sighed once or twice, and proceeded to grow new tails. The serpents possessed their peculiar power by virtue of a strange compound on which Peters fed them. Nakomas bought Peters' recipe for four ponies and a quart of whisky, and thereafter the Indian shuffled gaily along through life, a human marvel.

It should be noted in passing that Peters' whips were great stuff, and gained an enormous reputation throughout Kansas, Oklahoma and the Territory. For instance, when a quartet of mild-eyed sorrel mules decided that they had done as much work as the Union scale called for, and were plodding along with no apparent aim in life, the gentleman who was guiding their star of destiny dragged his rattle-snake whip out from under the seat, shook the cracker of it once or twice in the discouraged ears of his animals, and fractured the circumambient atmosphere in a thousand places. The animals, hearing the well-known danger signal, lit out in a way that caused chain lightning to go to the President of the Athletic Association and ask for a handicap.

Peters' business finally fell a prey to the meshes of the law. The oftener he trimmed his snakes, the bigger their rattles grew,—just as a kid's whiskers grow blacker and stiffer the oftener he peels them off. Finally when the rattles had attained the size of Baldwin apples, any energetic mule-skinner who used the rattlesnake whip shook up the country like the 20th Century Limited going through Delta, Ohio.

As Indian Territory was a new country at that time where almost everyone played poker all night and slept all day, the leading citizens resented the disturbance of their rest, and got out a permanent injunction restraining Peters from selling his specialty for ever and ever. The discouraged harness-maker disposed of his snakes at a great sacrifice to the Pittsburg Zoological Gardens.

Notwithstanding all his harrowing experiences, Nakomas was in an excellent state of preservation when he drifted into Lincoln in the Spring of 1906; he seemed good for a hundred years more of life and he certainly did enjoy it. He chewed tobacco with an earnest thought and an eager energy that beat everything I ever saw in that line previously. I used to sit behind him in the railroad trains for the express purpose of seeing him get busy with the two inches of Climax which he ordinarily separated from the parent plug as a moderate sized chew. Nakomas would open the window, rub his jaws once or twice to be sure they were in good working order, and then turn loose one of the livliest exhibitions of mastication I ever beheld. He specked and spangled the landscape as the train sped by. Occasionally his eagle eye would light on a ragged loafer holding up the sunny end of a country depot. As the train pulled out, Nakomas would carefully locate the object of his humorous experiments, open his face and emit a cataract that looked like the tail of an amber comet. When kind citizens carefully dug the loafer out, he usually looked around wildly, asked what caused the boiler explosion, and how many people were killed in the accident.

I remember that one time we were traveling through southern Wisconsin, in a region where times were hard and business so slow that the trains ran only four miles an hour. There were numerous old-timers there who had used tobacco all their lives, and whose hides were literally soaked with nicotine, but who had become so reduced in circumstances that they were unable to buy their usual chewing. Some of these old boys trotted along beside our train for days, close beneath Nakomas' window. They enjoyed the miniature cataracts which Nakomas produced as much as a thirsty sparrow does a shower bath, and the beatific expression on their faces as they followed us from town to town was one which I shall never forget. When they reached the Iowa State line, the Hawkeye authorities refused to allow these aged relics to cross the boundary, fearing they would become public charges, and their parting from Nakomas was a very sad one.

With all his laughable characteristics and his many admirable traits, Nakomas had some habits which caused me a great deal of trouble. For instance, he was always late to trains. He usually reached one end of the platform just as the rear car kissed the other end goodbye. When this happened, Nakomas raised enough disturbance to furnish a local sewing society with conversational topics for a month to come. He seemed to think the town and railway system had conspired to do him a great wrong, and he proceeded to shoot, carve and bruise everything within his range of vision. About three times a week I was compelled to go back and rescue Nakomas from the long, sharp talons of the law.

He Was Always Late at Trains

The severance of his connection with the team was brought about in a very peculiar manner. We played a game in Hartland, Minnesota, a place where no one but Swedes are allowed to live. Nakomas missed his train, and the first person he saw on whom to vent his rage was a big Scandinavian about the size of a Standard Oil Tank. Nakomas hit this Swede just once, and then the north-man woke up and the flags on the Royal Palace in Stockholm began to flap their folds with joy because of the beautiful showing that King Oscar's subject was making in a new land. Ole sank his teeth in Nakomas' neck, wrapped around him a couple of arms which looked like sections of the Washington Monument, and settled down for a long stay. A wrecking gang finally pried the Swede loose along about sunset. Like a decapitated snake he retained his enthusiasm as long as there was daylight. A local tailor sewed up the gap in the Indian's neck and shipped him on to me. The wound healed nicely and for a time we thought no more of it, but as a matter of fact the Swedish venom injected into Nakomas' system destroyed his usefulness as a member of the Nebraska Indians. He was inoculated with Scandinavian habits and characteristics. In a few weeks he abandoned his tobacco and went to chewing snuff and drinking it in alcohol. He insisted on wearing a leather coat and carrying a hard square grip trimmed in hoop iron and beautified with a wallpaper design. At Hotels he commenced asking for lingonberries and lutfisk. But the limit was reached when I found him on the bench one day in the presence of a big crowd reading a copy of the *Svenska Amerikanska Tribunen*. I could not convince people that a man reading that variety of literature was an Indian, so I very reluctantly propelled Nakomas back to the reservation.

STRANGE PLAYERS

One time in Apple River, Illinois, I ran across a ball player who had neither arms nor legs, but who played with artificial limbs exclusively. When he batted he stuck the ash in the pocket of his shirt and turned somersaults. This movement was so disconcerting to the opposing pitchers that the limbless wonder had as good an average as any of his team-mates.

Over at Sewal, Iowa, there was at one time a first baseman who usually caught hot grounders in the hip pockets of his ball pants. He was the surest fielder on the team.

I never possessed a player like either of the two above, but I had a glass-eyed performer one season that caused me lots of amusement. I noticed an expression of wild-eyed wonder on his countenance when I hired him, but I never for a moment suspicioned that this was due to an artificial window in his face. I was paying my hotel bill in Wahoo, Nebraska, one day when I heard a crash of falling glass. Thinking that a horse had run through a window, I looked around with considerable trepidation only to discover that my pitcher's glass optic had dropped out and was rolling along the marble floor. I then knew why so many local players had complained to me that this pitcher for no apparent reason looked at 'em as though he had something "agin 'em."

Rip, the Glass-Eyed Pitcher

Personally I don't consider a glass-eyed pitcher a valuable asset for any team; you never know when an accident is going to fill his system so full of splintered crystals that he will jingle when he walks. Then again his eye may drop out at any time, leaving him with a hole in his face that looks like an abandoned dug-out. This very thing happened to my man at Galva, Illinois. He was investigating the city water works when the only eye he had with him fell down the well, was pumped into the city mains, drawn by Jonas Olson from his hydrant, and drunk and digested by Mr. Olson before an alarm could be raised. A traveling man from Vermont,—a marble salesman—was stopping at the Baker House with us at the time of this mishap. He claimed to have a sample of marble with him which would take as fine a polish as the human eye, and he persuaded Rip, the pitcher, to trim down a small piece of this, polish it, and use it until a new glass-eye could be obtained from Chicago. Rip worked all night cutting this chunk of marble into shape, and came down to breakfast in the morning wearing a very pretty marble imitation in his face. Then the scoundrelly drummer discovered he had given Rip the piece of marble that contained his cost mark; he took his present back, and my player was left disconsolate.

Rip was very particular about his glass eye. He always carried a chamois-skin and a bottle of whiting in his uniform, and it was his custom between innings to go out behind the backstop and polish his eye. As the season advanced, he devoted more and more time to this manicuring process, until he would sometimes delay the game as much as an hour while he renovated his artificial optic. I of course could not tolerate this, and so one day I paid Rip off and sent him on his way. He went to Hot Springs, Arkansas, in the hope that the powerful waters of the resort would grow him a new eye.

A FOOT RACE

Randolph, New York, is in the southern part of the Empire state, in the midst of a country inhabited by the five civilized tribes. When we played there, every Indian in that region who was able to crawl, see or "holler" came into town to see the game. They were enthusiastic rooters, and added mightily to our support. During my stay among our New York brethren, I saw a pretty incident. The local Manager was an original cuss, and carried around with him a brain which was a seething mass of new ideas. He asked me, for instance, if we carried our own players' bench with us, and when I told him "Yes," he patiently waited for some humped back Indian to come over the brow of the hill lugging the needed piece of ball-park furniture. The bench did not arrive by the time the game started, and I consoled my Randolph friend by telling him I should fine my human dray-wagon a week's pay for being late.

After the game the Randolph magnate was grabbed and thrown by another idea. He told me that a tramp, who imagined he was a foot-racer, had drifted into town, and that the hobo wanted to try his limbs against one of my redskins. The manager raised a purse of $4.99 for this contest of speed,

Carrying Our Players' Bench

and I delegated Willie Weaver, a Chippewa Indian, who was about as fast as a country fire-department, to go up on the main street and show what he could do in the line of sprinting. Willie had nothing but his regular uniform and an ordinary pair of ball shoes to run in, but when the tramp (?) came out on the track he sported a pair of running pants and some spiked shoes that at once showed us there were some ingredients in our package not noted on the label.

Strange as it may seem, the tramp dug real money out of his rags and proceeded to bet this in lavish amounts with various local redskins who were standing about. Willie never wrote his folks the result of that race. The white sprinter collected his bets, and then thoughtlessly stayed in town instead of shaking hands and telling us how much he regretted to leave. The Randolph Indians didn't have much money left, but they retained a sufficient amount to buy a few strong drinks. By the time their insides were nicely calcimined with the fire-water, they knew for a certainty that the invading white man had committed one more great crime against the aborigine, so they engaged in eager search for said white man. They found him on a truck at the depot, pensively surveying the setting sun and dreaming of future conquests. He didn't dream long when he saw the storm cloud that was approaching. He leaped into the air, lit running, and tried to erase his name from the local census list. The Indians rose out of the ground, dropped from the clouds, swarmed out of back-alleys, appeared from corn-fields, sprouted from weeds that lined the roadside, and in less time than it takes to tell it, the ambitious foot-racer was a human mat for the prettiest war-dance that was ever

He Lit Running

pulled off in southern New York. The next day he was buried at county expense in a sunny corner of the local cemetery. Randolph has never seen a good foot-race since.

AMONG STRANGERS

People never entirely rid themselves of the feeling which, in ancient times, impelled them, at the approach of a stranger, to raise the drawbridge and flood the moat. We naturally think our friends are a little bit better than the rest of creation and that our daily companions are more to be trusted than the stranger who tarries within the gate for only a short time. In Auburn, New York, the hotel man told me the following incident: A prominent citizen visited the Auburn penitentiary and attended a religious gathering in which all the prisoners participated. During the exercises a light-fingered convict annexed the visitor's watch. The loss was soon discovered and the victim of the theft complained to the warden. The warden was surprised and grieved and said, "You must have lost that watch somewhere else. I don't think any of *my* boys would take it."

Every town in the country thinks "its boys" are all right and that everyone else is wrong. That's the reason I dislike to hear of a violation of the law in a city while we are visiting it. The chances are strongly in favor of the local sleuths convening in solemn conclave and deciding that "them darned Injuns" are the guilty parties.

After a visit we made to Indianola, Iowa, a prominent taxpayer missed a slab of bacon from his smoke house. He telephoned to the city marshal at Lucas, whither we had gone, accurately describing his bacon, telling which end of the chunk was worm-eaten, and giving the age of the hog which furnished the succulent breakfast dish. The anxious meat curer ended by asking the Lucas officer to go through my cook's grip, as he thought the meat was secreted in that roomy receptacle and we were only awaiting a favorable opportunity to permanently destroy its commercial value in the frying pan. The Lucas officer declined this bit of work as the reward offered for the return of the goods was not large enough.

In Murphysboro, Illinois, a young child strayed from home into the woods while we were unfortunate enough to be filling and engagement in that vicinity. The frantic mother, who had filled her brain with weird Indian tales, at once jumped to the conclusion that the savage red men had kidnapped her "che-ild." A fat "copper" came to camp to investigate, but after he had looked through a couple of trunks and stuck his face in the third baseman's dirty clothes bag, news was brought from the parents of the lost cherub that "little precious" had come back to them full of sand-burs and huckleberry stains. If the distracted mother had only known how many small boys I dissuade from a travelling life of adventure with the Nebraska Indians, she would have had no fears concerning the safety of her offspring.

In Center Point, Iowa, the Mayor appointed a large force of special police before we arrived in town, and these brave minions guarded the sleeping citizens through the perilous night, while an occasional voter put in the lone hours with a trusty gun across his knee waiting for an uprising. The funny part of all this was that we did not learn of it until we were at the Depot ready to leave town. We had been in the midst of all these alarms profoundly ignorant of them.

At Collinsville, Illinois, we camped a long way from town in a little grove. Collinsville is not a large town, but our camp was so located that it was hard for one unacquainted with the locality to find it. One of my players started for the tents late in the evening, and after walking several blocks he decided he was out of the way and turned his steps toward a convenient residence with the object of making inquiries to set himself right. He no sooner entered the gate than the door of the house was thrown open and he found himself looking into the muzzle of a revolver, while a stern voice said, "Don't stir or say a word." In vain the Indian tried to explain, but his captor would not permit it. The householder left his wife guarding the player while he ran for the police, his tongue hanging out of his mouth so far that he stepped on it at every jump. At the station he told a strange story of a big burglary and came prancing back to the scene of war with a lot of officers panting at his heels. Then the Indian, who sat dumb with amazement through all the excitement, was dragged away to the bastile. In the morning the whole proceeding assumed such a ridiculous aspect that my player was released without even the formality of a hearing. The Indian who went through this experience was a nice appearing, well educated young half-breed, a graduate of one of the leading Indian schools, and he never had trouble with any one in his life. He would think of committing suicide about as soon as he would think of burglary. But he was a stranger, and strangers are always safe objects of suspicion.

A most remarkable incident happened in Kokomo, Indiana, the comic opera town of the hiccough name. During the season of 1902, we stopped all night in Kokomo on our way from Tipton to Galveston. I was writing letters in the hotel office all that evening and personally saw that all the members of the team went to bed at an early hour. The next day I read in the Indianapolis paper a long and glowing account of an attempted hold-up at Kokomo the night before. The dispatch said that the Nebraska Indians were the bold criminals who tried to accomplish the crime but that they escaped from the officers. This story was so absurd that I wrote to the Chief of Police at Kokomo in regard to it, and this is the reply I received, *verbatim et literatim*:

Kokomo, Ind., Sept 3, 1902.
Guy W. Green

Dear Sir
in reply to yours of the 1st, inst?
will say thair was none of your Men arrested in our city, some of them should have binn, tha did try to hold a party up, but tha run and got a

way. i think in justes to your self and all corlsernes your red Men should be called down, and called proper.

Yery Resp,t Yours
R.M. Taylor
Supt. of. Police

I have always suspected that some roisterer was unsteadily taking his jag home with him on the night we stayed in Kokomo, and among other things, imagined he saw an attempted Indian hold-up, which he reported to the Police. I cannot understand how Chief Taylor got his information otherwise.

One morning we rose at an unholy hour in New Prague, Minnesota, and strolled down to the depot to catch a train. We had no breakfast and no prospect of getting any and felt generally gloomy, disagreeable and ready for war. At this unpropitious time the local drayman approached me and said he had not been paid enough for the job of hauling he had done for me, and that he would have to be given more money. I knew my baggage-man had overpaid him and I felt righteously indignant. The drayman was a small individual and I thought I could whip him. So I jumped at him like an angry trout for a fly and told him I was going to start a massacre right on

At New Prague, Minn

the platform in front of the passenger station. The native backed off and precipitately retreated up town. In a few moments he returned with an officer at his heels. The officer had a policeman's club in one hand, a small billy in the other, and a huge revolver conspicuously protruding from his hip pocket. Up to the time the train left, my drayman friend walked up and down the platform with the policeman following close behind him as a sort of body guard. I think they were anticipating bloodshed any minute. Nothing happened however, and as we pulled out of town I saw them going back to the principal saloon to take a drink of congratulation on their escape with their lives.

A game we once played at White Bear Lake, Minnesota, was finished in a hurry. We had so short a time to catch the train back to St. Paul that I sent two of my men up to the room where the team had dressed with instructions to gather up all the citizens' clothes and bring them to the train. The boys followed instructions and reached the train with the apparel just in time to jump on the cars. My men changed clothes in a room in the St. Paul Union Depot, and after they were dressed they discovered an extra suit. It appeared that unbeknown to us, one of the White Bear Lake players had changed in our room, hung his clothes up with ours, and they had been brought to St. Paul in the hurry. We turned the suit, which would have been dear at five dollars, over to the station authorities with a request that they hold it until it was called for. A few minutes after we had done this a squad of policemen from the central station swept into the depot with a crowd at their heels and three of my boys in tow, whom they had picked up on their way down. They announced that they had received a telegram from the White Bear Lake management requesting them to arrest the whole team on the charge of purloining a valuable suit of clothes. The station authorities told the officers what had happened and the officers explained to the White Bear Lake magnate that he was evidently mistaken in the assumption that the Indians had stolen his clothes. Then the Police force went on its way and so did we.

JUZICANEA

In all my experience, I have had but one Yaqui ball player. The Yaquis are a savage tribe living in the extreme southwestern part of the United

Juzicanea

States, and I hesitated a long time before I added Juzicanea to my team. He was the meanest looking Indian I have ever seen. He wore his hair long, surveyed everything suspiciously with piercing black eyes, and when he came down the street people moved to the edge of the sidewalk and apprehensively watched him pass. Juzicanea would not sleep in a bed. He could rest comfortably only on the floor or the ground. In the morning we were as liable to find him in the back yard under a tree as anywhere else. I remember that at Bluffton, Indiana, Juzicanea slept on the floor, and the landlord of the hotel, considering this a reflection on his beds, threatened to throw the entire team out of his hostelry.

Another of Juzicanea's peculiarities was his craving for raw meat; he demanded from one to two pounds of this delicacy each day, and unless he obtained it he was as surly as a caged tiger. I used to fill my pockets with raw meat when we went out to the grounds, and after Juzicanea made a particularly brilliant catch or a long hit, I fed him a liberal chunk of the succulent delicacy, which invariably caused him intense delight, and greatly amused the natives who watched him perform. I was compelled to line my pockets with oilcloth in order to provide suitable receptacles for Juzicanea's gory lunches. I made it a rule, soon after we entered each hotel, to inform either the land-

Raw Meat Caused Him Intense Delight

lord or the waiters of Juzicanea's peculiar appetite; otherwise his sudden demands for raw meat were liable to cause a series of embarassing resignations among the dining room force. At Burlington, Kentucky, however, I neglected my usual precautions. The waiters there were colored, and when one of them approached Juzicanea's chair, the savage tossed his tangled hair out of his eyes, growled ominously, and in broken English cried, "Bring me a pound of raw meat." The colored boy dropped his tray with a crash, and without waiting for his hat, his pay or anything else, plunged headfirst through the window screen and was gone. He never came back, and people who saw him several miles out from the village told me he was still travelling. His Ethiopian intellect was hopelessly unhinged.

Greatly Amused the Natives

Bring Me a Pound of Raw Meat

PLAYERS GOOD AND BAD

I have had some mighty good ball players in my time, and also some mighty poor ones. One of the funniest performers to whom I ever paid money was a lad by the name of Powless from Minnesota. He played right-field, and seemed to think it was part of his duties to fall down every time a ball came into his territory. If he ran fifty feet to catch a fly, he skated ten more on his face after he had nabbed the horse hide. If he ran backward for a long drive, he invariably sat down and caught the ball on his mouth, in his stomach, or on his spikes, but very seldom in his hands. His fame went ahead of him, and things became so bad after awhile that baseball associations which possessed a nicely sodded outfield compelled me to give bond before the game started guaranteeing to replace the sod which Powless plowed up. At Shreve, Ohio, a small stream ran through the grounds in deep left field. Powless caught a fly, made his usual gymnastic tumble, lit in the water

Speared a Fly with His Spikes

and floated down the stream a quarter of a mile before we could fish him out. Then I transferred him to right-field, where there was a wire fence. He caught a fly, very promptly fell down, mixed himself with the fence, and the efforts of a telephone gang were required to extricate him from his perilous position. Finally in Wooster, Ohio, he lay gracefully on his back and speared a fly with is spikes; the umpire refused to allow the catch. Powless insisted that it should be allowed, kicked vigorously and a riot ensued, from which we escaped with great difficulty, thankful to get away with our lives.

Finally, out of consideration for the unfortunate player, I bought him a pneumatic rubber suit which he inflated each day and put on beneath his uniform. This saved him many painful bruises, but when he fell down, one could never tell which way he was going to bounce, and his base running was a source of terror and amusement to opposing players. The end of his usefulness to me came in an unexpected manner.

We were playing a game at Plattsmouth, Nebraska, against Louisville. Old Buck Adams, a tramp ball player, was catching for Louisville. I heard him telling of the incident afterwards, and I shall give the account of it in his words:

"You see it was dis way," said Buck; "We was playin' a game agin de Nebrasky Injuns one Sunday in Plattsmouth. All de geeks an' spivies in de country was dere an' dey all had dough bet on de game. We was one run to de good in de last half o' de nint' innin' an' de Injuns was battin' wid two men out an' a man on first. De runner, a fellow named Powless, started to swipe de secon' sack but w'en he was half way down he stubbed his toe, bounced ten feet in de air, an' w'en he lit he dropt out o' sight like de eart' had eat 'im. Dere was not'in' but a hole to show where de guy had bin. We gedered 'roun' an' sent fer shovels an' ropes to get de jay outer de hole. De trouble was, dere had bin an ol' well in de path between de two sacks an' de boards wot had covered it had all rotted trew.

Powless Back Home

So wen Powless stepped on 'em dere was Hell to pay. Dis accident happened about four o'clock in de afternoon an' long about six we pulled de Injun outer de well. Jes as his head come above de groun' our secon' baseman, wot had de ball all de time, put it on him an' yelled, ''Ow's dat?' De empire said, 'Out,' an' de game was over. You see de empire hadn't called tome w'en we begun to dig fer dis Injun an' nacherly dere was not'in' ter prevent puttin' 'im out w'en he come in reach. Of course de Injuns roared dere heads off, but w'at was de use? We had de game an' we drawed de spon wot was bet on it."*

You can well imagine that such an incident as that described above cast a gloom over the team and my boys were convinced that Powless was a hodoo; so I sent him home to smoke his pipe quietly in the shade of his tepee.

SOMETHING FOR NOTHING

If it were not for the fact that the ordinary man wants something for nothing, get rich quick swindlers would go out of business. The baseball manager's path would also be strewn with roses. The number of people who will put forth five dollars' worth of effort in order to see a twenty-five cent ball game without paying the admission price, is surprising. A few incidents will illustrate my point.

At Sharpsville, Pennsylvania, the ball park was over run with people, half of whom had passes to the grounds which had been issued to them in prehistoric times for manual labor said to have been performed on an alleged race-track. I was young in the business then, and recognized these passes, but I never have been guilty of such a bit of foolishness since. At White Bear Lake, Minnesota, the diamond was half a mile from a wire fence which was supposed to keep people out of the grounds. A satisfactory view of the game from outside this fence could be obtained only by the use of a long range telescope, and yet the "sports" and "bloods" of the town put on their patent leather shoes and their clean collars, and bringing their best girls out to see the game, lined

*Editor's note: For the sake of amusement, Green has revised Buck Adams' story in *The Nebraska Indians: A Complete History* (96–97) to depict the hapless Powless as the unlucky base runner. Originally, the Nebraska Indians were not mentioned in the story.

up outside the fence, and patiently broiled in the hot sun all the afternoon. The young fellows of White Bear Lake are evidently liberal minded, and believe in showing their *inamoratas* a good time regardless of expense.

At River Falls, Wisconsin, the Mayor and Chief of Police decided that it was a "darned shame" for anyone to pay to see a baseball game. So they issued a public proclamation advising the deadbeats and deadheads of the town to line up in the road just outside of the park and get all they could for nothing. I waited until a nice crowd of these gentry had gathered, then I refunded the money to those who had paid, and my team went down town and removed their uniforms. River Falls is still wearing crepe on account of this disappointment.

For a good many years the people of Maxwell, Iowa, enjoyed their baseball for nothing. I was booked in that town for October 3d, 1901. Farmers drove in for miles to see the exhibition, bringing their wives and children with them. They lined up outside the grounds and patiently waited for such glimpses of the free exhibition as they could get. As soon as I grasped the situation, I mounted a dry-goods box, gathered a bunch of Iowa aristocrats around me and made them a speech on the error of their ways; then my team went back up town and the liberal minded citizens who had driven twenty miles to enjoy a ball game drove back home without seeing it.

Madison, Indiana, is another city which has never awakened to the fact that it takes money to pay board. The baseball ground at Madison is situated inside the fair ground. Old women, seventy years of age, crawled a mile and a half through the weeds in order to sift through holes in the fence; well dressed men ruined $50.00 suits worming their way through the grass in search of points of vantage from which they could see the game for nothing.

Bedford, Indiana, is fit to rank with Madison. We played in the fair grounds there also, and I am willing to bet that three people sneaked in for every one that paid. In this town I understood that Sunday School teachers brought their entire classes out and care-guided their little feet through various and sundry orifices in the fence.

At Wilmington, Illinois, the park was surrounded by a chattering mob of foreigners of the lowest grade, none of whom paid a cent, and all of whom were in danger of ruining their eye-sight on account of the persistency with which they glued their eyes to the knotholes in the fence. Yet these people are regarded as human beings and some of them even vote.

At Mahony City, Pa.

At Burnside, Kentucky, most of the spectators occupied points of vantage on the mountain side. A few people paid, but they did so by accident.

But Crisfield, Maryland, is entitled to the premium as the "cheapest" town in the United States. I suppose the leading citizens of that end of the oyster commonwealth ruined a thousand dollars' worth of corn in a field adjacent to the park, and destroyed enough wardrobe to stock a big clothing store, in their crawlings, creepings and contrivings to see Indians perform without exchanging the proper amount of coin for the privilege. Of course I did not play in this village, and thereby did the natives a great wrong.

Mahony City, Pennsylvania, should not be forgotten; a choice art-gallery of chronically "short" individuals stuck their physiognomies over the top of the fence and swore, smoked, chewed and spit, but never so far forgot themselves as to buy a ticket at the box-office.

It is just such towns as the ones enumerated above that put gray hairs in a manager's head and send him tottering to his grave long before his time.

UMPIRES

During the time that I have managed my baseball organization I have seen a great many different varieties of umpires. Almost every town has a man to preside over the destinies of its games who is considered a king-pin in his particular department, and most of these diamond autocrats are perfectly competent. But occasionally I run across gentlemen who are very peculiarly constituted. Sometimes they are ignorant; sometimes wilfully unfair; and sometimes so inflated with ideas of their own importance that the spectator in the grandstand is treated to an exhibition that would cost him a dollar in any first-class theatre in the country.

I always use two umpires, one of whom I furnish myself. I am thus sure of a square deal at least half of the time. For this reason I look upon umpiratical exhibitions with a great deal of complacency, and see only the amusing features of them.

The season of 1902 was exceptionally prolific of unusual umpires. At Covington, Tennessee, the home umpire was a brother of the local pitcher. It was necessary for Romulus to make a good record on the slab and so Remus helped him out as much as possible. No matter where Romulus threw the ball, Remus called it a strike. Some of the pitches plowed up dirt in front of the home plate; some of them were so wide the catcher could not connect with them; some of them were so high that they sailed over the backstop like balloons. But brother Remus called them all strikes, and so well did he do his work that it was only by the most extraordinary efforts that we kept Covington from scoring.

Hopkinsville, Kentucky, had another remarkable autocrat. My second baseman made a wide throw during a little warm up while we were waiting for a local man to go up to bat. The ball went far over the first baseman's head and into the crowd. The second baseman ran after the ball instead of waiting for the first baseman to get it. To our surprise the local judge of play immediately waved my first baseman off the diamond and ordered him out of the game.

"Why is that?" everyone asked. "Because," proudly said the umpire, as he looked wisely about him, "every player must chase his own passed balls. That ball went over the first baseman's head and the first baseman's duty was to get it. Because he didn't do it I must put him out of the game. That's the rule as given in the last Guide."

My captain went out to remonstrate. The umpire produced a knife about a foot long and threatened to cut somebody's "innards" out while the crowd yelled, "Stick 'im, Stick 'im; we'll stand by you."

It is needless to say that captain Taboshekeshick very precipitately retreated. Finally however, the local solon consented to modify his decision and the game went on.

But it remained for Bellvue, Iowa, to produce the rarest bird of the entire aviary of umpires. He was a barber, Bragg by name. Bragg took a small dose of stimulant before he marched onto the diamond and as he looked about him he felt very much like Alexander the Great. We had a large crowd and there was no place for my battery to warm up except in front of the grandstand. Bragg told them to go back to the stand, but nothing was there except a wilderness of unhusked corn. So the boys moved over toward the crowd as far out of the way as they could get.

"You are fined five dollars apiece," shouted Bragg. "What's that?" asked the battery. "Five dollars more," answered Bragg. At this point I "chipped in." I inquired how the fines were going to be collected. "Hold 'em out of the gate receipts," was the reply. I cried, "Whoa!" and hunted up the local manager. I was afraid that when the contest was over my share of the proceeds would be devoured by fines, and I would discover myself in debt to the Bellvue Baseball Association. The local manager assured me that everything was all right and the battle began.

Mr. Bragg was pretty yellow on balls and strikes, but one can't object seriously to errors of judgment and nobody said a word. Then occurred a remarkable decision. I had a man on second and a man at bat. The batsman hit a sharp grounder to the shortstop and as he did so the base runner on second started for third. The runner did not interfere with the ball in any way,— in fact he did not come within three feet of it — but Bragg called him out.

"What's that decision for?" we queried. "The base runner didn't touch the ball." "No, but he might have touched it from where he was," was the swift response, "and so I call him out for that. The place for your runner was behind the shortstop, not in front of him."

As the Bellvue shortstop was playing very deep, I have often wondered how far out in left field Bragg's interpretation of the rules would have required the base runner to go.

Speaking of umpires, we had another funny experience in Ripley, Tennessee. Olson was umpiring for me. We had the bases full when my man hit a sharp grounder two or three feet inside the third sack. Olson called the hit fair and two runs came in. An uproar at once arose. Olson walked over to a crowd assembled around third base, and said the decision would have to stand as made. Then he saw several enthusiastic individuals begin to drag out long, keen shiny knives.

"Ole" held up his hand for silence and said, "Wait a minute, gentlemen. There is always a possibility of an umpire being mistaken." Then he squinted carefully along the foul line and remarked, "Upon investigation I think perhaps that ball was foul and I shall call it so. Back to the bases, you runners."

The owners of the cutlery exhibition sighed regretfully as they realized that they could have no fresh Indian meat for supper, and the game went on. But at intervals throughout the afternoon the Swede umpire from Wahoo shed enough perspiration to float half the battleships in the navies of the world.

At Carrollton, Missouri, the village "bad man" umpired. He took his shooting irons out to the grounds with him, and before the game started exhibited his arsenal, and cheerfully informed my men that they must not expect to win because he would not allow it. He called my players out because they walked bow-legged when they went to bat, and did various other little stunts of amusing character. He certainly made good his threat to steal the game.

A FUNNY ACCIDENT

They say that when a man sticks his hand in an inoffensive prairie dog's hole and pulls out a quart of rattlesnakes he is a pretty much surprised community. I have never seen a wild, western incident of this kind, but one day I observed a youth who appeared as much astonished as the investigating naturalist who picks up a mess of serpents.

During the progress of a game in Ottawa, Illinois, a dapper young rooter occupied a nice, sunny spot in front of the grandstand. In fact he stood down by the players' bench, leaning against the wooden backstop. Suddenly a line foul winged its way to interested little Willie. As he dodged and uttered a girlish little squeal, the ball struck him in the side of the coat, hammering the cloth up against the boards with a resounding whack. Willie continued to smoke his cigarette, and as he did so, the people who watched him noticed a wisp of smoke curling up from his coat pocket almost exactly matching the one which was rising from his mouth. This phenomenon excited considerable interest and this interest developed very rapidly when the coat suddenly burst into a blaze that glowed like a miniature Vesuvius. Willie hurriedly removed his coat and stamped it into quiescence. Then he explained the mystery to a curious populace. He carried a box of matches in his pocket, and the concussion of the foul ball against his coat and the boards of the backstop had ignited the firesticks. When Willie discovered the trouble his coat was ruined beyond redemption and one more peril had been added to the list that accompanies cigarette smoking.

BRUTE LUCK

"What is the biggest piece of brute luck you ever saw in a base ball game?" This question is sometimes asked me. I think that one of the luckiest accidents I ever observed on a ball field occurred at Sewal, Iowa, a little town in the southern part of the Hawkeye state. We were playing a very close game and every run was valuable. Finally however, we succeeded in getting the bases full with two men out and a hard hitter at bat. The batsman lined out an unusually fast ground ball which traveled toward the Sewal first baseman. The husky guardian of the initial sack saw the ball coming, and with visions of sudden death before him, turned his back to it. In imagination I saw two runs coming across the pan. Then the horsehide struck the doughty first baseman in a very expansive Grecian bend and actually stuck in his hip pocket, snuggling down into its newly found nest like a bird coming back to its home shelter. The Sewal warrior leisurely reached his hand around behind him, removed the ball from his clothes and retired the runner and the side, while the crowd jarred the welkin with applause of the great play.

I don't know though, that this play was any luckier than a streak of pay dirt into which the Marion, Illinois, team ran while we were playing them. The Marion field is marred by a lone tree which stands some distance back of first base. At a crisis in the game when runs were a mighty scarce commodity with my team, one of my batters lined a nice hit over first base that looked good for two sacks. But the drive struck the tree, bounced accurately back into the first baseman's hands, and one little runner was out. My next hitter reached first safely, and immediately started to steal second. He had the task easily accomplished, when he twisted his ankle, snapped a tendon and fell in his tracks unable to move. He was easily touched out, as the accident happened just before he reached second base. I am still waiting for some member of the congregation to rise in his place and tell the waiting brethren a tale of consecutive bad luck equal to the story of these two put-outs.

OVER ADVERTISING

We played two games in Kahoka, Missouri, one time; it is a beautiful little town in the northern part of the state. The ball park was a very fine one, and the team was said to be the best in that section. A big crowd was out to see the first game, and we smothered the Missourians by the score of 20 to 5. They had saved their star box-artist however, for the concluding

Tied Himself in a Bow Knot

game; Coke was his name. They chalked the side walk with the magnetic words, "Coke will pitch." Everyone who could raise the money came out to see Coke perform; he was an old professional and was said to be invincible. Kahoka went into the field, and Coke stepped into the box. Ogee, the Indian shortstop went to bat. The grandstand was packed to suffocation, and as Coke rubbed his hands over the ball and smiled gleefully, some enthusiast on the seats sang out, "Don't waste a one, Jimmy." Jimmy tied himself in a double bow-not smiled confidently and said, "I won't." Then he turned his first ball loose. Ogee hit it so far no one ever went after it. The second Indian came to bat, and he wrought some more ruin by losing another nice, white $1.25 ball. The third redskin stepped up and touched Coke's delivery so hard that nobody ever saw the pellet again. At the conclusion of the game the score was 34 to 7 in favor of the red men, and several precincts had not yet been heard from. Coke threw his arm away in a useless effort to stem the tide; he was simply the victim of over-advertisement.

He Threw His Arm Away

In 1905 we played a series of three games with Kentucky University at Lexington. We won the first engagement 11 to 0. At its conclusion Tobey stepped out into the middle of the diamond, and proudly introduced Gayzhebawesa, our pitcher for the next game, as the greatest Indian twirler alive. We all felt proud and happy, and every Kentuckian there expected something to drop on the blue-grass metropolis the next afternoon. But the College boys used Gayzhebawesa for a human door mat, and we were beaten so easily that I blush now when I tell about it. Poor Geyzhebawesa was simply the victim of over-advertising.

NOT SO BAD AS THEY SEEMED

Our game with the Tonawanda Indians at Akron, New York, was a peculiar one. The redskins had been playing all the best teams in their region for several years and had never lost a contest. Their method of procedure was a very simple one. The moment their opponents appeared on the grounds the entire tribe gathered on the side lines and began a series of blood-curdling yells and whoops. They would threaten to cut the hearts out of their pale-faced adversaries, and do various other unpleasant things. By this method the Tonawanda braves produced a reign of terror that took all the courage out of the teams which opposed them, and the dusky sons of the forest were invariably returned winners. They tried these tactics with us but my men had been there before and laughed at the efforts of their Tonawanda brethren. We took the lead in the very first inning and were never headed. I remember that before the game one little fat Indian sat up on top of the water-keg like a Chinese idol on a pillar, and tore the atmosphere into shreds with his vociferations and savage yells. After the first round of the battle he wilted like a sensitive plant in the breath of a simoon and didn't utter another word. In fact the whole tribe subsided, and became the most docile lot of aborigines I ever saw.

During our first season while we were yet traveling in wagons, we were overtaken one night by a rain storm and slept in a schoolhouse between Boone and Jewell Junction, Iowa. The Indians were in good spirits and decided that the surroundings were favorable to a few festivities. So they stripped, each participant improvised a breechclout,* and for three hours they made the walls rattle with their savage songs and dances. There was no light in the room save the illumination which came from an occasional lightning flash and the contorting savages made a weird picture. As I looked from the schoolhouse window I could see a light appear occasionally in some neighboring house, but I afterwards learned that the citizens were afraid to approach the seat of the disturbance. It happened that a short time previous an old acquaintance of my baggageman had asked permission to join my people and he had been traveling with us for several days. He had never enjoyed a very close acquaintance with the idiosyncrasies of the red men and during their midnight demonstration his terror was pitiable. He was seemingly expecting every minute to cross the divide into the next world. Morning finally came and with the first flush of dawn our friend departed never to return. He had experienced one night a savage life and that was enough.

ACCIDENTS

Everyone knows that pitchers are notoriously weak hitters. In 1901 we were playing a game at Manchester, Iowa. The contest was very close and was tied 4 to 4 up to the tenth inning. We failed to score in our half and retired two of the Manchester men in their half without trouble. Then Brown, the Manchester pitcher came up. He had not made a hit in two years and we began to plan on winning out in the eleventh. Suddenly something broke and Brown for the first time in his life connected for four sacks and won the game.

As bad an accident as I have ever seen befall players in a contest occured at Nora Springs, Iowa, during a game we played there in June, 1901. A player by the name of Wiley was on first base for Nora Springs and a man named Dexter was catching. A high foul rose between first base and home plate, and both players went after it. They came together with a crash and the two men dropped to the earth senseless. When they were picked up they were covered with blood, and Dexter had his jaw broken, five teeth knocked out and his forehead so badly cut that several stitches were necessary to draw the

*Editor's note: i.e., breech cloth.

gash together. Wiley's face was also badly cut. The strangest part of the whole matter was that Dexter caught the ball and hung onto it through all the trouble, thus securing a putout.

TWO PUTOUTS ENOUGH

We were playing a game in Northwood, Iowa, one time against the local team of that place. Some of the Northwood players were kickers, *par excellence.* I was scoring the game and our opponents looked on our count with a very suspicious eye. Finally in the seventh inning we began to tally runs and made several scores after one man was out and before anyone else was retired. Northwood then disposed of another man and their right fielder came running in from his position in the high grass, bellowing like an ox, swearing that three men were out and that there would be a riot unless I agreed with his contention. He looked like he actually wanted to fight and we were so far in the lead that the matter was not a serious one to us. Besides, my accident insurance had lapsed. So I looked at the score sheet again, told my belligerent friend he was wrong, but that we sometimes played under the new rules that prescribed only two put-outs for the Indians and three for the other fellows, and my men trotted out to the field.

THEY JOINED THE PROCESSION

Everyone has heard the expression, "Keep up with the procession." I never realized its full significance until after a little incident that occured in

New York City during our 1900 tour. When we jumped from Philadelphia to Brooklyn the cook table was left behind to come on a following train as there was no room for it in the baggage car which accompanied us. When the table finally reached New York we made arrangements with a transfer company to haul it over to Brooklyn, but the company neglected its duty, and we were forced to do without the piece of furniture during our stay in Brooklyn. We were still without it when we went north to Mt. Vernon. I left my handsome and accomplished partner, Mr. John DeY. Smith, and the courteous and efficient baggage man, S. Tennyson Leach, in New York City to find the table and bring it on. The rest of us went ahead to play the afternoon game. John and Sandy finally found the table in Brooklyn, where it had been taken after we left. As there was no transfer office within a mile they persuaded the driver of a pickling works wagon to haul the table and themselves to the Grand Central Station on the other side of the river. The wagon bore in big gilded letters on its sides the inscription, "Pickled Pig's Feet, Tongues and Ox Mouths." When the table and several half barrels of preserved dainties were loaded into the bed of this chariot, and the driver, Smith and Leach, occupied the seat the vehicle was just about full. It had iron tires and every time it crossed a car track the rattling could be heard a mile. Everything went swimmingly until New York was entered. Then the pilot drove squarely into a long funeral procession which was crawling across his pathway at right angles to the direction he chanced to be going at the time. The driver, however, was a wise lad, always ready to take advantage of every opportunity and he figured that if he joined the procession he would be free from interruption and danger, and would be able to take a even nice gait which would not tire his horse. So he turned in directly behind the hearse and just ahead of the mourners' carriage. In this manner the procession went through New York's crowded streets. First the hearse, then the tripe wagon with Smith and Leach perched upon the seat with the driver smoking cob pipes, and then the mourners. All the vehicles in the procession with the exception of the tripe wagon, were rubber-tired, and this wagon alone made enough noise to awaken the corpse had there been any possibility of doing so. Finally the animal Smith and Leach were driving cast a shoe and they bade goodbye to the procession. They are still returning thanks because they encountered no one who knew them.

GETTING ACQUAINTED WITH STRANGERS

The longer I live, the more thoroughly am I convinced that it never pays one stranger to grow "miscellaneous" with another on short acquaintance. A few incidents will furnish a correct map of my meaning.

For some years I have had with me a pitcher by the name of Tobey, a very blonde white man, who twirls his share of the games and acts as assistant manager of the team. On one occasion Tobey was pitching a hard game at Attica, Indiana. The opposing rotater was the pride of that section; his picture appeared in the weekly newspaper the day before we played in Attica, and all his relatives from his grandfather down, were out to see the game. The grandfather was ninety-two years of age, and was wheeled out to the grounds in an invalid chair. During the game, Tobey sat down by him, not knowing who he was, and proceeded to visit with the veteran. "Don't you think," said the old man, in a cracked voice, "that the boy is pitching mighty fine ball?" "Sure he is pitching fine ball," answered Tobey, "it's the finest ball I ever saw; it's a new $1.50 Spalding." Then Vesuvius erupted. The poor old crippled nonagenarian climbed out of his invalid chair and rained right and left handers on Tobey's physiognomy so thick and fast the "Blondy" thought he had been caught in a hail storm with no shelter in sight. He finally went down for the count, and old grandpa tottered back to his nurse. A bucket of water dashed in Tobey's face soon restored him to consciousness and the game went on, but the good effects of this lesson remained with him forever.

We were driving one night from Woodsfield to Barnesville, Ohio. One of my pitchers, Thorgy by name, was riding with the Woodsfield driver. This driver had been a great reader of wild-west stories, and had a wholesome respect for the prowess of the Indians. We stopped at a tollgate, and Thorgy descended to get a drink, leaving his coat on the seat. The driver either accidentally or intentionally shoved the garment off on the ground. Then Thorgy reached for him. The Woodsfield scion dropped off on the other side of the wagon and was moving when he hit the ground. We heard the thud of his foot-steps as he disappeared down the road in the direction of his home. The hour was ten o'clock at night and the road was dark as pitch and as lonesome as a Texas Republican. The scared driver faded away like a town marshall in the presence of a crime, and never stopped going until he struck his family roof-tree twelve miles distant. His subsequent treatment of strangers was greatly improved.

HE ALMOST DROPPED DEAD

Mr. D. W. Tobey acted as road manager for my Japanese Ball Team in 1906. He surprised me one day by sending me the following letter. I have no doubt the incident described is true in every particular. The question is — could Tobey have been held as the murderer of this hotel keeper had he actually dropped dead, and would I have been regarded as an accessory because I furnished the money which killed him.

"Manhattan, Kans., Apr. 22nd, 1906.

"Now Guy, the following is certainly the truth. I have one eye witness to this, Kissell. When I paid my hotel bill last night at Riley, $18.75, the proprietor fell into a swoon; his heart failed him and it was several minutes before he was able to sign receipt. Guy, I tell you I was scared. I counted out the eighteen bones and I was getting the seventy-five cents when I noticed he was acting very strange. He started to bend over like a person having a fit; he kicked the desk a hell of a jolt and closed his eyes, his face all wrinkled up. I tell you I thought his day had come. I yelled to Kissell. He was on the porch. He came in and was badly scared and wanted to know what I had done to the man. He came to after a short while, signed the receipt, then he told us he was subject to heart failure. I shall never forget this affair as long as I live. You know you and I used to say we knew of or about people dropping dead when we paid a hotel bill. Well, this was close enough for me. It was a rotten hotel, no towels, no water and no grub to speak of. I do believe the $18.75 was a life-saver to him; yes, I am sure it was."

THE TRAMP PITCHER

In the larger towns I often advertise my games by a ballyho stunt. Tobey puts on a clown costume which I carry with me, and in company with the

Indians in savage dress, announces the games upon the streets. One season we had been playing the smaller towns of central Illinois for several weeks and opportunity for a good ballyho had been sadly lacking. The clown suit was moldering away in the trunk and becoming lonesome from disuse. We were booked for a game in Illiopolis, and were anxious to win it in such an impressive way that the victory would never be forgotten, because Illiopolis, which had only a little country team, had previously beaten us twice by close scores. Tobey was seized by a bright idea which we proceeded to put into execution. We secured a disreputable old tramp suit, a pair of shoes which gapped in a dozen places and a grip which would have disgraced a suburban ash-pile. Tobey carefully packed his clown suit in his grip, donned his tramp attire, and by the consent of the conductor of our train, rode into Illiopolis on the blind baggage. He dropped off the cars and went up town by way of back alleys and unfrequented streets. The rest of us repaired to our hotel. Shortly after, I was in consultation with the Illiopolis manager, who was the leading druggist of the town, when a tough looking specimen of the *genus* hobo, carrying a battered old satchel, shuffled into the store, deposited his cigarette butt carefully on the counter and asked for the local ball man. Having secured his ear, Tobey unfolded a tale of woe a mile long. He told how he had been travelling as a clown with a little circus which had recently stranded on the other side of Decatur, how he was a ball player and a good pitcher, and would like a chance to work that afternoon against the Nebraska Indians. The Illiopolis man questioned him closely and then turned him down, saying he did not want to monkey with any tramps. Then Tobey turned to me, and with tears choking his voice, asked if there was any chance to get on with me, and ended by begging for something to eat. I gave him a quarter and told him to eat at a restaurant but not to come fooling around our hotel. Then I asked him if he had a ball suit, but he said he had nothing left but his clown clothes which he had brought with him from the circus. He proudly said, however, that he owned a pair of ball shoes. Finally I told him to put on such costume as he happened to have and come out to the grounds in the afternoon. Then he limped disconsolately away, bought him a meal in a cheap restaurant and with the aid of some small boys found a barn in which to dress.

Before the hour for the game arrived, everyone in town knew of the tramp ball player who was in the village, and when Tobey came onto the grounds a little late, dressed in his clown suit, every farmer present pointed his finger at him and said, "That's the feller that travelled with the busted show, and claims to be a ball player. I hope the Injun manager lets him pitch this afternoon, and we'll show 'im what our boys can do to 'im." None of my players would have anything to do with Tobey, and he was compelled to warm up with a high school lad who borrowed a big mitt from one of the Illiopolis players. The game finally started and Tobey went into the box for me. For five innings he shut out the Illiopolis team. Then he shed his clown blouse, exposed the Indian shirt which he was wearing underneath it, rid himself of his clown hat and put on his Indian cap and the secret was out. A roar went up from the spectators when they realized the clever ruse that had been worked. We won the game eleven to two.

SANDY

One of the most peculiar characters that has ever been connected with my organization was Sandy Leach, for several years my property man. He was a big strapping lad, as strong as a bull, who juggled trunks as if they were play things. As harmless as a kitten in reality, he had a ferocious appearance which awed the obstreperous and induced would-be bad men to think twice before they started trouble. It was his delight to work on the gate loaded down with a piece of artillery which weighed twelve pounds *avoirdupois*, and decorated with a cartridge belt filled with deadly lead pellets. I sent him ahead of me one time to prepare for my advent in a town where we expected to arrive late, and he was compelled to stay over night at Davenport, Iowa. He picked out a tough hotel close to the depot, a hostelry which had a reputation for midnight killings and robberies. On the way up to his room he dragged his artillery from his hip pocket, caressed it affectionately, and said to the night clerk, "See here, youse, I understan' dis dump is a tough joint, an' I want to say dat if I hear any disturbance roun' me room tonight, I'll make a mosquito bar* out o' some o' youse guys." Then he went peacefully to bed leaving a call for 5:30. He had so thoroughly cowed the

*Editor's note: i.e., a fly strip.

hotel clerk that that individual was afraid to rap on his door in the morning and it was only by accident that Sandy awoke and made his train.

I remember that on one occasion Sandy, who is very near sighted, distinguished himself by stealing his own trousers. We were camping out at that time, and for some reason Sandy in the afternoon had taken off his best clothes, and had been working around the trunks in overalls and jumpers. Some of the local players changed clothes in our tents that day, and after they were gone Sandy discovered what appeared to him to be an elegant pair of pantaloons peacefully reposing in one corner of his tent. It did not occur to him that the garments were his own, as he thought he had carefully put his clothes away when he changed to his working duds. So Sandy, in his near-sighted innocence, quietly approached his quarry, grabbed it quickly when no one was looking, and salted it away in his grip for future reference. Later in the evening when everyone had left the vicinity of the tents, and all was still, Sandy opened his grip, determined to examine carefully his new find. Then he discovered to his chagrin that he had stolen his own pants.

TWO LITTLE BOYS

The following succinct paragraph appears on the back of my letterheads: "Under no circumstances will we play for a smaller general admission price than twenty-five cents. This must be paid by everyone both men and women. If the game is worth seeing it is worth paying for."

I always try to enforce the above provision to the letter but on one occasion I was unable to do so. I arranged a game by wire with Ada, Ohio, on very short notice. The local manager had only one day in which to advertise, and so he issued bills of his own which bore the magic words, "Ladies free." The first thing I saw upon arriving at Ada was one of these fatal bills. It was too late, however, to avert the threatened blow, and so I drew a long breath and decided to take my medicine like a man. The turnout of women in Ada was remarkable. They came by dozens and twenties from all points of the compass. The town emptied itself of its female population, and then country cousins and ladies from the suburbs began to arrive, having been notified by telephone and grape-vine telegraph of the free feast which awaited them. A few citizens of the masculine persuasion passed through the gate and contributed the admission price, but they were few, Oh! So few! I looked over the baseball yard and decided that every woman in that part of Ohio was within the enclosure, when suddenly my eyes beheld sailing down the road a majestic galeon. She was a fond mother who was hurrying to get into port before it was too late, and she was convoyed on either side by two strapping boys, one of whom looked to be about nineteen years of age and the other twenty-four. I figured that I was sure of fifty cents more with which to buy bread when the ample lady started to brush by me at the gate, her boys sticking close to either side. "Madam," I said, "the men will have to buy tickets." She fixed me with a look of haughty surprise, and then ejaculated, "What! do I have to pay for my two little boys?" "Yes, madam," I responded, "all boys have to pay as soon as they begin to grow whiskers." "Then," said the offended goddess, "I shall not patronize your game. You're nothing but a sharper going through the country robbing poor people and making mothers pay for children who should be admitted free." I stood firm, however, and the lady and her two "little boys" backed out of the gate and wended their way toward town. Question: How much did I lose by refusing to admit free this fond mamma and her two "little boys?"

THE OLD LADY CAUGHT ON

A cheery-faced, sociable, loquacious, finely dressed old southern lady and her no less interesting and entertaining husband boarded at the same hotel where we stayed during one of our visits to Lexington, Kentucky. The old lady was much interested in the Indians, and I persuaded her to go out and see one of the games which we played against the Kentucky University team. That evening at supper I asked my newly made friend how she enjoyed the contest. "Oh, I liked it very much," she replied, "and I think it was awfully exciting; but I want to speak to your catcher."

Taboshekeshick, the catcher, was sitting beside me at the time. The old lady shook a warning finger at him and continued, "Do you know, sir, you didn't treat our boys fair? Maybe you thought you were concealing it, and that nobody could notice what you were doing, but my old eyes are pretty sharp, and I know, sir, that you were making signs behind the bat and putting up a scheme to fool our boys. You may call that a cute trick, but I can't see anything about it but cheating, and I don't care to have anything to do with men who are guilty of that kind of work." Then the old lady closed up as tight as a clam and not another word would she say to us during our stay in Lexington.

HE WANTED A GOOD PLACE

When my team went into the field for the second inning at Stevens Point, Wisconsin, I was astonished to see a very large and very black colored man walk majestically out behind second base, select a nice grassy spot, settle himself on his camp-stool, raise his umbrella, and assume an attitude of quiet expectancy. I waited a few minutes, thinking that if the man were violently insane he would begin to show signs of his affliction, but he said nothing — simply gazed soberly straight ahead and waited for the festivities to continue. Then I went out and touched him on the arm. I asked him what his business was in that locality. He replied, "I am out heah to see the game, sah; theah is such a crown up along the sides that I can't see nothin' at all. The men up theah told me to come out heah wheah theah was more room." I explained to him that the second sack wasn't exactly the place for the spectators, and after much argument persuaded him to retire from the diamond amid the uproar of the hilarious crowd of spectators who had put up the job.

LOCAL MANAGERS WHO WERE FOOLED

It used to be a common thing for local managers to come to me soon after we reached a town and with tears in their eyes and apprehension in their voices, tell me they had booked my team contrary to the judgment of many of the town's best citizens. Then they would beg me to put up as good an exhibition as possible, because their people were used to fast baseball, and they were afraid that a poor game with a travelling organization would ruin future prospects in the village.

The manager at Mt. Vernon, N. Y., took me back to the grand stand for a confidential talk, lowered his voice to a hoarse whisper and addressed me thus: "Now I have a very strong team here, and they have been playing good ball. In fact, our people have been used to close contests, and I hope you will do your best and at least try to give my boys a run for their money. Of course I realize that you cannot win, but I don't want you to get discouraged, but play for all there is in you. Put in your very best pitcher, for I have a team of sluggers." We beat Mt. Vernon fifteen to nothing, my pitcher allowing the local team one hit.

W. J. Swift, at one time manager of the Kenosha, Wisconsin, team, told me before our appearance in his city, that he had no faith in the Nebraska Indians, and that he hoped I would give him the very best I had in stock, because he didn't want to disappoint his supporters by booking a fake. He said his town had been beating everyone and that he wanted us to make the game as close as we could. We jumped in from the start, and ran the Kenosha team to death. We batted and biffed and banged them until good brother Swift's crown grew discouraged and began to leave in the sixth inning. The score was fourteen to one. That was pretty good for a fake traveling team, wasn't it?

THE SMALL CROWD LEFT

I have heard the following story a good many times in several different forms, and I smile every time anyone tells it to me.

We were playing in Greenup, Illinois, for the benefit of the smallest crowd that it was ever our misfortune to give an exhibition before. I was working on the gate. A Sabbath stillness pervaded the air. I had not heard a sound from the diamond, but I judged that the game had advanced to about the third inning. I was aroused from a semi-doze by the voice of a little boy who was just making his way out of the enclosure. "Hello, son," said I, "aren't they playing the game?" "Yes, sir," he replied. "What's the matter? Don't you like it?" I continued. "Yes sir, it's all right," the little lad responded, "but I'm afraid to stay in there all alone with nobody but the umpire and them eighteen big rough ball players." Then the lad ambled down the road, and although the crowd had departed, the players went on and finished the game.

A FOOL QUESTION

We were waiting for a train at a small Junction in Indiana. Our trunks and grips were scattered around over the depot platform. A couple of rural individuals came over to the station from a neighboring hay-field and eyed us curiously. They read the big white inscriptions on the trunks which said that the party was "Green's Nebraska Indian Base Ball Team." They read the records of games lost and won for ten years past. They examined the bats, and balls, and mitts, and mask. Having done all this, they sidled up to me and overcome by a desire to worry me by fool questions, they asked, "What kind of a party is this, Mister?" I replied, "From the looks of things you might suspicion that it is a base ball team, but that is only a disguise. As a matter of fact, this is a crowd of itinerant revivalists. We carry a big tent in sections in those trunks, and we are going out to Jackson's grove three miles in the country to hold a two weeks' series of meetings. Try and get out yourselves, and tell all you friends to come."

My inquisitive brothers expelled their breath with a hissing sound, and went away dazed.

PART II

TEN YEARS' RECORDS

1897

We opened our 1897 season, which by the way was our first one, at Wahoo, Nebraska, on June 21st. We were beaten in the first game the Nebraska Indians ever played by a score of 12–0. We closed the season at Delmar, Iowa, on August 14th, losing the final engagement 17–13. During the season we played in but two states — Nebraska and Iowa. We won 21 games and lost 26. The scores follow:

Teams Defeated by the Nebraska Indians During 1897

Ackley, Iowa, 10–9.
Avoca, Iowa, 9–1.
Boone, Iowa, 13–7; 11–3.
Dayton, Iowa, 10–8.
Earling, Iowa, 22–11.
Fremont, Nebraska, 20–15.
Hamburg, Iowa, 28–7.
Harlan, Iowa, 28–6.
Independence, Iowa, 4–1.
Jewell Junction, Iowa, 21–14.
Lost Nation, Iowa, 11–5.
Manchester, Iowa, 6–1.
Oxford Junction, Iowa, 5–4.
Perry, Iowa, 7–6.
Sidney, Iowa, 18–13.
Stratford, Iowa, 59–4.
Tabor, Iowa, 15–9; 19–7.
University of Nebraska, Lincoln, 17–11.
Whitten, Iowa, 11–4.

Teams Which Defeated the Nebraska Indians During 1897

Anamosa, Iowa, 19–6; 9–1.
Avoca, Iowa, 21–5.
Carroll, Iowa, 15–5; 8–7.
Carson, Iowa, 9–7; 12–1.
Central City, Iowa, 23–13.
Coon Rapids, Iowa, 4–1.

Delmar, Iowa, 17–13.
Eldora, Iowa, 10–6; 7–2.
Fort Crook, Nebr., 15–6.
Fremont, Nebr., 32–12.
Hampton, Iowa, 5–2.
Lehigh, Iowa, 17–15.
Louisville, Nebr., 32–12.
Manchester, Iowa, 10–7.
New Hampton, Iowa, 9–1; 14–7.
Sidney, Iowa, 12–11.
Springfield, Nebr., 18–0.
Tabor, Iowa, 17–7.
University of Nebraska, Lincoln, 15–6.
Wahoo, Nebr., 12–0; 10–5.

1898

We opened our 1898 season on Friday, June 19th, in Lincoln, Nebraska, against the State University, whom we defeated 8–5 and 13–1. We played continuously for a few days more than four months, closing on Monday, October 10th, at Coon Rapids, Ia. Of a total of 103 games we won 81 and lost 22. The season was notable from the fact that we won at one time 37 straight games through Iowa, Missouri and Illinois.

Teams Defeated by the Nebraska Indians During 1898

Allerton, Iowa, 16–9.
Ashland, Nebr., 17–1.
Auburn Parks of Chicago, 8–5.
Bayard, Iowa, 6–2; 22–9.
Bradford, Ill., 10–2.
Cable, Ill., 16–6.
Calamus, Iowa, 2–0; 20–2.
Center Point, Iowa, 8–7.
Charles City, Iowa, 12–4; 24–3.
Clarinda, Iowa, 21–10.
Corning, Iowa, 12–4; 35–4; 35–8.
Corydon, Iowa, 38–10.
Creston, Iowa, 6–1; 22–3; 14–8.
Crete, Nebr., 3–0.
Exeter, Nebr., 13–1.
Forest City, Iowa, 18–5.
Fort Madison, Iowa, 40–4.
Geneseo, Ill., 12–7.
Gilchrist, Ill., 5–0.
Henry, Ill., 20–5.
Humeston, Iowa, 13–1; 14–4.
Jamaica, Iowa, 22–11.
Kahoka, Mo., 20–5; 34–7.
Kewanee, Ill., 7–6; 24–3.
Lacon, Ill., 11–9.
Lake Mills, Iowa, 9–3.

Leon, Iowa, 15–3; 21–0.
Lisbon, Iowa, 25–2.
Louisville, Nebr., 7–1; 7–3; 12–7.
Mason City, Iowa, 20–3.
Mechanicsville, Iowa, 20–4.
Morris, Ill., 19–2.
Neponset, Ill., 20–2.
Oneida, Ill., 7–4.
Orion, Ill., 6–3.
Osceola, Iowa, 10–0; 13–3.
Princeville, Ill., 20–3.
Schuyler, Nebr., 12–3.
Seward, Nebr., 11–4.
Seymour, Iowa, 41–6.
Sheffield, Ill., 14–5; 5–3.
Slater, Iowa, 11–6.
Staplehurst, Nebr., 18–0.
Stronghurst, Ill., 20–2; 16–8.
Surprise, Nebr., 24–6.
Tabor, Iowa, 24–12; 26–7.
Toluca, Ill., 9–3; 11–4.
Unionville, Mo., 16–3; 20–2.
University of Nebraska, Lincoln, 8–5; 13–1.
Varna, Ill., 22–4; 5–2.
Villisca, Iowa, 17–1.
Wilmington, Ill., 10–8; 7–6.
Woodhull, Ill., 10–1.
Woodward, Iowa, 23–8.
Wyoming, Ill., 13–2; 14–4.
Walker, Iowa, 9–1; 14–4.
York, Nebr., 17–0.

Games Lost by the Nebraska Indians During 1898

Cambridge, Ill., 5–3; 4–2.
Center Point, Iowa, 10–7.
Charles City, Iowa, 11–10.
El Paso, Ill., 8–3; 12–9.
Forest City, Iowa, 6–3.
Galesburg, Ill., 13–2.
Gilchrist, Ill., 13–9; 7–5; 12–5; 9–8.
Joliet, Ill., 15–6.
Keithsburg, Ill., 3–2.
Morris, Ill., 11–8 (10 innings).
New Hampton, Iowa, 9–2; 6–1.
Princeville, Ill., 5–3.
Sheffield, Ill., 17–16.
Toluca, Ill., 4–3.
Wymore, Nebr., 11–10; 8–2.

1899

Our playing season in 1899 began on May 10th. This was one month earlier than we began in 1898. Several of my players were late in getting into Lincoln, and the first game was played under many disadvantages. The University of Nebraska defeated us by a score of 18–5. We closed our season at Sheffield, Illinois, on Friday, October 13th. We played 143 games, of which we won 108. We covered more than two thousand miles in our travels, and played in eight different states. Read the scores:

Games Won by Nebraska Indians in 1899

Akron, Ohio, 8–1; 18–2.
Alexandria, Ind., 7–4.
Apple River, Ill., 13–3; 15–0.
Audubon, Iowa, 34–5.
Avoca, Iowa, 20–2.
Bellefontaine, Ohio, 16–6.
Bluffton, Ind., 8–3; 12–6; 9–6.
Bremen, Ind., 11–3; 12–1; 8–0.
Belmond, Iowa, 8–1.
Camden, Ohio, 4–0.
Canton, Ohio, 6–5.
Carey, Ohio, 11–4.
Cedar Falls, Iowa, State Normal, 20–11.
Celina, Ohio, 8–3.
Crestline, Ohio, 12–10; 13–0.
Dayton, Iowa, 8–4.
Dixon, Ill., 4–2; 3–2.
Dubuque, Iowa, 12–5; 7–6; 7–1.
DeGraff, Ohio, 14–3.
Eagle Grove, Iowa, 21–2; 11–1.
Elyria, Ohio, 16–3.
Fayette, Iowa, Upper Iowa Uni., 3–0; 11–3.
Fairbanks, Iowa, 9–0.
Findlay, Ohio, 6–4.
Fort Recovery, Ohio, 18–3; 14–6.
Fortville, Ind., 24–11.
Freeport, Ill., 4–0; 6–1; 12–11.
Gowrie, Iowa, 7–4.
Greenville, Pa., 3–2.
Havelock, Nebr., 13–8.
Hinckley, Ill., 13–6; 23–9.
Hopkinton, Iowa, Lenox College, 12–2.
Indianola, Iowa, Simpson College, 13–2; 5–1.
Iowa Falls, Iowa, 22–2; 6–2.
Janesville, Iowa, 16–1.
Jamestown, N. Y., 5–2.
Kendallville, Ind., 10–7.
LaFountaine, Ind., 15–4; 14–3.
Lisbon, Ohio, 17–6.
Manchester, Iowa, 16–4; 9–4.
Marion, Ind., 8–5; 27–11.
Medina, Ohio, 18–13.
Mercer, Pa., 20–4.
Matthews, Ind., 3–2.
Michigan City, Ind., 5–3.
Millford Center, Ohio, 17–5; 10–3.
Morris, Ill., 7–4; 15–13.
Mt. Victory, Ohio, 13–6; 17–6; 10–2.
Nevada, Ohio, 8–6.
New Madison, Ohio, 7–4; 10–8.
New Waterford, Ohio, 8–6.
Paulding, Ohio, 22–3.
Paw Paw, Ill., 17–5.

Payne, Ohio, 8–3.
Plymouth, Ohio, 12–3.
Platteville, Wis., State Normal, 13–2.
Portland, Ind., 7–1.
Perry, Iowa, 17–8; 16–7.
Randolph, N. Y., 5–1.
Redkey, Ind., 17–3.
Richmond, Ind., 11–5.
Rochelle, Ill., 11–4.
Rochester, Ind., 8–4.
Salem, Ohio, 11–9.
South Bend, Ind., 7–5.
Sterling, Ill., 10–9; 5–3.
Sharpsville, Pa., 21–6.
Sheffield, Ill., 14–7.
Union City, Ind., 20–8.
Urbana, Ohio, 17–12.
Versailles, Ohio, 8–1; 8–6.
Wadsworth, Ohio, 11–7.
Warren, Ind., 36–15.
Warren, Pa., 17–0.
Waverly, Iowa, 8–1.
Winamac, Ind., 8–0.
Woodstock, Ohio, 18–5; 10–4.
Wyanet, Ill., 15–5.

Games Lost by the Nebraska Indians in 1899

Ashtabula, Ohio, 5–1; 8–4
Auburn Parks of Chicago,
Canton, Ohio, 10–9; 7–3.
Chicago Unions, 3–2.
Erie, Pa., 5–2; 9–8.
Fayette, Iowa, Upper Iowa Uni., 9–7.
Fortville, Ind., 4–3.
Findlay, Ohio, 10–6.
Freeport, Ill., 8–2; 15–9; 3–2; 12–2.
Gowrie, Iowa, 11–5.
Greenville, Pa., 10–4.
Kendallville, Ind., 13–11.
LaFountaine, Ind., 7–6.
Michigan City, Ind., 13–6.
Nevada, Ohio, 13–6.
Painesville, Ohio, 5–1; 17–12.
Paulding, Ohio, 8–7.
Paw Paw, Ill., 17–16.
Richmond, Ind., 5–2.
Ridgeville, Ind., 7–6.
Rochester, Ind., 14–6.
Salamanca, N. Y., 9–6.
South Bend, Ind., 6–3; 5–1.
University of Nebraska, Lincoln, 18–5.
Warren, Ohio, 6–3.
Winamac, Ind., 8–7; 9–8.

1900

I began my 1900 season at Lincoln, Nebraska on Friday, April 15th defeating the University of Nebraska team on that date by a score of 10 to

9. We closed at Hudson, Michigan, on September 19th. During the tour we played 144 contests, of which we won 90, lost 53, and tied 1.

Games Won by the Nebraska Indians in 1900

Adel, Iowa, 14–5.
Akron, N. Y., Tonawanda Indians, 9–3.
Akron, Ohio, 10–2; 12–5.
Albia, Iowa, 5–4.
Avoca, N. Y., 7–3.
Aylmer, Ont., Can., 13–0.
Alliance, Ohio, 11–1.
Belleville, Ohio, 16–4.
Bloomington, Ind., State University, 21–7.
Brewster, N. Y., 21–5.
Brooklyn, N. Y. Skellys, 8–6.
Burlington, N. J., 8–5; 5–3.
Chatham, N. Y., 11–3.
Chester, Pa., 12–9
Cicero, Ind., 5–0; 5–2.
Cleveland, Ia., 18–17.
Clifton Springs, N. Y., 3–2.
Clinton, Mich., 10–3.
Coldwater, Michigan, 7–1; 9–0.
Corning, N. Y., 9–3.
Dunnville, Ont., Can., 9–8; 11–10.
East Palestine, Ohio, 19–3; 13–7; 11–7.
Eureka, Ill., College, 22–11.
Fairbury, Ill., 28–3; 19–1.
Germantown, Pa., 8–4; 9–5.
Hammondsport, N. Y., 9–6.
Hoopeston, Ill., 24–5.
Homer, Mich., 16–1.
Hudson, N. Y., 8–0.
Huntington, Pa., 10–3; 6–3.
Indianapolis, Ind., Reserves, 8–3.
Indianola, Iowa, Simpson College, 14–2.
Ingalls, Ind., 5–1.
Iowa City, Iowa, State University, 5–4; 4–2.
Kent, Ohio, 11–6.
Kewanee, Ill., 25–13; 23–10.
Lapel, Ind., 13–1.
Lancaster, Pa., 11–10.
Leamington, Ont., Can., 27–8.
Lewiston, Pa., 8–2; 7–4.
Lisbon, Ohio, 23–0.
Lincoln, Nebr., State University, 10–9.
Livonia, N. Y., 20–8.
Marengo, Iowa, 9–3.
Medina, Ohio, 11–4.
Millvale, Pa., 6–1.
Monmouth, Ill., College, 10–0.
Mt. Vernon, N. Y., 15–0.
Newman, Ill., 24–0.
New Philadelphia, Ohio, 12–7.
North Philadelphia, Pa., 14–3; 6–0.
Oak Harbor, Ohio, 19–8.
Oakland, Ill., 17–4; 13–3.
Rock Island, Ill., 10–5; 16–4.
St. Johnsville, N. Y., 3–0.
Saybrook, Ill., 24–10.

Seneca Falls, N. Y., 24–6.
Sidell, Ill., 11–2.
South Bend, Ind., 10–3.
Spiceland, Ind., 14–6.
Sturgis, Mich., 13–9.
Toluca, Ill., 22–3.
Uniontown, Pa., 8–7; 8–7.
Wabash, Ind., College, 16–4.
Wadsworth, Ohio, 12–3.
Wakeman, Ohio, 7–4.
Washington, Iowa, 18–8; 32–19.
Warren, Ohio, 9–6.
Waterford, N. Y., 6–3.
Weedsport, N. Y., 8–0.
York, Pa., 8–4; 17–11.

Games Lost by the Nebraska Indians in 1900

Akron, Ohio, 6–4.
Altoona, Pa., 4–3.
Beaver Falls, Pa., 9–3.
Brooklyn, N. Y., Skelleys, 13–4.
Burr Oak, Mich., 5–2.
Cambridge, Ill., 18–17.
Canton, Ohio, 11–4.
Chester, Pa., 13–4
Columbia Giants, Chicago, Ill., 4–3; 11–3; 4–3; 17–5; 11–5; 7–0; 9–8; 8–6; 8–5; 1–0; 11–5; 8–1; 8–4.
Corning, N. Y., 7–6.
Dapauw, Ind., University, 9–5.
Des Moines, Iowa, Western League, 14–2.
Downingtown, Pa., 6–2; 3–1.
Etna, Pa., 8–7.
Homestead, Pa., 14–4.
Hudson, Mich., 8–2; 6–3.
Ilion, N. Y., 4–3.
Ingalls, Ind., 10–9.
Iowa City, Iowa, State University, 20–0.
Kent, Ohio, 4–3.
Manheim, Pa., 11–6.
Marengo, Iowa, 7–5.
Middletown, Pa., 12–8.
Millvale, Pa., 11–1.
Monmouth, Ill., College, 9–8.
Natrona, Pa., 6–5.
New Philadelphia, Ohio, 12–3.
Notre Dame, Ind., 16–13.
Omaha, Nebr., Western League, 6–2.
Port Clinton, Ohio, 6–5.
Richmond, Ind., 4–2; 6–3.
South Bend, Ind., 6–3; 15–6.
Tecumseh, Mich., 11–4.
Waverly, N. Y., 9–4; 6–5.
Weedsport, N. Y., 4–2.

Tie Game in 1900.

Dunnville, Ont., Can., 1–1 (14 innings)

1901

Our 1901 tour began on Monday, April 22nd, at Wahoo, Nebraska. We won our first game by a score of 12 to 8. During the season of 1901 we made the best record we had ever attained up to that time. We played 162 games. Of these we won 135, lost 26, and tied 1. During the season immediately previous we had beaten the hitherto invincible Tonawanda Indian team at Akron, N. Y., and in 1901 we beat the Genoa Indians at Genoa, Nebraska. We closed our season on October 9th, at Jamaica, Ia.

Games Won by the Nebraska Indians During 1901

Anoka, Minn., 9–1; 15–6.
Atalissa, Iowa, 10–5.
Bayard, Iowa, 8–7.
Beacon, Iowa, 6–4; 28–1.
Bedford, Iowa, 12–2.
Belleville, Kan., 21–1.
Belvidere, Nebr., 27–9; 21–3.
Black River Falls, Wis., 29–5; 24–7.
Bloomfield, Iowa, 24–5.
Boone, Iowa, 23–4.
Bourbonnais, Ill., 6–3.
Burlington, Iowa, 15–6.
Burlington, Wis., 25–10; 21–5.
Cedarburg, Wis., 17–6.
Centerville, Iowa, 11–6; 12–6; 4–3.
Chippewa Falls, Wis., 23–0.
Clermont, Iowa, 17–2.
Cleveland, Iowa, 2–1.
College Springs, Iowa, 27–13; 27–4.
Collins, Iowa, 19–5.
Delano, Minn., 15–5.
Durand, Wis., 6–1; 4–2.
Dwight, Ill., 16–6.
Earlville, Ill., 28–13.
Earlville, Iowa, 9–8.
East Troy, Wis., 25–11.
Elk River, Minn., 36–3.
Ellsworth, Wis., 15–3; 9–6.
Elroy, Wis., 18–0.
Essex, Iowa, 27–0.
Exeter, Nebraska, 11–2.
Farmington, Minn., 20–7.
Gardner, Ill., 15–5.
Genoa, Nebr., Indian School, 10–6; 7–6.
Grand Rapids, Wis., 17–5; 6–4.
Gilchrist, Ill., 5–1.
Greeley, Iowa, 25–1.
Hammond, Wis., 12–7.
Hanover, Kan., 11–3.
Hartland, Minn., 18–2.
Hebron, Ill., 49–5.
Hiawatha, Kan., 24–4.
Hines, Iowa, 16–8.

Hiteman, Iowa, 13–5.
Hopkinton, Iowa, 28–11.
Jamaica, Iowa, 5–4.
Kenosha, Wis., 7–6; 14–1.
Kent, Iowa, 20–0.
Lancaster, Mo., 19–10.
Leaf River, Ill., 17–8.
Madrid, Iowa, 22–0.
Manhattan, Ill., 26–5.
Manteno, Ill., 9–1.
Maynard, Iowa, 25–2.
Mediapolis, Ia., 13–6.
Mendota, Ill., 13–4.
Moline, Ill., 24–8.
Momence, Ill., 18–4; 11–5.
Merillan, Wis., 24–9.
Menomonie, Wis., 13–8.
Mondovi, Wis., 17–8.
Morrison, Ill., 22–1.
Muscatine, Iowa, 6–5; 9–6.
Nashua, Iowa, 19–9.
New Lisbon, Wis., 15–7; 18–2.
New Prague, Minn., 8–1.
New Richmond, Wis., 14–2.
Nora Springs, Iowa, 30–6; 29–3.
Northwood, Iowa, 11–4.
Ohio, Ill., 11–5.
Oregon, Ill., 14–2; 26–2.
Ottawa, Ill., 11–2.
Peotone, Ill., 24–5.
Plainfield, Ill., 34–11.
Pleasantville, Iowa, 12–1.
Plymouth, Wis., 21–10.
Portage, Wis., 9–7.
Port Byron, Ill., 17–6; 11–3.
Port Washington, Wis., 8–1.
Pulaski, Iowa, 27–7.
Richland, Iowa, 23–4.
River Falls, Wis., 34–5.
Rosemont, Minn., 14–0.
Savanna, Ill., 27–2.
Sewal, Iowa, 16–3; 4–2.
Seymour, Iowa, 24–5; 29–8.
Sharon, Wis., 7–1.
Somonouk, Ill., 15–11.
South Milwaukee, Wis., 20–4.
Strawberry Point, Iowa, 15–3.
Stevens' Point, Wis., 12–6.
Stromsburg, Nebr., 27–16.
Sublet, Ill., 23–4.
Tecumseh, Nebr., 13–10.
Two Rivers, Wisconsin, 18–2; 13–1.
Ulysses, Nebr., 11–9.
Volga, Iowa, 14–5.
Vernon Center, Minn., 16–5.
Wahoo, Nebr., 13–3.
Wapello, Iowa, 13–6.
Waseca, Minn., 5–4.
Waukon, Iowa, 13–9; 12–8.
Waupaca, Wis., 5–4.
Waverly, Minn., 10–1; 34–2.
West Bend, Wis., 18–4.
Westfield, Wis., 18–0.
West Union, Iowa, 30–1.
Winfield, Iowa, 50–5.
Winnebago City, Minn., 10–8; 12–8.
Woodward, Iowa, 18–4.

Games Lost by the Nebraska Indians During 1901

Albert Lea, Minn., 15–4.
Bedford, Iowa, 1–0.
Bonaparte, Iowa, 22–19.
Burlington, Iowa, 10–7.
Centerville, Iowa, 9–6.
Clinton, Wis., 15–12.
Cleveland, Iowa, 1–0.
Dyersville, Iowa, 11–4.
Elgin, Ill., 2–1.
Elkader, Iowa, 12–8.
Exeter, Nebr., 11–4.
Kaukauna, Wis., 24–8.
Keokuk, Iowa, 12–10; 18–6.
Manchester, Iowa, 5–4.
Monroe Center, Ill., 10–6.
Nebraska City, Nebr., 17–14; 10–2.
Ottawa, Ill., 24–8.
Paw Paw, Ill., 14–13.
Sterling, Ill., 15–0.
Tecumseh, Nebr., 14–5.
Ulysses, Nebr., 6–5.
Wahoo, Nebr., 12–11.
Waseca, Minn., 4–2; 14–0.

Tie Game in 1901

White Bear Lake, Minn., 1–1 (11 innings).

1902

The Nebraska Indians began the 1902 tour on Friday, April 18th, at Havelock, Nebraska. They were beaten 11 to 7. They closed the season at Cedar Falls, Iowa, on Thursday, October 2d. They won the last game of the season 14 to 0. In their concluding contest, each of the Indian players pitched one inning, as had been done at the close of the campaign of 1901. During the season the team played through Nebraska, Iowa, Illinois, Indiana, Missouri, Kentucky and Tennessee. They took part in 152 games, of which they won 136. They lost 15 and tied one. The drawn engagement occurred at Fairfield, Illinois, on Saturday, July 19th. We played only one extra inning game during 1902. This lasted twelve innings at Galena, Illinois, on Thursday, September 25th. We won 2 to 1.

During 1902 we invaded the south for the first time, playing sixteen games in Kentucky and Tennessee, of which we won 13.

During 1902 we shut out our opponents 29 times. We were shut out once. We lost only one game out of the last 43 played.

The following table gives a complete list of the games played together with the scores:

Teams Defeated by the Nebraska Indians During 1902

Alexis, Ill., 14–2.
Arcola, Ill., 10–5.
Ashmore, Ill., 24–5.
Aurora, Nebr., 15–7.
Anna, Ill., 13–4.
Ashkum, Ill., 7–1
Beacon, Ia., 19–0.
Bedford, Iowa, 10–6; 13–1.
Bedford, Ind., 14–5.
Bellevue, Iowa, 14–5.
Bloomfield, Iowa, 24–14.
Bonaparte, Iowa, 17–5; 10–9.
Braceville, Ill., 6–0.
Brazil, Ind., 16–2.
Brownville, Tenn., 4–1.
Cadiz, Ky., 19–5.
Cairo, Ill., 11–2.
Cape Girardeau, Mo., 4–0.
Carlisle, Ind., 17–3.
Carmi, Ill., 22–1.
Cedar Falls, Iowa, 14–0.
Centerville, Ia., 17–2; 4–0.
Cicero, Ind., 7–0.
Clarksville, Tenn., 23–8.
Clay City, Ill., 9–8.
Cleveland, Iowa, 6–0.
Coin, Iowa, 15–0.
College Springs, Iowa, 11–6.
Collinsville, Ill., 13–4.
Covington, Tenn., 8–0.
Darlington, Ind., 9–5.
Donnelson, Iowa, 14–3.
Dyersville, Iowa, 15–3.
Delphi, Ind., 14–6; 3–1.
Dwight, Ill., 10–6; 23–8.
Earlville, Ill., 17–4.
Earlville, Iowa, 6–0.
Evansville, Ill., 25–4.
Eddyville, Ky. 14–4.
Eureka, Ill., 11–5.
Exeter, Nebr., 13–5.
Flanagan, Ill., 15–0.
Flora, Ill., 9–5.
Frankfort, Ind., 10–5.
Friend, Nebr., 12–10.
Galena, Ill., 2–1 (12 innings).
Galveston, Ind., 20–2.
Girard, Ill., 12–0.
Gresham, Nebr., 14–0.
Galva, Ill., 22–2.
Giltner, Nebr., 12–5.
Greenup, Ill., 19–3.
Hartford, Ky., 9–4.
Hazelton, Ind., 9–0.
Hillsboro, Iowa, 10–1.
Huntington, Tenn., 14–1.

Harrisburg, Ill., 6–0.
Herrick, Ill., 30–2.
Hopkinsville, Ky., 13–7.
Iowa Wesleyan University, Mt. Pleasant, Iowa, 6–0.
Jerome, Iowa, 25–6.
Kent, Iowa, 68–8.
Kewanee, Ill., 12–6.
Keokuk, Iowa, 4–3.
Knox College, Galesburg, Ill., 8–3.
Ladoga, Ind., 8–1.
Manchester, Iowa, 15–3.
Marion, Ill., 11–9.
Marshall, Ill., 22–1.
Mascoutah, Ill., 21–7.
Momence, Ill., 5–3.
Mt. Vernon, Ind., 7–6.
Murphysboro, Ill., 23–6.
Manteno, Ill., 20–10.
Marion, Ky., 18–1.
Martin, Tenn., 10–3.
Mediapolis, Iowa, 16–1.
Mt. Vernon, Ill., 12–0.
Moweaqua, Ill., 11–3.
Nashville, Ill., 12–0.
Oakland, Ind., 23–2.
Odell, Ill., 22–1
Oakville, Iowa 23–2
Odon, Ind., 20–3.
Oskaloosa, Iowa, 12–6.
Owensboro, Ky., 7–0; 19–1.
Otley, Iowa, 24–5.
Pesotum, Ill., 13–2.
Poseyville, Ind., 19–5.
Princeton, Ind., 7–1.
Pontiac, Ill., 17–5.
Prairie City, Iowa, 14–10.
Pulaski, Iowa, 17–0; 8–0.
Ramsey, Ill., 13–6.
Ripley, Tenn., 18–7.
Roseville, Ill., 15–0.
Reddick, Ill., 15–10.
Robinson, Ill., 4–3.
Salem, Ill., 15–2.
Saybrook, Ill., 17–3.
Sorento, Ill., 8–2.
Streator, Ill., 9–5.
Sullivan, Ind., 15–0.
Sandoval, Ill., 24–0.
Seatonville, Ill., 16–1.
Sparta, Ill., 19–9; 7–3.
Sullivan, Ill., 11–2; 5–0.
Thorntown, Ind., 27–5.
Tiskilwa, Ill., 23–2.
Toluca, Ill., 11–2.
Tipton, Ind., 29–0.
Tolono, Ill., 15–2.
Tuscola, Ill., 18–5.
Ulysses, Nebr., 6–4.
Valley, Nebr., 34–12.
Vincennes, Ind., 6–4; 3–1.
Veedersburg, Ind., 4–0.
Wahoo, Nebr., 5–3; 19–14.
West Lebanon, Ind., 17–3.
Winterset, Iowa, 12–0.
Wyanet, Ill., 13–4.
Westfield, Ill., 8–0; 29–5.
Williamsport, Ind., 9–3.
Winthrop, Iowa, 14–0.

Teams Which Defeated the Nebraska Indians During 1902

Benton, Ill., 10–4.
Creighton University, Omaha, Nebr., 22–5.
Havelock, Nebr., 11–7.
Loda, Ill., 2–1.
Ottawa, Ill., 11–4.
Saybrook, Ill., 6–4.
Trenton, Ill., 8–7.
University of Nebraska, Lincoln, Nebr., 13–5.
Collinsville, Ill., 5–4.
Dyersburg, Tenn., 9–8.
Harvard, Nebr., 16–15.
Linton, Ind., 6–3.
Memphis, Tenn., Chickasaws, 8–1; 7–0.
Staplehurst, Nebr., 10–5.

Tie Game

Fairfield, Illinois, 15–15.

1903

During the season of 1903 I ran two teams, an eastern and a western. The western team was under the management of one of my pitchers, Mr. Dan W. Tobey, and played only in Iowa, Illinois, Wisconsin and Missouri. This team won 123 games, lost 24, and tied 1; the boys shut out their opponents 36 times.

My eastern team was under my individual management, and we played through Nebraska, Missouri, Iowa, Illinois, Indiana, Kentucky, Ohio, West Virginia and Pennsylvania. We won 144 games, lost 33, and shut out our opponents 28 times.

The scores of all games played by both organizations are as follows:

Teams Defeated by the Nebraska Indians During 1903

Abington, Ill., 6–4.
Ada, Ohio, 7–0.
Albany, Mo., 9–7.
Alta, Ia., 2–1.

Anamosa, Iowa, 5–0.
Argenta, Ill., 10–0.
Arlington, Iowa, 5–0.
Athens, Ohio, 14–2.
Attica, Ind., 7–5.
Augusta, Ill., 5–0.
Augusta, Ky., 6–5.
Aurora, Ind., 5–4.
Ava, Mo., 11–10.
Ashley, Ohio, 11–4.
Albion, Ill., 12–0.
Arthur, Ill., 16–1.
Baraboo, Wis., 12–6.
Barneston, Ohio, 18–0.
Barry, Ill., 6–4.
Bement, Ill., 18–2.
Benton, Ill., 18–1.
Bethany, Ill., 16–0.
Bethesda, Ohio, 5–4.
Blanchard, Ohio, 13–1.
Bloomfield, Iowa, 8–0.
Bowling Green, Ohio, 4–1.
Bradford, Ill., 6–2.
Bridgeport, Ill., 21–5.
Bucklin, Mo., 7–2.
Burlington, Iowa, 9–1.
Butler, Ky., 26–5.
Calamus, Iowa, 14–1.
California, Mo., 15–1.
Campbellsville, Ky., 24–5.
Camp Point, Ill., 7–0.
Canton, Mo., 19–5; 10–7.
Canton, Ohio, 8–5.
Cape Girardeau, Mo., 5–2.
Carmi, Ill., 26–3.
Carrollton, Ky., 16–2.
Chadwick, Ill., 17–0.
Charleston, Mo., 14–4; 8–2.
Cincinnati, Ohio, "Bellevue Browns," 4–0.
Clarence, Mo., 2–1.
Clay City, Ky., 10–5; 13–4; 6–1.
Clarinda, Iowa, 10–2.
Clinton, Iowa, 3–2.
Clinton, Mo., 7–1.
College Springs, Iowa, 12–0.
Colfax, Iowa, 12–5; 3–0.
Columbus, Ohio, "Inter Urbans," 8–1.
Columbus, Wis., 5–0.
Corydon, Ind., 8–3.
Coshocton, Ohio, 14–6.
Cowden, Ill., 6–0.
Cynthiana, Ky., 11–1.
DeKalb, Ill., 7–1.
Donaldson, Iowa, 9–0.
Dunkirk, Ohio, 12–4.
DuQuoin, Ill., 18–0.
Dyersville, Iowa, 9–0; 14–5.
Earling, Iowa, 3–0.
Earlville, Ill., 15–8.
East Palestine, Ohio, 14–3.
Edina, Mo., 10–7.
Effingham, Ill., 17–7.
Eldon, Iowa, 6–0; 5–0; 12–10.
Eldorado, Ill., 7–3.
Enfield, Ill., 21–0.
Equality, Ill., 27–8.
Eureka, Ill., College, 11–8.
Fairfield, Ia., 9–0.
Falmouth, Ky., 19–8.
Farmington, Mo., 7–6; 4–5.

Farnhamville, Iowa, 9–0.
Flemingsburg, Ky., 15–2.
Ford, Ky., 11–0.
Fowler, Ind., 6–5.
Frankfort, Ind., 5–4.
Freeport, Ill., 5–0.
Fulton, Mo., 19–1.
Galena, Ill., 9–3; 2–0.
Galva, Ill., 6–5.
Georgetown, Ky., College, 6–1.
Germantown, Ohio, 14–4.
Gilchrist, Ill., 7–4.
Girard, Ill., 17–4.
Glasgow, Mo., 11–1.
Goshen, Ohio, 5–4.
Gowrie, Iowa, 11–0.
Grayville, Ill., 9–6; 9–2; 17–2.
Greeley, Iowa, 5–0.
Greenfield, Mo., 8–3.
Greenup, Ill., 11–5; 25–2.
Grundy Center, Iowa, 6–1.
Harrisburg, Ill., 6–1.
Harrodsburg, Ky., 5–0.
Haubstadt, Ind., 11–1.
Havelock, Nebr., 17–3.; 9–2.
Hawkeye, Iowa, 9–0.
Henderson, Ill, 10–0.
Heyworth, Ill., 23–7.
Hillsboro, Iowa, 6–1.
Hillsboro, Wis., 18–5.
Houston, Mo., 12–3.
Hubbard, Iowa, 8–2.
Huntingsburg, Ind., 7–2; 6–1.
Iuka, Ill., 11–6.
Jackson Center, Ohio, 4–3.
Jamesport, Mo., 11–2.
Jamestown, Ind., 14–2.
Jasper, Ind., 8–4.
Kansas, Ill., 24–2.
Keithsburg, Ill., 4–0.
Kempton, Ind., 13–0.
Keokuk, Iowa, 10–9.
Kenney, Ill., 3–0; 13–2.
Lafayette, Ind., 11–3.
LaGrange, Ky., 7–1.
Lamar, Mo., 14–9.
Lancaster, Mo., 18–3.
LaPlata, Mo., 20–5.
Lawrenceburg, Ky., 15–0.
Lehigh, Ia., 22–4; 9–0; 15–0.
LeRoy, Ill., 28–3.
Lewisburg, Ohio, 22–3.
Loda, Ill, 4–3.
Louisville, Ky., Reccius, 3–2.
Macomb, Ill, 28–1.
Marion, Ill, 4–1.
Marion, Ohio, 19–8.
Maroa, Ill, 4–0.
Marshall, Ill., 17–2.
Marshalltown, Iowa, 6–0.
Maynard, Iowa, 10–0.
Maysville, Ky., 11–2.
McArthur, Ohio, 28–9.
Media, Ill., 9–2.
Mellott, Ind., 9–1.
Memphis, Nebr., 3–1; 9–1.
Middleport, Ohio, 2–0.
Midway, Ky., 14–2.
Milton, Iowa, 5–0.
Minier, Ill., 24–11.
Minerton, Ohio, 14–0.
Monona, Iowa, 3–1.

Monticello, Iowa, 10–2.
Montford, Wis., 9–5.
Mt. Vernon, Ill., 6–3.
Mt. Vernon, Ind., 12–4.
Murray City, Ohio, 16–2.
Nashville, Ill., 6–0.
Nicholasville, Ky., 16–7.
New London, Ia., 14–0.
New London, Ohio, 20–5.
New Waterford, Ohio, 4–2.
North English, Iowa, 18–5.
North Salem, Ind., 24–2.
Oakland City, Ind., 7–3.
Odebolt, Iowa, 17–7.
Odell, Ill., 14–7.
Odin, Ill., 12–7.
Oelwein, Iowa, 5–0.
Olney, Ill., 28–5.
Oregon, Ill., 9–0; 9–4.
Osgood, Ind., 9–6.
Ottumwa, Iowa, 10–4.
Oxford Junction, Iowa, 7–5.
Pana, Ill., 10–4.
Parkersburg, W. Va., 8–0.
Paris, Ill., 11–1.
Peoria, Ill., 14–0.
Petersburg, Ill., 16–0.
Piketon, Ohio, 6–3; 19–0.
Plainfield, Ill., 20–7.
Plymouth, Ill., 33–11.
Poplar Bluff, Mo., 3–0.
Port Byron, Ill., 3–0; 4–0.
Poseyville, Ind., 8–2.
Postville, Iowa, 8–4.
Princeton, Ind., 6–5.
Quasqueton, Iowa, 10–5.
Radcliffe, Iowa, 19–4.
Ramsey, Ill., 14–1.
Redbud, Ill., 7–4.
Richmond, Ky., 19–1; 23–3.
Riverside, Iowa, 2–1.
Roachdale, Ind., 5–0.
Rockford, Ohio, 8–0.
Rockville, Mo., 20–1.
Sabula, Iowa, 8–6; 6–4.
St. Elmo, Ill., 13–3; 11–3.
St. Genevieve, Mo., 7–5.
Salem, Ill., 8–6.
Schaller, Iowa, 22–5.
Scio, Ohio, 11–2.
Sebring, Ohio, 7–2.
Senecaville, Ohio, 9–5.
Shabbona, Ill., 14–2.
Shelbyville, Mo., 11–6.
Shreve, Ohio, 8–6.
Sigourney, Iowa, 10–2; 18–3; 3–1.
Sikeston, Mo., 6–1.
Springfield, Ky., 35–6.
Staunton, Ill., 4–3.
Story City, Iowa, 4–0.
Stoughton, Wis., 8–6.
Sumner, Ill., 18–3.
Tampico, Ill., 15–5; 30–8.
Tarkio, Mo., College, 6–1.
Tell City, Ind., 6–0.
Tiffin, Ohio, 5–3.
Tippecanoe, Ohio, 10–1.
Tomah, Wis., 14–2.
Tremont, Ill., 7–4.
Tripoli, Iowa, 10–2.
University Place, Nebr., Wesleyan, 15–4.

Urbana, Ill., 8–3.
Valley, Nebr., 9–2.
Vandalia, Ill., 9–0.
Vincennes, Ind., 6–1.
Vinton, Iowa, 5–4.
Wahoo, Nebr., 11–2; 11–0.
Wapello, Iowa, 20–2.
Washington, Ind., 12–0; 12–1.
Waynestown, Ind., 12–1.
West Point, Mo., 17–10; 16–4; 7–0.
Wheatland, Ind., 21–6.
Wheatland, Iowa, 8–2.
Whitten, Iowa, 4–2; 2–1.
Williamsburg, Iowa, 11–8.
Winchester, Ky., 27–4; 33–4.
Winthrop, Iowa, 11–5.
Wooster, Ohio, 6–2.
Wyanet, Ill., 10–5.

Games Lost by the Nebraska Indians During 1903

Algona, Iowa, "Brownies," 4–2.
Ash Grove, Mo., 6–5.
Atwood, Ill., 6–2.
Augusta, Ill., 9–8.
Barnesville, Ohio, 2–1; 6–4.
Beaver Falls, Pa., 7–5.
Bedford, Iowa, 5–3; 6–3.
Bowling Green Ohio, 3–2.
Brookfield, Mo., 2–1.
Bucyrus, Ohio, 5–4.
Chillicothe, Mo., 13–2.
Clinton, Iowa, 8–2; 5–0; 6–4.
Craig, Mo., 1–0.
Danville, Ky., "Central Un.," 3–0; 1–0.
Findlay, Ohio, 10–0.
Fowler, Ind., 6–5.
Freeport, Ill., 6–5.
Gallatin, Mo., 10–2.
Galesburg, Ill., "Knox College," 8–6.
Galesburg, Ill., "Lombard College," 4–3.
Gilchrist, Ill., 8–4.
Greenfield, Mo., 17–12.
Hannibal, Mo., 5–1; 4–3.
Havelock, Nebr., 9–2.
Homestead, Pa., 18–1.
Hoopeston, Ill., 3–2.
Illiopolis, Ill., 1–0; 2–1.
Juneau, Wis., 7–6.
Keosauqua, Iowa, 5–4.
Kewanee, Ill., 13–8.
Kirksville, Mo., 4–3.
LaCrosse, Wis., 11–9; 3–2.
Lehigh, Iowa, 5–4.
Lincoln, Nebr., State Uni., 8–5; 14–2.
Louisville, Ky., "Frontenacs," 7–4.
Manning, Iowa, 7–6.
Monmouth, Ill., College, 10–0.
Moweaqua, Ill., 10–2.
Ozark, Mo., 12–8.
Poplar Bluff, Mo., 3–2.
Quincy, Ill., 7–3; 4–3.
Sebring, Ohio, 8–6.

Somonauk, Ill., 6–5.
Sparta, Ill., 3–2.
Urbana, Ohio, 12–5.
Virden, Ill., 8–7.
Wilkinsburg, Pa., 12–5.

Tie Game in 1903

Lone Rock, Wis., 2–2.

1904

In 1904, I played through Nebraska, Missouri, Illinois, Indiana, Kentucky, Ohio, Michigan and Wisconsin, going as far north as the copper country of the upper peninsula of Michigan. We won 149 games, lost 25, and tied 1.

Some of our records this season were remarkable. For instance, we won every game played from April 17th to June 4th, inclusive, or 42 straight contests. We shut out our opponents 48 times. While playing against the strongest independent teams of southern Michigan, we won 7 straight shutout games; in other words we were not scored against for 63 consecutive innings.

Games Won During 1904

Ada, Ohio, 11–0.
Ansonia, Ohio, 13–3.
Ashland, Ohio, 15–3.
Ashley, Ohio, 16–2; 10–0.
Athens, Mich., 16–0.
Aurora, Ind., 9–0.
Beatrice, Nebr., 11–5.
Bangor, Mich., 8–0.
Battle Creek, Mich., 8–0.
Berlin, Wis., 31–4.
Bloomville, Ohio, 17–0.
Brown City, Mich., 11–3.
Buchtel, Ohio, 18–2; 11–8; 13–3.
Canal Dover, Ohio, 16–0.
Carroll, Ohio, 8–3.
Carrollton, Ohio, 6–1.
Centerburg, Ohio, 13–4.
Chelsea, Mich., 7–1.
Chenoa, Ill., 3–2.
Chicago, Ill., "Gunthers," 9–5.
Chicago Jct., Ohio, 4–2.
Clay City, Ill., 14–2.
Coldwater, Ohio, 14–4.
Columbiana, Ohio, 11–4.

Connersville, Ind., 8–0; 4–1.
Copemish, Mich., 20–0.
Danville, Ind., 16–2.
Danville, Ky., Central Uni., 4–0; 20–7; 12–2.
Dayton, Ohio, "Nationals," 15–7.
Decatur, Mich., 7–0.
Dennison, Ohio, 5–0.
East Jordan, Mich., 8–7; 5–3.
East Liverpool, Ohio, 2–0.
Edina, Mo., 9–2.
Equality, Ill., 13–0.
Escanaba, Mich., 10–0.
Fairmont, Ind., 11–1.
Falls City, Nebr., 15–0.
Franklin, Ind., 2–0.
Garrett, Ind., 15–2; 13–4.
Germantown, Nebr., 9–0.
Golconda, Ill., 5–0.
Grass Lake, Mich., 19–0.
Greensburg, Ind., 3–2; 3–2.
Hale, Mo., 18–2.
Hannibal, Mo., 5–2.
Harbor Springs, Mich., 6–3.
Harrisburg, Ill., 11–0; 11–1.
Hartford, Mich., 21–5.
Hartford, Wis., 14–5.
Hazelton, Ind., 13–0.
Holly, Mich., 8–0.
Hymera, Ind., 10–1.
Illiopolis, Ill., 11–2.
Ishpeming, Mich., 7–4.
Jamestown, Ind., 8–0.
Johnstown, Ohio, 13–4.
Kenton, Ohio, 7–6.
Kirksville, Mo., 18–5.
Lapeer, Mich., 5–0.
Lexington, Ill., 8–0.
Lexington, Mo., 14–1.
Ligonier, Ind., 4–3.
Lima, Ohio, 21–1.
Loraine, Ohio, 15–7.
Mackinaw City, Mich., 11–0.
Madison, Ind., 5–2.
Malmo, Nebr., 9–5.
Manteno, Ill., 14–12.
Marion, Ill., 12–3.
Marion, Ind., 7–2.
Marquette, Mich., 7–0.
Marshall, Mich., 6–0.
Martinton, Ill., 11–3.
Matthews, Ind., 10–0.
Menomonie, Mich., 11–0; 7–0; 11–4.
Mentone, Ind., 16–2.
Metropolis, Ill., 7–1.
Middletown, Ohio, 4–1.
Milan, Mo., 25–4.
Millersburg, Ohio, 7–3; 6–0.
Montpelier, Ohio, 18–1.
Marlette, Mich., 2–0.
Moweaqua, Ill., 1–0.
Mt. Gilead, Ohio, 3–2.
Munising, Mich., 4–1.
Nokomis, Ill., 9–2; 9–2.
Nashville, Ill., 23–5.
New Bremen, Ohio, 5–4.
New Washington, Ohio, 5–3.
North Salem, Ind., 7–2.
North Vernon, Ind., 12–1.
Oblong, Ill., 13–0.
Okawville, Ill., 12–1.
Omro, Wis., 20–4.

Osgood, Ind., 10–5.
Ostrander, Ohio, 23–4.
Palestine, Ill., 9–0.
Palmyra, Nebr., 18–2.
Piper City, Ill., 5–3.
Pontiac, Mich., 11–6.
Portland, Ind., 18–0.
Prospect, Ohio, 7–2.
Rushville, Ind., 6–2.
Ridgeway, Ill., 20–0.
Saginaw, Mich., 1–0.
St. Marys, Ohio, 20–5.
Salineville, Ohio, 4–0; 7–5.
Sault Ste. Marie, Mich., 5–1.
Schoolcraft, Mich., 4–0.
Shawnee, Ohio, 10–3.
Sherrodsville, Ohio, 9–2.
Shoals, Ind., 6–1.
Sparta, Ill., 2–1.
Springport, Mich., 8–0.
South Frankfort, Mich., 2–0.
Sterling, Nebr., 28–4.
Sullivan, Ill, 4–1.
Tecumseh, Nebr., 14–3.
Tiffin, Ohio, 4–1.
Troy, Mo., 5–1.
Uhrichsville, Ohio, 5–1.
Union City, Ind., 13–0.
Valparaiso, Ind., 5–1.
Vienna, Ill., 15–0.
Verdon, Nebr., 5–1.
Warsaw, Ind., 23–0.
Waterloo, Ind., 21–1.
Weldon, Ill., 7–4.
West Bend, Wis., 20–4.
White Water, Wis., 4–0.
Wyandotte, Mich., 8–2.
West Branch, Mich., 8–2.
Yale, Mich., 19–1.

Games Lost During 1904

Benton, Ill., 4–2.
Bucyus, Ohio, 8–7.
Calumet, Mich., 9–8.
Cincinnati, Ohio, "Gym Shamrocks," 4–1.
Crystal Falls, Mich., 5–4.
Defiance, Ohio, 2–1.
Delaware, Ohio, 3–1.
Dollar Bay, Mich., 6–3.
Fowler, Ind., 4–0.
Franklin, Ind., 6–5.
Garrett, Ind., 9–2.
Houghton, Mich., 7–2.
Kent, Ohio, 2–0.
Lexington, Ky., University, 2–1; 10–9.
Lincoln, Nebr., University, 10–7; 7–1.
Ludington, Mich., 8–2.
Ogden, Ill., 8–2.
Paxton, Ill., 4–2.
Petoskey, Mich., 6–3; 2–0.
Sault Ste. Marie, Mich., 5–1.
Washington, Ind., 2–1.
Wyandotte, Mich., 2–1.

Tie Game During 1904

Loogootee, Ind., 2–2; 11 innings.

1905

Our percentage of victories in 1904 was .852. In 1905 it was .858, that is to say, we won 163 games, lost 27, and tied 1. I should mention incidentally that we shut out our opponents 43 times, and were ourselves shut out but twice. These are excellent records when you remember that we played the strongest independent teams just as they came through Nebraska, Iowa, Missouri, Illinois, Indiana, Kentucky, Ohio, Pennsylvania and Michigan.

Games Won in 1905

Addison, Mich., 11–3.
Atlantic, Iowa, 10–0.
Angola, Ind., 4–1.
Albion, Ind., 10–3.
Augusta, Ill., 16–2.
Avilla, Ind., 18–3.
Batavia, Ill., 6–3.
Batavia, Iowa, 17–0; 2–1.
Beaver Dam, Ky., 7–3.
Beaver Falls, Pa., 4–1.
Birmingham, Iowa, 51–1.
Bloomfield, Ky., 2–0.
Bloomville, Ohio, 17–0.
Bonaparte, Iowa, 7–0.
Braceville, Ill., 16–1.
Bunker Hill, Ill., 18–5.
Burlington, Ky., 6–2.
Bussey, Iowa, 4–1.
Calhoun, Ky., 23–0.
Cambridge, Ohio, 12–4.
Carlisle, Ky., 8–2.
Cave City, Ky., 8–2.
Chapin, Ill., 16–1.
Chicago Jct., Ohio, 7–3.
Clare, Iowa, 12–3.
Columbia, Ky., 19–3.
Congo, Ohio, 8–4.
Connersville, Ind., 6–4.
Corydon, Ky., 20–0.
Crete, Nebr., "Doane," 16–3.
Crooksville, Ohio, 6–2.
Crosswell, Mich., 11–7.
Dayton, Iowa, 7–0.
Delta, Ohio, 2–0.
Dixon, Ky., 14–2.
Dunkirk, Ind., 8–4; 6–1.
Earling, Iowa, 6–4.
Edon, Ohio, 9–4.
Elkton, Ky., 7–3.
Elkton, Mich., 10–0.

Eminence, Ky., 10–3.
Farnhamville, Iowa, 9–1.
Flemingsburg, Ky., 8–2.
Frankfort, Ky., 12–1.
Frankfort, Ind., 7–3.
Frankton, Ind., 6–5.
Fraser, Iowa, 23–4; 9–1.
Geneva, Ind., 8–0.
Genoa, Ill., 11–0.
Gilmore, Iowa, 23–0.
Grant, Ky., 15–0.
Greensburg, Ky., 9–2.
Griggsville, Ill., 15–2.
Hamilton, Ind., 4–1.
Hampshire, Ill., 6–4.
Hartford, Ky., 9–0.
Hartford City, Ind., 13–0.
Havelock, Nebr., 16–1.
Huntley, Ill., 6–2.
Imlay City, Mich., 12–3.
Jeromeville, Ohio, 15–4.
Jonesville, Mich., 10–2.
Kentland, Ind., 7–0.
LaGrange, Ky., 8–2.
LaGrange, Mo., 18–0.
Lexington, Ky., Kentucky Uni., 11–0; 11–2.
Louisville, Ky., "Butchertowns," 14–1.
Macomb, Ill., 17–2.
Madisonville, Ky., 14–2.
Madrid, Iowa, 5–0.
Magnolia, Ohio, 13–1.
Malvern, Ohio, 14–0.
Marblehead, Ohio, 15–5.
Marlette, Mich., 9–2.
Meredosia, Ill., 14–1.
Midland, Mich., 4–2.
Milford, Nebr., 17–3.
Millersburg, Ky., 13–7.
Mingo Jct., Ohio, 3–0.
Montgomery, Mich., 16–5.
Montpelier, Ohio, 7–6.
Morganfield, Ky., 5–2.
Mt. Sterling, Ky., 5–3.
Mystic, Iowa, 10–2; 34–0.
Nelsonville, Ohio, 4–0.
New Albany, Ind., 8–4.
New Berlin, Ohio, 9–1.
New London, Ohio, 19–2.
Newton, Ill., 13–2.
Nicholasville, Ky., 7–1.
North Branch, Mich., 8–0.
North Manchester, Ind., 5–4.
Oakville, Ind., 17–0.
Oquawka, Ill., 10–3.
Orion, Ill., 7–1.
Orland, Ind., 15–0.
Orrville, Ohio, 5–1.
Ottawa, Ohio, 11–0; 12–7.
Owensville, Ind., 20–2.
Oxford, Ind., 8–4.
Oxford, Ohio, Miami Uni., 18–1.
Palmyra, Nebr., 24–4.
Paris, Ky., 19–4.
Pella, Iowa, 13–4.
Perry, Iowa, 10–4.
Pitcairn, Pa., 8–2; 5–0.
Pleasant City, Ohio, 19–2.
Pleasant Lake, Ind., 8–1.
Pleasantville, Iowa, 10–1.
Plymouth, Ill., 8–1.

Polo, Ill., 10–0.
Poseyville, Ind., 5–3.
Princeton, Ky., 10–2.
Reese, Mich., 10–3.
Rising Sun, Ind., 16–2.
Runnells, Iowa, 9–3.
Rushville, Ind., 6–1.
St. Charles, Mich., 6–0.
Saginaw, Mich., 10–3.
Salem, Ohio, 6–5.
Salt Lick, Ky., 8–1.
Sebree, Ky., 11–0.
Sewal, Iowa, 7–4.
Shelby, Ohio, 3–0.
Shelbyville, Ill., 17–0.
Sherrodsville, Ohio, 5–3.
Shreve, Ohio, 24–4.
Sigourney, Iowa, 13–0.
Smithton, Pa., 17–0.
Staunton, Ill., 3–1.
Sterling, Ill., 4–2.
Stillman Valley, Ill., 3–0.
Stockport, Iowa, 21–1.
Stronghurst, Ill., 17–0.
Sturgis, Ky., 15–0.
Sunfield, Mich., 13–0.
Tiffin, Ohio, 6–5.
Toledo, Ill., 7–3.
Toledo, Iowa, Western College, 3–2.
Toledo, Ohio, "Campbells," 18–3.
Uniontown, Pa., 11–1.
Utica, Nebr., 18–0.
Versailles, Ky., 5–2.
Virden, Ill., 5–1.
Walton, Ky., 23–1.
Warsaw, Ky., 14–2.
Wauseon, Ohio, 9–3.
West Baden, Ind., 11–0; 11–0.
West Union, Ohio, 7–1.
What Cheer, Iowa, 14–1.
Williamstown, Ky., 19–2.
Wilmington, Ill., 17–1.
Windsor, Ill., 30–2.
Woodsfield, Ohio, 9–5; 12–4.

Games Lost in 1905

Adrian, Mich., 8–4.
Auburn, Ind., 5–0.
Augusta, Ky., 6–5.
Chicago, Ill., Leland Giants, 4–3.
Cincinnati, Ohio, "Shamrocks," 3–2.
Chicago Jct., Ohio, 5–3.
Connersville, Ind., 4–1; 4–3.
Garrett, Ind., 3–1; 5–4.
Greensburg, Ind., 3–1.
Harbor Beach, Mich., 7–5.
Ironton, Ohio, 4–2.
Jackson, Mich., 7–4; 8–4.
Kalamazoo, Mich., 2–1.
Lincoln, Nebr., State Uni., 5–4; 7–6.
Lexington, Ky., Kentucky Uni., 6–4.
Mattoon, Ill., 16–1.
Oxford, Mich., 5–4.

Portsmouth, Ohio, 6–5.
Saginaw, Mich., 5–4.
Steubenville, Ohio, 4–1; 4–0.
Washington, Pa., 3–2.
Waynesburg, Pa., 4–1.

Tie Game in 1905

Wooster, Ohio, 0–0.

1906

In 1906 we undertook the most ambitious tour that we ever attempted. We not only included our regular territory of the Central states, but we went as far east as the Atlantic Coast, playing all the largest cities and summer resorts, and opening the eyes of the natives of New York, New Jersey, and adjacent states. We visited Nebraska, Kansas, Iowa, Missouri, Pennsylvania, Illinois, Indiana, Ohio, Maryland, New Jersey, Delaware, New York, West Virginia, Kentucky and Tennessee — a total of fifteen states. We won 151 games, lost 31, and tied 2. We shut out our opponents 44 times, and ourselves drew zeros 9 times.

Games Won in 1906

Albany, Mo., 10–0.
Ashland, Ohio, 4–0; 12–0.
Astoria, Ill., 14–0.
Attica, Ohio, 18–1.
Avon, Ill., 26–0.
Batesville, Ind., 12–0.
Bellvue, Ky., 102.
Barberton, Ohio, 6–5.
Blanchard, Iowa, 4–1.
Bloomfield, Ky., 4–2.
Bluffton, Ohio, 18–1.
Bosworth, Mo., 15–1.
Bowling Green, Ky., 8–0; 11–1.
Brooklyn, N. Y., "Brightons," 8–4.
Bruin, Pa., 13–4.
Brunswick, Md., 4–0.
Buda, Ill., 35–0.
Burlington, Ky., 12–0.
Burnside, Ky., 11–2.
Caledonia, Ohio, 11–2.
Camden, N. J., 11–2.
Camp Point, Ill., 8–1.
Canton, Ill., 7–3.
Canton, Mo., 19–8.
Carmel, Ind., 13–3.
Carnegie, Pa., 6–2.

Carrollton, Ky., 26–5.
Centerburg, Ohio, 3–0.
Chicago, Ill., "Lawndales," 5–4.
Chicago Jct., Ohio, 8–6.
Chillicothe, Mo., 24–4.
Cicero, Ind., 12–0.
Clarinda, Iowa, 11–4.
Clearfield, Pa., 2–0.
Coffeyburg, Mo., 24–6.
Coldwater, Ohio, 12–2.
Columbia, Tenn., 10–5.
Columbus Grove, Ohio, 9–1; 16–7.
Danville, Pa., 5–3.
Davenport, Nebr., 11–0.
Decatur, Ind., 3–0.
DeWitt, Nebr., 33–3.
Douglas, Nebr., 8–0.
Dunkirk, Ind., 6–3.
Dunkirk, Ohio, 7–1.
Earling, Iowa, 8–0.
Easton, Md., 9–3.
Ellenboro, W. Va., 8–5.
Elmwood, Ill., 11–6.
Emlenton, Pa., 4–1.
Ethel, Mo., 26–3.
Fairmont, W. Va., 3–2; 8–0.
Fayetteville, Tenn., 15–1.
Federalsburg, Md., 9–0.
Flora, Ind., 6–3.
Fort Hancock, N. J., 8–0.
Frankfort, Ind., 5–3.
Franklin, Pa., 6–0.
Gallatin, Tenn., 14–3.
Garrettsville, Ohio, 11–0.
Georgetown, Ky., College, 6–1.
Georgetown, Ohio, 14–0.
Greenville, Tenn., 9–4.
Grove City, Pa., 5–0.
Harrodsburg, Ky., 12–3.
Hebron, Ind., 12–4.
Hickman, Nebr., 14–4.
Indianapolis, Ind., A. B. C's., 4–0.
Indianapolis, Ind., Duesseldorfers, 2–1; 8–2.
Jeromeville, Ohio, 8–3.
Jersey Shore, Pa., 4–1.
Kirksville, Mo., 7–1.
Knoxville, Tenn., 3–2; 5–2.
LaCrosse, Ind., 6–3.
Lancaster, Mo., 36–5.
Lansford, Pa., 5–2.
Lincoln, Nebr., State Uni., 15–13; 8–3.
Louisville, Ky., "Reccius," 1–0.
Louisville, Ohio, 4–1.
LaRue, Ohio, 19–4.
Navarre, Ohio, 6–4.
Nicholasville, Ky., 7–1.
Nodaway, Iowa, 15–0.
Norborne, Mo., 23–2.
North Judson, Ind., 10–9.
North Liberty, Ind., 10–0.
Madison, N. J., 8–0.
Mahanoy City, Pa., 5–0; 8–4.
Maitland, Mo., 9–3.
Mantua, Ohio, 12–2.
Marietta, Ohio, 15–0.
McKeesport, Pa., 14–3.
Memphis, Mo., 24–1.
Mendon, Ohio, 6–3.
Middlefield, Ohio, 5–2.
Midway, Ky., 12–1.

Morristown, Tenn., 8–5.
Mt. Carmel, Pa., 9–1.
Mt. Pleasant, Ohio, 11–0.
Mt. Sterling, Ill., 16–1.
Mt. Vernon, Ohio, 7–0.
Oketo, Kans., 14–4.
Oak Hill, Ohio, 7–1.
Pawnee City, Nebr., 20–2.
Pen Argyl, Pa., 10–4.
Persia, Iowa, 15–2.
Petersburg, Ky., 14–4.
Plattsburg, Mo., 10–4.
Portsmouth, Ohio, 11–0.
Princess Anne, Md., 12–1.
Rowlesburg, W. Va., 20–4.
Sabina, Ohio, 3–2.
Sanders, Ky., 8–3; 23–0.
Seaford, Del., 11–2.
Sharpsville, Ind., 5–3.
Sheridan, Ind., 7–0; 14–2.
Shinnston, W. Va., 12–0.
Slatington, Pa., 3–2.
Somerset, Ky., 5–1.
Syracuse, Nebr., 13–2.
Table Grove, Ill., 17–1.
Tarkio, Mo., 24–1.
Terra Alta, W. Va., 10–4.
Toledo, Ohio, "Pope Toledos," 7–2.
Toms River, N. J., 8–0.
Tuckerton, N. J., 5–0.
Union Mills, Ind., 19–4.
Union Star, Mo., 5–2.
Vibbard, Mo., 13–2.
Walton, Ky., 6–0.
Waverly, Ohio, 6–0.
Wellston, Ohio, 5–0.
West Farmington, Ohio, 13–1.
West Middlesex, Pa., 6–1.
West Mansfield, Ohio, 13–3.
West Salem, Ohio, 8–0.
Wharton, Ohio, 18–1.
Whitestown, Ind., 14–2.
Williamstown, W. Va., 14–2.
Wilmington, Ohio, 9–4.
Xenia, Ohio, 22–2.

Games Lost During 1906

Baltimore, Md., City League, "All Stars," 7–0; 2–1.
Bethel, Ohio, 2–1.
Bluffton, Ind., 4–2.
Brooklyn, N. Y., "Paramounts," 3–2.
Carmel, Ind., 4–0.
Carrollton, Mo., 6–4.
Chicago, Ill., "Gunthers," 15–3.
Connersville, Ind., 8–1.
Cuban X-Giants, 5–2.
Dillsboro, Ind., 5–4.
Elizabeth, N. J., 2–1.
Frankfort, Ind., 6–1.
Geneva, Ind., 2–0.
Hazelton, Pa., 8–6.
Indianapolis, Ind., A. B. C's., 9–6; 3–0; 9–8.
Lincoln, Nebr., Western League, 6–2.

Milton, Pa., 5–0.
Nesquehoning, Pa., 6–0.
Newport, Ky., "Colonels," 1–0.
New Richard, Ohio, 3–0.
New Rochelle, N. Y., 2–1.
Noblesville, Ind., 4–3.
North Vernon, Ind., 1–0.
Notre Dame, Ind., 5–3.
Philadelphia, Pa., "Giants," 5–3.
Quincy, Ill., 6–4.
Shamokin, Pa., 3–2.
Wooster, Ohio, 11–2.

Tie Games in 1906

Asbury Park, N. J., 0–0.
Connersville, Ind., 2–2 —14 innings.

APPENDIX

"Experiences with an Indian Ball Team"

Guy Wilder Green
***Nebraska State Journal*, Dec. 20, 1908: C6**

Guy Green has managed an Indian baseball team and if there are troubles connected with that business that he has not encountered information concerning them need not be forwarded. Green tells his experience in these words:

> In 1895 I was working in Stromsburg, this state. Stromsburg had a typical country baseball team. I did not play regularly. The leading civilians wouldn't let me. My duties were to tear through the sunflowers of the Blue River Bottom and retrieve foul balls. I got so used to this retrieve act that I used to bark in my sleep like a bird dog. After my father had climbed out in the middle of the night, a couple of times and prowled around the house with his trusty shotgun to see who was disturbing the domestic animals, he discovered that I was making the nocturnal row and he chained me up until my nervous system regained its equilibrium.
>
> About this time a fortuitous thing happened for me. The manager of the local baseball team was sent to the penitentiary for horse stealing and, since I seemed to possess a good many of the departed citizen's characteristics, the players asked me to take his place — not in the penitentiary, but as manager of the Stromsburg team. This was in July of 1895. My first act was to book the Genoa Indians school team for a game in Stromsburg. I branched out as a big advertiser and sent glowing notices of the approaching game to every paper in my part of the country. The people came out in hordes. Cripples, who had not been out of the house since the Smith hanging in Osceola in '88, paid their money to see the game, Old timers were there who have taken no interest in any event from that day to this, with the exception of the election last fall, when the democratic state central committee dug them out and persuaded them to vote the straight ticket. When I counted my money after that game the idea of the Nebraska Indians was born. The team did not go on the road, however, until 1897.

Rocky Trail in Wagons

We first took to the rocky trail of public amusement in wagons. I had two lumber wagons, six horses, a bale of hay and a dog as my complete traveling outfit. Four of the horses were hitched side-by-side to one wagon. This arrangement was all right ordinarily, but when we struck a narrow bridge we had to flatten and stretch our steeds out like a rubber band until part of them was crossing a bridge in one county while the head end was contentedly browsing out of a strange pasture over beyond the next meridian.

During our first year we made some terrific jumps, considering the fact that our method of travel was by means of horse power. In case we played on two successive days in two towns thirty miles apart, it was necessary to travel all night. I slept in the bottom of the wagon on these night jumps mixed up promiscuously with horse fodder, the cook table and various culinary impedimenta and gastronomic delicacies. Sometimes when we reached a new town the mayor came out to meet us on a big white horse, backed up by the village band and a large part of the floating population. When he asked for the owner of the team I crawled out from the back end of our Studebaker covered with hay and hominy, the local dignitary often fainting from surprise and let his horse trample him to death before help could reach him. I remember distinctly that an accident like this happened one Sunday morning, in Carroll, Ia. That first season finally ended and when the record was made up I found that my peerless aggregation of talent had won twenty-one games and lost twenty-six. I waited for some time, expecting a few offers to manage teams from the National league, but as none came, I took to the road again the next year and the team has been gratifying the American people ever since. We have used no wagons, however, since the first season.

Incidents of Twelve Years

A lot of things have happened in the course of these twelve years. One of them was called to my mind the other day. Waseca (Emil Hauser), of the Carlisle football team, came into the office and I asked him if he remembered his dime novel experience in Carrollton, Ky., in 1906. Hauser broke his ankle in Carrollton, and after the local drayman had hauled him to the hotel and the Bourdon surgeons were through working on him, it became evident Emil would have to stay right in the choice little Kentucky hostelry for some time and live on fried apples, corn pone and fried bacon until his underpinning recovered its pristine elasticity. So we sailed away leaving Waseca in his Ohio River haven of delight. During his second day there a sweet little society lady who had been writing papers on the noble red man for the woman's club, dropped in to see how the aborigine was prospering. She carefully untied the "Four X" flour sacks with which Emil's foot was wrapped, soaked it copiously with tears of sympathy and a horse liniment which cost three dollars a gallon at the corner drug store, and went away. The next day she returned to again look after the patient, and this continued until Hauser wore a haunted expression most of the time and trembled whenever he saw a man go by with a gun. One day as Hauser was enjoying his afternoon doze, and endeavoring to digest the Kentucky provender with which his insides were calcimined, the big husband of the Indian's admirer burst into the room with an assortment of bright new oaths and a consignment of firearms that made a civil war museum look as tame as an exhibit of agricultural implements. He shoved a gun, the barrel of which looked big enough to sleep in, up against Emil's palpitating dinner and told him to fly fast and far. Emil flew. He flew on foot, by wagon, by horseback, mule back, steamboat and trail until he reached us where we were sojourning somewhere down in Tennessee. And he has never even written. Every time he sees the name of the town on the map someone has to administer smelling salts.

Tom Cockrill's Challenge

Kentucky is prolific of adventure and strange sensations. In Winchester one day I was strolling along the street looking at tobacco warehouses and waiting for the train to go up to Clay City, where we were to play on the morrow. I stopped in front of a commission house in front of which a long, gangling, red-headed young fellow was propped back in a chair contemplatively chewing tobacco and warming himself in the sun. He hailed me and told me just exactly how good the Clay City team was and how poor my fellows were. Then he offered to bet a small roll of money on the result of the next day's engagement. I was gathering my energies preparatory to telling this officious stranger just exactly what I thought of unknowns who "butted in" to foreign affairs when someone came up behind and in a whisper suggested that I keep quiet. Then I found that the red-headed boy was Tom Cockrill, one of the leaders of the Cockrill-Hargis feud, the brother of Jim Cockrill, who had been murdered by Curt Jett up in Jackson shortly before and the killer of two or three of the Hargis-Jett tribe himself. So instead of opening the vials of my wrath, I gently subsided into a chair beside Tom and visited with him and listened to his story of the feud while peace and amity hovered so closely about us that it could have been cut and corded up for future use.

The next day Tom went up to Clay City with us. It was the Fourth of July and hot. Cockrill and I went out to the grounds together. Cockrill had on no coat or vest and seemed unarmed, carefree and happy. Clay City was right in the edge of the mountains on the border of the Hargis principality.

"Suppose," said I to Cockrill, "trouble should start this afternoon. What would you do? You haven't a sign of a gun."

Then Thomas reached inside of his shirt with his right hand and pulled from under his left arm the biggest revolver I ever saw. He was carrying it in a holster out of sight where he could get at it handily in case of need and in my ignorance of local usage I had imagined him harmless. No one was shot that afternoon. True, one man was hit over the head with a two-by-four and killed and dragged out just before the game started, but he met his death in a little private disturbance and was a comparatively obscure citizen anyhow, and no one seemed to miss him much.

It Was a Quiet Affair

This Clay City Fourth of July was a very quiet affair. An excursion train came down from Beattyville and Jackson bringing a load of mountaineers and in anticipation of their coming the city fathers of Clay City passed a special ordinance forbidding the explosion of fireworks of even the simplest character. There was nothing for the ebullient visitors to do but drink whiskey and control their spirits. There was one little saloon in the town. This place sold $1,200 worth of stuff by 2 o'clock and closed its doors. Its entire stock of goods was gone. But that evening, when the visitors finally climbed on board their train and started for home, they unlimbered their firearms and shot the cars so full of holes that they went to the repair shop the next day. Bubbling mountain spirits cannot be forever suppressed.

In Buffalo Valley, Tenn., last year the umpire who represented the southerners called my players to the middle of the diamond just before the game started and shifting his gun to a convenient position said, "Now, damn ye, unload them balls, all of ye."

My men looked at the official in amazement. "Unload, I mean it," he cried, "We know all about you fellers. Every one of ye has his shirt full of baseballs right now. You can't fool our boys. Don't think for a minute you can go out there and throw in them extra balls whenever you fell like It." No little persuasion was required to convince the fiery Tennessean that no extra balls were concealed about the persons of my gladiators.

Nakomas the Half-Breed

I used to have a player with me by the name of Nakomas. Nakomas was a half-breed, a mixture of Irish and Indian. He is one of the few men I have seen who loved a fight for the fight's sake. When he was not playing I put him where trouble was most likely to take up its abode. Just before the game at Franklin, Penn., which town by the way is the habitat of Bill Dwyer who will manage Des Moines this season, the manager of the Franklin team confided to me that he had been having a lot of trouble on one of his gates from people who insisted on entering the grounds without the formality of paying the admission price. Had I a man who was nervy enough to stop this? If so, would I please put him over in the troublesome spot? I whistled to Nakomas, who came up with a glad look in his eyes. He scented trouble and wanted to be in it. The situation was explained to Nakomas and he went happily to his post of duty. In about three minutes there arose a caterwauling that could be heard clear down town and Nakomas came loping across the park dragging a dapper little man by the scruff of the neck and breathing soft Indian expletives down the bosom of his shirt the while he caressed him gently with his spikes on his new broadcloth pantaloons. Nakomas dropped his burden at the feet of the Franklin manager and smiled beatifically. The manager looked at the disheveled wreck and leaned against the box office for support. Nakomas had captured the owner of the Franklin team, one of the leading manufacturres and business men of the city. But he had done his duty.

A Snag Dan Tobey Struck

Dan Tobey, whom practically everybody in Lincoln knows, has worked for me for many years. He pitches for the Pasadena team of the California league during the winter, and acts as road manager of the Nebraska Indians during the summer. Tobey is a mine of energy. He drops into a town at 10 o'clock in the morning, is acquainted with everybody inside of an hour, and at noon is liable to be eating lunch with the mayor or a leading preacher. I remember one occurrence, however, when his conversational powers involved him in an unexpected accident. Tobey was pitching a hard game at Attica, Ind. The opposing rotater was the pride of that section, and all his relations from his grandfather down to his little sister were out to see the game. The grandfather was ninety years of age, and was wheeled out to the grounds in an invalid chair. During the game Tobey sat down by him and proceeded to visit with the veteran. "Don't you think," said the old man in a cracked voice, "that this Attica boy is pitching a mighty fine ball?" "Sure he is," answered Tobey, "it's the finest ball I ever saw, a new $1.50 Spalding." Then Vesuvius erupted. The poor old crippled nonogenarian climbed out of his invalid chair and rained right and left-handers on Tobey's physiognomy so thick and fast that the humane society was obliged to stop the slaughter. Tobey went down for the count, and grandpa tottered back to his nurse. A bucket of water dashed in Dan's face soon restored him to consciousness, and the game went on, but the good effects of this lesson have remained with my manager to this day.

A Glass-Eyed Performer

Elmer Johnson, of Wahoo, was responsible for my hiring one of the most peculiar players I have ever paid a salary to. This man was nothing less than a glass-eyed performer, who caused me lots of amusement. I noticed a peculiar expression of wonder on his countenance when I engaged him, but I never for a moment suspicioned that this was due to an artificial organ in his face, until I was one day paying my hotel bill in Dyersville, Ia. Then I heard a crash of falling glass. I looked around with considerable trepidation only to discover that my pitcher's glass optic had dropped out and was splintered on the floor. I then knew why so many local players had complained to me that this pitcher for no apparent reason "looked at 'em as though he had something again 'em." Personally, I don't consider a glass-eyed pitcher a valuable asset for any team. You never know when an accident is going to fill his system so full of crystals that he will jingle when he walks. Then again he may lose his eye at inopportune times. This very thing happened to my man in Galva, Ill. He was investigating the city water works when the only eye he had with him fell down the well, was pumped into the city main, drawn by the mayor from a hydrant and drunk and digested before an alarm could be turned in or a physician summoned.

A traveling man from Vermont, a marble salesman, was stopping at the Baker House with us at the time of this mishap. He claimed to have a sample of marble with him that would take so fine a polish that it would look like the human eye, and he persuaded my pitcher to trim down a small piece of this, polish it, and use it until a new-glass-eye could be obtained from Chicago. "Rip" worked all night getting this chunk of marble into shape, and came down to breakfast the next morning wearing a very fair imitation of marble in his face. Then the scoundrelly drummer discovered that he had given Rip the piece of sample marble that contained his cost mark. He took his present back, and my player was left disconsolate. Rip was very particular about his artificial eye. He always carried a chamois skin and a bottle of whiting in his uniform, and it was his custom between innings to go out behind the backstop and polish his imitation optic. As the season advanced he devoted more and more time to the process until he sometimes delayed the game as much as an hour. I, of course, could not tolerate this and so one day I paid him off and sent him on his way.

Instinctive Fear of Strangers

People never entirely rid themselves of the feeling which, in ancient times, impelled them at the approach of a stranger, to raise the drawbridge and flood the moat. We naturally think our friends are a little bit better than the rest of creation, and that our daily companions are more to be trusted than the stranger who tarries within the gate for only a short time. In Auburn, New York, the hotel man told me the following incident. A prominent citizen visited the Auburn penitentiary and attended a religious gathering in which all the prisoners participated. During the exercises a light-fingered convict annexed the visitor's watch. The loss was soon discovered and the victim of the theft complained to the warden. The warden was surprised and grieved and said, "You must have lost that watch somewhere else. I don't think any of MY boys would take it," Every town in the country thinks "its boys" are all right, and that everyone else is wrong. That's the reason I dislike to hear of a violation of the law in a city while we are visiting it. The chances are strongly in favor of the local sleuths convening in solemn conclave and deciding that "them darned Injuns" are the guilty parties.

After the visit we made to Indianola. Iowa, a prominent taxpayer missed a slab of bacon from his smoke house. He telephoned to the city marshal at Lucas, whither we had gone, accurately describing his bacon, telling which end of the chunk was worm-eaten, and giving the age of the hog which furnished the succulent breakfast dish. The anxious meat-curer ended by asking the Lucas officer to go through my cook's grip, as he thought the meat was secreted in that roomy receptacle and we were only waiting a favorable opportunity to permanently destroy its commercial value in the frying pan. The Lucas officer declined this bit of work as the reward offered for the return of the goods was not large enough.

Kidnapped, Her "Che-ild"

In Murphysboro, Illinois, a young child strayed from home into the woods while we were unfortunate enough to be filling an engagement in that vicinity. The frantic mother, who had filled her brain with weird Indian tales, at once jumped to the conclusion that the savage red men had kidnapped her "che-ild." A fat "copper" came to the camp to investigate, but after he had looked through a couple of trunks and stuck his face in the third baseman's dirty clothes-bag, news was brought from the parents of the lost cherub that "little precious" had come back to them full of sandburs and huckleberry stains. If the distracted mother had only known how many small boys I dissuade from a traveling life of adventure with the Nebraska Indians, she would have had no fears concerning the safety of her offspring.

In Center Point, Iowa, the mayor appointed a large force of special police before we arrived in town and these brave minions guarded the sleeping citizens through the perilous night, while an occasional voter put in the lone hours with a trusty gun across his knees waiting for an uprising. The funny part of all this was that we did not learn of it until we were at the depot ready to leave town. We had been in the midst of all these alarms profoundly ignorant of them.

At Collinsville, Illinois, we camped a long way from town in a little grove. Collinsville is not a large town, but our camp was so located that it was hard for one unacquainted with the locality to find it. One of the players started for the tents late in the evening, and after walking several blocks he decided he was out of the way and turned his steps toward a convenient residence with the object of making inquiries to set himself straight. He had no sooner entered the gate than the door of the house was thrown open and he found himself looking into the muzzle of a revolver, while a stern voice said, "Don't stir or say a word." In vain the Indian tried to explain, but his captor would not permit it. The householder left his wife guarding the player while he ran to the police, his tongue hanging out of his mouth so far that he stepped on it at every jump. At the station he told a strange story of a big burglary and came prancing back to this scène of war with a lot of officers panting at this heels. Then the Indian, who sat dumb with amazement through all the excitement, was dragged away to the bastile. In the morning the whole proceeding assumed such a ridiculous aspect that my player was released without even the formality of a hearing. The Indian who went through this experience was a nice appearing, well-educated, young half-breed, a graduate of one of the leading Indian schools, and he never had trouble with anyone in this life. He would think of committing suicide about as soon as he would think of burglary. But he was a stranger, and strangers are always safe objects of suspicion.

Memory of White Bear Lake

A game we once played at White Bear Lake, Minnesota, was finished in a hurry. We had so short a time to catch the train back to St. Paul that I sent two of my men up to the room where the team had dressed with instructions to gather up all the street clothes and bring them to the train. The boys followed instructions and reached the train with the apparel just in time to jump on the cars. My men changed clothes in a room in the St. Paul union depot, and after they were dressed they discovered an extra suit. It appeared that unbeknown to us, one of the White Bear Lake players had changed in our room, hung his clothes up with ours, and they had been brought to St. Paul in a hurry. We turned the suit, which would have been dear at five dollars, over to the station authorities with a request that they hold it until it was called for. A few minutes after we had done this a squad of policemen from the central station swept into the depot with a crowd at their heels and three of my boys in tow, whom they had picked up on the way down. They announced that they had received a telegram from the White Bear Lake management requesting them to arrest the whole team, on the charge of purloining a valuable suit of clothes. The station authorities told the officers what had happened, and the officers explained to the White Bear Lake magnate that he was evidently mistaken in the assumption that the Indians had stolen his clothes. Then the police force went on its way and so did we.

Was Only One Yaqui

In all my experience, I have had but one Yaqui ball player. The Yaquis are a savage tribe living in the extreme southwestern part of the United States, and I hesitated a long time before I added Juzicanea to my team. He was the meanest looking Indian I have ever seen. He wore his hair long, surveyed everything suspiciously with piercing black eyes, and when he came down the street people moved to the edge of the sidewalk and apprehensively watched him pass. Juzicanea would not sleep in bed. He could rest comfortably only on the floor or the ground. In the morning we were as liable to find him in the back yard under a tree as anywhere else. I remember that at Bluffton, Ind., Juzicanea slept on the floor, and the landlord of the hotel, considering this a reflection on his beds, threatened to throw the entire team out of his hostelry.

Another of Juzicanea's peculiarities was his craving for raw meat he demanded from one to two pounds of this delicacy each day, and unless he obtained it he was as surly as a caged tiger. I used to fill my pocket with raw meat when we went out to the grounds, and after Juzicanea made a particularly brilliant catch or a long hit, I fed him a liberal chunk of the succulent delicacy which invariably caused him intense delight, and greatly amused the natives who watched him perform. I was compelled to line my pockets with oilcloth in order to provide suitable receptacles for Juzicanea's gory lunches. I made it a rule, soon after we entered the hotel, to either inform the landlord or the waiters of Juzicanea's peculiar appetite: otherwise his sudden demands for raw meat were liable to cause a series of embarrassing resignations among the dining room force. At Burlington, Ky., however, I neglected my usual precautions. The waiters there were colored, and when one of them approached Juzicanea's chair, the savage tossed his tangled hair out of his eyes, growled ominously and in broken English cried, "Bring me a pound of raw meat." The colored boy dropped his tray with a crash, and without waiting for his hat, his pay or anything else, plunged headfirst through the window screen and was gone. He never came back, and people who saw him several miles out from the village told me he was still traveling. His Ethiopian intellect was hopelessly unhinged.

Index

Prepared by Skip McAfee
Bibliography Committee, Society for American Baseball Research

Numbers in ***bold italics*** refer to pages with illustrations.